THE DUKE OF WELLINGTON AND THE BRITISH ARMY OF OCCUPATION IN FRANCE, 1815–1818

Recent Titles in
Contributions in Military Studies

Militarism and Politics in Latin America: Peru from Sánchez Cerro to
Sendero Luminoso
Daniel M. Masterson

Salzburg Under Siege: U.S. Occupation, 1945-1955
Donald R. Whitnah and Florentine E. Whitnah

Terrain and Tactics
Patrick O'Sullivan

The Vietnam War: Teaching Approaches and Resources
Marc Jason Gilbert, editor

Current French Security Policy: The Gaullist Legacy
Theodore Robert Posner

Treatise on Partisan Warfare
Johann Ewald; Translation, Introduction, and Annotation by
Robert A. Selig and David Curtis Skaggs

Controlling and Ending Conflict: Issues Before and After the Cold War
Stephen J. Cimbala and Sidney R. Waldman

Nordic Security at the Turn of the Twenty-First Century
Ciro Elliott Zoppo, editor

A History of Military Medicine
Volume I: From Ancient Times to the Middle Ages
Volume II: From the Renaissance Through Modern Times
Richard A. Gabriel and Karen S. Metz

The Duke of Wellington
and the
British Army
of
Occupation in France,
1815–1818

Thomas Dwight Veve

Contributions in Military Studies, Number 114

Greenwood Press
Westport, Connecticut • London

Library of Congress Cataloging-in-Publication Data

Veve, Thomas Dwight.
  The Duke of Wellington and the British army of occupation in
France, 1815-1818 / Thomas Dwight Veve.
    p. cm.—(Contributions in military studies, ISSN 0883-6884
; no. 114)
  Includes bibliographical references and index.
  ISBN 0-313-27941-1 (alk. paper)
  1. Wellington, Arthur Wellesley, Duke of, 1769-1852. 2. Great
Britain. Army—History—19th century. 3. Great Britain—History,
Military—19th century. 4. Great Britain—Foreign
relations—1800-1837. 5. Great Britain—Foreign relations—France.
6. France—Foreign relations—Great Britain. 7. France—History—
Louis XVIII, 1814-1824. 8. France—Foreign relations—1814-1830.
9. Napoleonic Wars, 1800-1815—Peace. I. Title. II. Series.
DA68.12.W4V48   1992
941.07′092—dc20   91-13559

British Library Cataloguing in Publication Data is available.

Library of Congress Catalog Card Number: 91-13559
ISBN: 0-313-27941-1
ISSN: 0883-6884

First published in 1992

Greenwood Press, 88 Post Road West, Westport, CT 06881
An imprint of Greenwood Publishing Group, Inc.

Printed in the United States of America

The paper used in this book complies with the
Permanent Paper Standard issued by the National
Information Standards Organization (Z39.48-1984).

10 9 8 7 6 5 4 3 2 1

Contents

Appendices

Maps

Preface

This study of the Duke of Wellington and the allied army of occupation of 1815–1818 had its genesis in 1985, when Professor John W. Rooney, Jr., first suggested to me that the role of the allied army left in France after the *Second Treaty of Paris* and its part in the European peace arrangements after the Battle of Waterloo required examination. He indicated that this subject had never been discussed and that the allied army had never received due credit for its peacekeeping role. As I began reading and researching on the issue, it became obvious to me that the Duke of Wellington played the key role in the success of this operation, and this aspect of the story warranted scholarly investigation.

Though the biographies of Wellington are fewer in number than those about Napoleon, the duke's military career has been exhaustively studied. Yet, new biographies continue to appear about him. Studies concerning his performances in India, in Spain, and at Waterloo are complete. One thing that all these studies have in common is the lack of careful consideration of his three-year command of the allied occupation army in France. Biographies, such as those by Stephen G. P. Ward, Philip Guedella, Oliver Brett, and Richard Aldington, have relegated Wellington's command between 1815 and 1818 to a few paragraphs, and they fail to examine the major role that Wellington played, not only as a military officer, but as a statesman, during his tenure as commander-in-chief of the occupation army. Elizabeth Longford's more recent book does the same. No specialized studies of these three years exist. Wellington's command in France is not simply the final chapter of a successful military career. It serves as an important transition to his future political career.

Wellington never wavered from the mission assigned to him and the army by the European powers. The army was to provide for the future security of Europe by curbing residual French expansionist tendencies, while allowing Louis XVIII the time to reconsolidate his rule. Wellington was guided in his decision-making processes by these goals. It was through his command that European objectives were met. Wellington set the standard for individual behavior. He decided when the allied troop reduction was going to take place. He was responsible for the inspection of the Dutch barrier fortress renovation program. Without this barrier system, the allied army would have been unable to depart France prior to the end of the planned five-year stay. Finally, he guided the process by which the allies decided they would terminate the occupation.

This work is also a study of the British army as part of the allied army of occupation. The allied army was history's first multinational peacekeeping operation. There had been no manuals written which described how this operation should work, and so this army should have established precedent for future similar endeavors. Under Wellington's leadership, the allied army maintained its neutrality. It served both the victorious European powers and France. It provided time for Louis XVIII to reestablish the Bourbons on the French throne. Wellington actually never employed the army to enforce allied decisions on the French nor protect the French king. The final test of the success of the duke and his army lies in events after the departure of the allies. General war, which had engulfed Europe for a generation, was not renewed for another century.

The collections of documents on Wellington and the British army exist in several locations in France and Great Britain. Wellington's papers at the University of Southampton which cover this period are well organized. Many letters to Wellington located there are not in his published papers found in *The Supplementary Despatches, Correspondence and Memorandum of Field Marshal the Duke of Wellington.* I found the papers of Sir George Murray, located in the National Library of Scotland, to be well cataloged. Murray served as Wellington's chief of staff in France, and accordingly was *de facto* chief of staff of the entire allied army. The relevant papers of Sir Richard Hussay Vivian, at the National Army Museum, are also well organized and most helpful in my study. Lord Vivian served Wellington as a cavalry brigade commander in France and kept detailed records.

For the French point of view, I examined the foreign ministry papers at the Quai d'Orsay which covered the day-to-day activities of supporting an occupying force. These papers are chronological in sequence, and cover a multitude of issues. The bulk of these files concentrate on the day-to-day relations between the French government and all the occupying nations. The French army papers are kept in the Musée de l'Armée de Terre located in the Château de Vincennes just outside Paris. They are not as well organized, but they are voluminous. Anyone concerned with the day-to-day operations of the French army during the Second Restoration should examine these files.

Works such as this are not completed without the assistance of many people. Professor John W. Rooney encouraged me to pursue work in military history. It was with his support that I entered the field of Napoleonic history where I first encountered the Duke of Wellington. This current study is a natural combination of the military and diplomatic events of the era. I wish to thank Dr. Rooney for his full support over the last years. I wish also to acknowledge Professor David E. Gardinier of Marquette for careful and conscientiously reviewing the entire manuscript. He too deserves many thanks for his criticisms which helped to rectify stylistic flaws. Dr. Frank L. Klement, Professor Emeritus at Marquette, has also given me great support in this effort. I also thank Dr. James Marten and Father Michael Zeps, S. J., for their keen insights and criticisms of the manuscript.

I also wish to acknowledge the generous assistance provided to me by my friend, Mr. John C. Horgan. John devoted both his time and energies in preparing the manuscript for publication. I also thank Mr. Jim Sumiec of Marquette for his assistance in putting together the four maps used in this work.

My archival research in the United Kingdom and France was made possible by a grant from the Cyril Smith Family Scholarship Foundation of San Francisco. I shall always be grateful to the Arthur J. Schmitt Foundation of Chicago for its generous financial assistance.

My research experiences overseas were pleasant ones and for this I thank the many archivists and historians who assisted me. Particularly, I wish to acknowledge the service given me by Mr. Julian Russell at the National Library of Scotland and Mr. C. M. Woolgar at the University of Southampton. At Southampton, Dr. Charles Esdaile provided great assistance while he conducted his own research on Wellington. I also cannot forget Mr. and Mrs. Keith Johnson of London for opening their home to me during my stay in the United Kingdom.

More than anyone I wish to thank my family. My biggest supporters have been my wife, Jennifer, my children, Shannon, David, and Christian, and my parents, Stephen and Reba Veve. It is they who have made the greatest sacrifices over the past five years, and to them I dedicate this work.

THE DUKE OF WELLINGTON
AND THE
BRITISH ARMY
OF
OCCUPATION IN FRANCE,
1815–1818

1

Introduction

The grand alliance against the Axis powers of the Second World War did not survive the war, and the period since 1945 has not seen the comfortable re-establishment of peace. While it is true that there has been no global conflagration, the postwar peace has been fragile. Based explicitly upon the principle of sovereignty, the United Nations, this century's greatest hope to prevent future war, has had only minimal successes. Its predecessor, the League of Nations, likewise failed. Such peace as has existed is due more to exhaustion of human and material strength of opponents and, as such, war frequently has loomed on the horizon, threatening whenever diplomats fail at the conference table; or it has been a peace based on mutual fear. Heretofore, all major peace initiatives have faltered prior to resolution.

Perhaps too much of this has been due to a lack of study of past situations which resulted in a more stable world. The world's nations are left with agreements designed only to reduce the level of terror. Too much attention has been given to the study of the causes and courses of war without equal attention having been given to those techniques which allowed nations to maintain peace effectively for an enduring period.

Historians such as Henry Kissinger, C. K. Webster, and Harold Nicholson have looked back at the post-Napoleonic era with some romanticism and have written of the Concert of Europe, or the years after the Vienna settlement, as an era of peace and international order. Certainly the peace efforts of 1814–1815 helped provide Europe with almost a century of general peace, though no one asserts that absolutely no fighting or confrontation existed among the major European powers. The Austrian foreign minister, Prince von Metternich, the British foreign minister, Lord Castlereagh, and the Russian czar, Alexander I, should receive credit for devising a system which produced the long-sought peace after a generation of revolution, rape, destruction, and revenge produced by the wars of the

French Revolution and Napoleon.

The Congress of Vienna successfully prevented general European war for a century, though many rebellions and military operations took place, some as early as 1820. Its success was based on many elements which, in themselves, would not have been enough to accomplish the lasting results experienced. This synergistic success may have started with what Talleyrand called "the sacred principle of legitimacy" whereby the hereditary rulers, especially the Bourbons in France, were returned to their thrones. Territorial aggrandizements were the reward of the victors to compensate themselves for their efforts against France. The allied powers eliminated many smaller European nations. By Article VI of the *Treaty of Alliance and Friendship*, signed on November 20, 1815, the allied powers agreed that they would meet in conference in the future to discuss the problems of the continent rather than to resort to war. The decision to meet via periodical and timely conferences served as a positive means to seek redress without conflict. The 1815 postwar era demonstrated the first known attempt on the part of European powers to create a means to perpetuate their system of values established by treaty.

As Henry Kissinger wrote, it was essential to peace that no power involved in creating international order come away from the settlement table dissatisfied.[1] The case of Germany after World War I demonstrates what occurs when dissatisfaction prevails to such a degree that revenge threatens the newly established peace. The allied generosity to the French nation in 1814 did not create widespread dissatisfaction, but Napoleon regained his throne rather easily in April, 1815, when the French army deserted Louis XVIII. Peace negotiators faced a difficult task. The allies decided France would have to provide greater concessions in 1815 than she had the previous year, while at the same time, the Bourbons could not endure a harsh settlement which would prevent French recovery and destabilize the king's position. In addition, the peace arrangements were negotiated in an atmosphere of vindictiveness on the part of those nations which had long endured the Napoleonic excesses.

Allied security was one important principle considered at Vienna. In order to maintain peace, France had to be kept within the new borders drawn for her and accepted by the Bourbons. Even with Napoleon safely enroute to permanent exile at St. Helena, the European powers had to keep revolutionary fervor and nationalism under control. Thus the Kingdom of the Netherlands gained Belgium, Prussia acquired territory on the west bank of the Rhine River, and to the southeast of France, Piedmont was enlarged. The allies agreed to aid in the reconstruction of the barrier fortresses along the border between France and the Netherlands. The fortress reconstruction program was central to the peace arrangements of 1815. The powers designated Arthur Wellesley, the first Duke of Wellington, to oversee the construction of the fortresses. The expected completion date of the barrier forts was early 1820 and, accordingly, a substitute designed to restrict France was required for the interim. The allies agreed to create a military force that would be established inside France to act as that substitute. Wellington's observations concerning the fortress rebuilding program was certain to affect the allied length of stay inside France.

The contemporary world might profit a great deal from the allied occupation experience, for the major European powers contributed soldiers to the army, a clear demonstration of their commitment to peace. Modern day peacekeeping operations have been left to small countries with little interest in the area in which they have been deployed. When participating peacekeeping countries have no national interests, their motives are not questioned. Such a system limits superpower involvement.[2]

In 1815, the allies learned from their experience of the Hundred Days of Napoleon that the loyalty of the French army to the Bourbons was suspect. If France was to be kept within her newly established borders, the diplomats needed to place restraints upon her. Moreover, the diplomats realized that to limit or control France's ambitions, internal conditions needed change. Only time, consistent policy, and careful leadership would result in the desired objectives and allow Louis XVIII to remain in power and reintroduce France as a responsible member of the European continent. Where the allies had failed to take any substantive measures to insure Louis' rule in 1814, they opted for those means in 1815 since they still considered him the best choice to keep France out of the internal affairs of other nations. Louis needed considerable time to establish his rule and, more importantly, he needed time to rebuild a French army void of Bonapartist ambitions. The army had too quickly rallied to Napoleon when he returned from Elba. Barely a shot had been fired in support of the king. The allies envisioned an occupation army assigned to maintain peace so that Louis could gain the time he needed to re-establish confidence in royal authority. In addition, the army would help maintain security in Europe by containing France within its borders.

The eventual success of the allied army of occupation was based on several factors, all of which were essential to the restoration of tranquillity in Europe. This allied occupation force set standards for all subsequent peacekeeping operations since it was the first multinational force created under unified command. A multinational force of its character faced the same problems and questions that are endemic to wartime coalitions. The issue of a commander was open. There remained the possibility that a member of the coalition would with-draw from participation, either from weariness, avoidance of assigned responsibilities, or having reached a bilateral agreement with France. The success of this effort offers many valuable lessons. The 1815–1818 occupation army suffered from many of the same problems that any similar force would face in any age. Once an allied coalition sub-dues its common enemy, national self-interests become paramount to nation-states regardless of their previously stated goals. In 1815, the allies enjoyed unity as long as France remained stronger than any single member of the coalition. But once a coalition member achieved its ends, allied unity faced dissolution. Allied differences were manifest in the contingents provided to the occupation army. That the Duke of Wellington overcame these differences remains an outstanding example for future students of peacekeeping operations.

The role of the Duke of Wellington, as commander-in-chief of the occupation forces, was central to the success of the allied army. Wellington's many biographers, including such historians as Richard Aldington, Stephen G. P. Ward, and Philip Guedalla, have concen-trated on three portions of the duke's life: his command of the British army in the Peninsular War of 1809–1814, his wonderful day at Wa-terloo, and his tenure as prime minister.[3] All have neglected his role of 1815–1818 as a commander-statesman!

Wellington's battlefield experiences in India served as the basis for his achievements in later years in Spain and in the Lowlands. Yet little, if anything, was known about Wellington's ability to serve as allied commander-in-chief in 1815. He fought alongside Spanish and Portuguese forces during the Peninsular campaign, but those joint operations often did not function very well.[4] The allied powers selected their occupation commander based largely on his battlefield victory at Waterloo.

As was the common British army practice of his day, Arthur Wellesley received his early promotions by purchase of rank. He did well in India under combat conditions against the Mahrattas. He learned the value of logistics during the long Peninsular campaign. But Wellington's experiences in Spain were difficult. When he added his name to the Convention of Cintra in 1808,[5] it became doubtful he would ever again command, let alone enjoy his later glory. After Wellesley's return to Spain upon Sir John Moore's death in 1809,[6] he campaigned on a limited basis in Portugal and Spain due to lack of commitment on the part of Parliament. Victories such as those at Bussaco and at Talavera were followed by retreats which did not endear Wellington to the parliamentary opposition nor increase the logistical support he received. In 1812, though Wellington captured

Madrid, after the failure of the siege at Burgos, he retreated all the way to the Portuguese frontier and was unable to resume the offensive until 1813. Only then did Wellington achieve his first lasting success. His victory at Vitoria in 1813 earned him his dukedom and the rank of field marshal. The duke drove French forces from Spain, and he invaded southern France in 1814 as Russian, Austrian, and Prussian armies entered Paris. Though Wellington played a major role in the demise of Napoleon's empire, it was the armies of the continental powers that conquered northern France and that faced Bonaparte in battle. It was only on June 18, 1815, that Wellington won the confidence and respect of the continental powers. Waterloo constituted a spectacular victory which the duke won in the same way he had won in the Peninsula, by perseverance, a solid defensive position, and the instilling of confidence into his soldiers. The victory made Wellington the pre-eminent general on the continent as he had beaten Napoleon in combat. His reputation was settled.

As a matter of state policy, Wellington fully supported the Bourbons at the time he was chosen to command the occupation army. In 1813 he had probably favored retaining Napoleon on the French throne if the latter would give up his conquests and accept borders consistent with pre-war boundaries. Wellington had not been a supporter of the Bourbons prior to his invasion of southern France in 1814. His thinking had begun to change when it had become apparent that Napoleon had no real intention of negotiating an end to the fighting. Wellington had been also exposed to the possibility of a Bourbon return when Louis-Antoine, Duke of Angoulême,[7] arrived and traveled with his army as it entered France. Angoulême sought support for a restoration of the Bourbons, and Wellington could not have avoided seeing the white cockades when he entered Bordeaux on March 12, 1814. In a carefully orchestrated operation, Angoulême had entered the welcoming city accompanied by British troops. A Bourbon at the head of allied troops who behaved better than the soldiers of the French Empire would gather support. The acclamation of the Bourbons in Bordeaux had strong repercussions in Paris when word reached the capital. Word of the abdication of Bonaparte reached the British army as it entered Toulouse, which also espoused the Bourbon cause. Wellington had realized that the restoration was a fact of life. In June, 1814, the duke was named as British ambassador to the court of Louis XVIII. He grew closer to the monarch in the short time he was in Paris. He was serving as the British plenipotentiary in Vienna when Napoleon returned from Elba. Wellington's departure from Paris for Vienna had resulted from his lack of popularity among the French and threat of assassination, not because of a break between himself and the Bourbons.

Wellington believed that the Bourbon departure from Paris after Napoleon's return would harm their image among the French. Louis XVIII believed that as well, but was persuaded at the last moment to depart. However, the duke still considered the Bourbons preferable to the other possible choices and he remained in close contact with the king at Ghent. After Waterloo, Wellington immediately wrote to Louis about the great victory and recommended that he return as rapidly as possible to Paris to reclaim his throne. Louis left immediately, going first to Mons and then to Cambrai. Louis demonstrated his reliance on the allies as he followed along the same route as the armies. Influenced by Wellington's advice, the king moved slowly towards the capital, and several fortresses surrendered in his presence, perhaps even due to it; for with disaster befalling Napoleon, French army units hesitated to resist in the presence of the monarch. Though Wellington was following instructions from his government, Louis personally liked him and got along well with him. When an army of occupation was decided upon in October, 1815, Louis could certainly have asked for no better commander-in-chief. With support of George, the Prince Regent, the allied powers, the Bourbons, along with the prestige of his victory at Waterloo, no other general was even considered for the post of allied commander. Lord Castlereagh stated that Czar Alexander made Wellington's command of the army an essential pre-condition for Russian participation in the occupation.[8] The decision to make the Duke of Wellington the commander-in-chief was a good one, based upon his reputation and his disciplined army. Under his leadership, the army of occupation achieved the goals established for it.

Many have ascribed the duke's preparatory training to his years in India or Spain, but it was in France between 1815 and 1818 that he confronted the delicate problems of diplomacy, dealing with heads of state or their plenipotentiaries, and balancing his decisions among the multinational contingents of the occupation army. Commanding an army in Spain and Portugal represents something far different than speaking the languages and nuances of the courts of Europe. Biographers[9] of Wellington have universally relegated Wellington's command of the occupation army to a few pages, mentioning the assassination attempts against him, while ignoring his three-year tenure as if it contained little of significance. While it is true that this period does not carry the glamour of the Peninsula or Waterloo campaigns, it must not be ignored, for it was the period wherein the duke learned the lessons he needed to enter into the political arena. This study will demonstrate that this command was more than merely the final active military command of the duke. Wellington successfully presided over an international force beset with internal squabbling

related to each country's national interests. Above all, he was faced
with the revenge motive in the participants' minds. In the interests
of peace and for the long-term future of the continent, Wellington
could not ignore allied differences as he had while commanding in the
field. Here his failures were obvious to all and could not be hidden
in dispatches to the war office. The three years that the duke commanded the occupation force were the major formative years when
he forged his character for his subsequent political career.

At the same time, Armand-Emmanuel du Plessis, the Duke
of Richelieu and foreign minister of France during the occupation,
played an important role from the French side. In this study, his role
is secondary to that of Wellington. Richelieu, in spite of his famous
name, was as unknown in France as Wellington was in England in
1808. An *émigré*, he had been absent for many years prior to being
named foreign minister and president of the council in 1815. He re-
luctantly accepted the positions with little knowledge of the changes
effected by the French Revolution and Napoleon upon France's internal affairs. His tenure in office began in September, 1815. His
first major act was to sign the *Treaty of Paris* of November 20, 1815,
a treaty which acknowledged the presence of an army of occupation.
His ministry's end coincided with the departure of the allied army
of occupation in 1818.

From November 21, 1815, Richelieu dedicated himself methodi-
cally to meeting the provisions of the treaty so that the allies would
end their occupation as soon as possible. This goal explains most of
his administrative actions. His dedication to France made it possible for the occupation to end two years early. His efforts resulted in
France again reclaiming her rightful place as an equal with the allied
powers in 1818. The tenures in power of Wellington and Richelieu
coincided almost to the day.

After the victory at Waterloo and Napoleon's second abdication, Louis XVIII was again restored to the throne of his ancestors.
The Hundred Days demonstrated to the allies the weaknesses of the
first restoration and the necessity of consolidating Louis' position
rather than merely restoring him as they had in 1814. In Louis the
allied governments saw, perhaps mistakenly, their best hope for the
security and stability of Europe. Napoleon had been defeated and
imprisoned but the allies had to face the revolution and the forces
it had released first hand. By comparison, their military problems
paled before the political, economic, and social ones. The decision
to create a multinational force was the first step in this regard, and
an essential one. Wellington's success as leader of the allied peacekeeping effort, an integral part of the peacemaking process, is the
central concern of this work.

NOTES

1. Henry Kissinger, *A World Restored: Metternich, Castlereagh and the Problems of Peace, 1812-22* (Boston: Houghton Mifflin Company), 1.

2. The United States actively participates in the successful Sinai peacekeeping force created in 1981. The U.S., along with its allies France, Great Britain, and Italy, failed with the peacekeeping force sent to Lebanon in 1982.

3. Richard Aldington, *The Duke* (New York: The Viking Press, 1943); Stephen G. P. Ward, *Wellington* (New York: Arco Publishing Company, 1965); Philip Guedalla, *Wellington* (New York: The Literary Guild, 1931).

4. For example, Wellington had little use for the Spanish general, Don Gregorio de la Cuesta. The duke considered any military operation which included the general unlikely to succeed. The Spanish failure to cooperate after the victory at Talavera led to a retreat by Wellington. The duke vowed never again to cooperate with Spanish troops. On the other hand, greater cooperation was achieved between Wellington and Portuguese forces. Portuguese forces were commanded by a British general, Sir William Beresford.

5. Wellington defeated the French at Vimiero in Portugal on August 22, 1808. He gave up his command to two senior officers, Generals Burrard and Dalrymple, who agreed to negotiate with the French forces. The convention terms allowed the French to evacuate twenty-six thousand men, complete with equipment, on British vessels. Wellington added his name to the agreement though he did not agree with its provisions. All three commanders were recalled and faced a court of inquiry for their actions, and all were exonerated from blame. The court added its recognition to Wellington's victory.

6. Sir John Moore (1761–1809), Lieutenant General, had a long military career and served with distinction in 1801 when Britain defeated the French army left behind in Egypt by Napoleon. He took command of British forces in Portugal after the Convention of Cintra. He invaded Spain in late 1808 and pushed all the way to Madrid when he discovered he had been cut off from Portugal. Moore retreated to Corunna where he turned and defeated the French, but was mortally wounded.

7. Louis-Antoine de Bourbon (1775–1844), Duke of Angoulême, eldest son of the Count of Artois and nephew of Louis XVIII. He lived as an *émigré* in England and joined up with Wellington's Peninsula army in 1814 as it crossed into France. He organized resistance to Napoleon in the south of France during the Hundred Days. He commanded the French army sent to Spain in 1823. He became heir

to the throne when his father became Charles X. He again went into exile during the 1830 Revolution, and later proclaimed himself Louis XIX.

8. C. K. Webster, editor, *British Diplomacy, 1813–1815. Select Documents Dealing with the Reconstruction of Europe* (London: G. Bell and Sons, Ltd., 1921), Castlereagh to Liverpool, August 12, 1815.

9. See Ward, *Wellington*, 100–3; Guedalla, *Wellington*, 295–312; and Aldington, *The Duke*, 242–52.

2

Establishment of the Army of Occupation

In July, 1815, the British Prime Minister, Lord Liverpool,[1] first suggested that the allies place an occupation force inside the now-defeated France. Liverpool deemed that the "magnanimous policy" introduced in 1814 had been a complete failure.[2] After re-evaluating their actions of the previous year and their generosity in the *Treaty of Paris* of May 30, 1814, the allies agreed with Liverpool's assessment. Since they had maintained that the war had been against Napoleon, not France, the 1814 treaty was non-punitive. From the start, the restored Bourbon throne gained a great advantage by the lack of extractions in 1814. Reparations were not allowed though Prussia desired some restitution for Napoleon's extractions. Britain was not repaid, as she was entitled, for support of French prisoners of war whom she had long maintained. The French were even allowed to keep the many art treasures they had taken during the prolonged war years. Liverpool stated that there would be "considerable disappointment" in Britain if France were left as she had been after the *Treaty of Paris*.[3]

The 1814 *Treaty of Paris* deprived France of her Rhine frontier but she was reduced only to her boundaries of 1792 which in effect were her ancient borders plus the significant additions of Avignon, Savoy, and several communes along the north and northeastern frontier. The terms of the treaty were lenient; the allies intended to avoid weakening the restored Bourbons or humiliating France so that Frenchmen could more easily accept the return of the Bourbons. Considering Napoleon's triumphant return from Elba, Liverpool's announcement that the policy of 1814 had been a failure can hardly be called inaccurate. In an abrupt change from the lenient policy of 1814, the British prime minister proposed that the allies primarily focus upon their own security rather than leaving it to the Bourbons. "The French nation is at the mercy of the allies, in consequence of a war occasioned by their violation of the most sacred treaties. The allies are fully entitled to indemnity and security."[4] Liverpool further suggested they should place an army of occupation in northern and eastern France. He advised that this force should remain in place until a suitable replacement could be found which could also maintain security requirements.[5]

> We feel that we have a right to retain such part of the king-
> dom as is necessary for the security of adjoining countries,
> until that security shall have been provided for in another
> manner, and the enemy has defrayed the expenses of it.[6]

Liverpool blamed the French nation for not answering the allied calls in the springtime to overthrow Bonaparte. Had they done so, the allies could have upheld the provisions of the 1814 *Treaty of Paris* and not sought permanent acquisitions from France. Instead, bloody battles were fought and Louis XVIII was restored only through force of arms. Liverpool claimed the allies were entitled to conquests for their own security. No French leader, including Louis, could guarantee allied security, which, in effect, necessitated a temporary military occupation by the allied armies.[7] British foreign secretary Viscount Castlereagh thought that the allies could enforce any proposed program onto France as long as their half million soldiers were present on French soil.[8]

Soon thereafter, the Duke of Wellington followed Liverpool's suggestions by presenting a detailed proposal which served as the basis upon which the ultimate allied decision was made. Wellington's proposal served as the framework for the design of the occupation army. Wellington based his plan upon his personal understanding of the situation. He contended that Napoleon was the source of most of Europe's problems. He asserted that upon Napoleon's return from Elba, the French had merely submitted to the emperor but never really backed him with the fervor of previous years. He argued that if the French had fully supported Napoleon's return from exile, the allies would never have been able to advance so deeply into France and enter Paris only two short weeks after Waterloo.

In July, 1815, Wellington recommended moderation, not revenge, from fear that any harsh demands placed upon France would compromise the allied objectives of quietly ending the French Revolution, controlling the fire of nationalism, insuring balance of power, and reducing military establishments. The duke approved the use of an occupation force to be located in critical points with all costs borne by the French government. Most important in the duke's mind was to give Louis XVIII the time and opportunity to strengthen his political position while building a loyal army. This plan would prevent recurrence of the internal situation which Napoleon had exploited in April. Also, the occupation would allow Frenchmen to adapt to peacetime conditions as rapidly as possible. Wellington planned to concentrate allied forces in northern France to control the French fortresses along the Franco-Netherlands border. This could be achieved, he thought, with an army of approximately 100 thousand men. He proposed that the occupation army remain until such time as the French paid whatever reparations that were demanded by the allies. Wellington's proposal became the foundation upon which the allied army was formed.[9]

It was the responsibility of the French government to make such counter proposals to the allies as it thought it would be able to enforce upon its populace. Once an agreement was reached, it was the French ministry's responsibility to convince the nation of its necessity and then secure the support of the chambers in carrying them out, while at the same time, gathering support for the crown. This rebuilding process occurred at the precise moment when the most discordant political elements in France were alive and active. The sword does not kill ideas; it kills people. Bonapartism and republicanism did not disappear after Waterloo. The ultra-royalists, consisting of *émigrés* and others who had remained and suffered humiliations under the republic and empire, wanted a restoration along the lines of the society of the Old Regime.

The task of restoring France's greatness and regaining her status among the European powers called for compromise, understanding, and diplomatic dexterity. The task went beyond the traits of even the wily French minister, Prince Talleyrand,[10] who had so well defended France's positions in 1814. Talleyrand, who seemed to have ties with every French faction, became abhorrent to the Russian czar, Alexander I, and Frederick William III of Prussia when he aligned France behind Britain and Austria over the Saxon question at the Congress of Vienna. Likewise, he was unacceptable to the *émigrés* and royalists who regarded him and his colleague Joseph Fouché[11] as too closely tied with republican and imperial interests. They simply refused to trust him. This unacceptability made it increasingly difficult for Talleyrand to retain the reins of the government.

Negotiations for the second *Treaty of Paris* began in early July, 1815. As the summer passed, the allied ministers moved closer to general agreement concerning the conditions of peace. On September 20, they delivered their views to the French government in the form of an ultimatum. The allied ultimatum listed six bases upon which future negotiations between the allies and France would proceed: 1. The *Treaty of Paris* of May 30, 1814 was confirmed, along with any of its provisions that might not be modified by any new agreement. 2. France would lose some additional territory: The Kingdom of the Netherlands would gain territory along its borders with France;

Savoy would totally be ceded to Sardinia; and the German frontier would be rectified. France would lose Philippeville, Marienbourg, Givet, Charlemont, and Sarrelouis in the north, and Landsau in the east along with a few adjoining cantons. 3. The fortifications of the Runingen were to be destroyed with the guarantee they would never be rebuilt. 4. A 800 million franc indemnity would be imposed to cover the costs of the late war. 5. Another 200 million francs would be collected from France to defray the costs of new fortifications that would be built in territories adjacent to the French frontier. 6. An allied army of 150 thousand men would occupy the northern and eastern departments of France for seven years with all costs paid for by France.[12]

On September 22, the French cabinet rejected the ultimatum as unreasonable and without precedent under international law. The government argued that France should not pay the cost of a usurper's acts. Louis XVIII, recognized by all as the legitimate sovereign, had opposed the return of Napoleon as much as any European monarch. The French cabinet questioned the requirement of territorial concessions from an ally. Napoleon had been branded an outlaw at Vienna on March 19, 1815, upon the recommendation of the French government. Outlaws had no protection under international law and Napoleon held no legitimate claim to the French throne. Under such circumstances, why should France be penalized and be required to make concessions of any sort.[13] Talleyrand's reply to the allies stated that although France should not be forced to make any territorial concessions beyond those in the *Treaty of Paris* of May 30, 1814, she was willing to negotiate.[14] France was willing to accept a provisional occupation for the purposes of maintaining order, but the duration, occupation areas, and size of the force should be the subject of further discussions. A seven-year occupation was completely unacceptable. Talleyrand acknowledged that Louis would consent to an indemnity, but noted that the king could not accept one which led to overtaxing the country's resources. If those resources were strained, it would make it difficult for the government to create the conditions for economic and political recovery.[15]

The allies responded to Talleyrand's objections: "It is evident that the necessity of guarantees for the future has become more perceptible and more urgent than it was at the time of the signing of the *Treaty of Paris*." The Hundred Days of Napoleon had forced additional sacrifices on the allies at a time when Europe thought itself at peace. This meant that France would have to offer "some further pledge of security," which should be in the shape of territorial concessions. The allies believed the extent of the concessions were "inconsiderable" and were not consistent with any type of conquest but "that the safety of the adjoining states was their sole and single aim in making these demands."[16] The allies justified their rationale in a second note which stated that the re-establishment of order and consolidation of royal authority in France should serve as the basis for negotiations between the French and allied plenipotentiaries. France would never enjoy a permanent peace if her neighbors harbored feelings of resentment and faced continual alarm. Therefore, they argued, France's attitude towards her neighbors should be one of just compensation for losses they had suffered defending themselves, and France should be willing to offer guarantees for their future safety. These principles were essential for a permanent peace.[17]

Opposition at home, combined with the allied unity on the issued ultimatum, meant the end of the Talleyrand-Fouché ministry. As a diplomat, Talleyrand had excelled when he could utilize divisions among his adversaries for French gains. Faced with an ultimatum flowing with allied unity and with rising criticism from the royalist deputies now arriving in Paris for the opening of the Chamber of Deputies, Talleyrand tendered his resignation on September 25. It was immediately accepted by the king.[18] The allies were glad to see him leave office.

The difficult job of resolving the impasse between the French government and the allies was offered to Armand-Emmanuel du Plessis, the Duke of Richelieu.[19] The choice of Richelieu as foreign minister and president of the council was especially agreeable to the Russian czar, for it offered an opportunity to extend Russian influence in the French government, something Alexander had long sought. Richelieu had held a close personal relationship with Alexander for twenty years, and the czar considered him "the only friend I have who will tell me the truth to my face." The Duke of Wellington also believed that in Richelieu Louis had made an excellent choice to lead the Restoration government: "His word is as good as a treaty."[20] Castlereagh wrote that Richelieu would be a "most valuable minister" in spite of his close ties with Russia.[21] With three of the most influential men in the allied coalition behind him, Richelieu, as president of the council, formed a ministry which enjoyed the support both of his own monarch and the European powers. In addition, he was acceptable to the ultra-royalist deputies who mistakenly believed he would assume the leadership of their cause. Certainly Talleyrand could never have expected such support. Even with this backing, Richelieu doubted his ability to carry out the task.

As early as July, 1815, Louis XVIII had named Richelieu to be Minister of the King's Household. Richelieu had declined the post then because he considered himself unqualified. He wrote to Talleyrand that he had been away from France for too long and was "ignorant of the manner in which [government] affairs are conducted." Absent from France for twenty-five years, he sensed that he was incapable of serving in a ministerial post and rejected Talleyrand's efforts to change his mind.[22]

In September, when Talleyrand resigned, the king named Richelieu as president of the council and assigned him the additional portfolio of foreign affairs. Once again Richelieu refused his appointment on the basis of his long absence from France and his unfamiliarity with persons and events. Talleyrand mockingly added that Richelieu was an excellent choice for the post since he was "The one man in France who knows most about the Crimea."[23]

All data confirms that Richelieu believed himself unqualified for the task offered him, but he was loyal to his country and was prepared to strive to achieve whatever was best for France. Czar Alexander I directly intervened to persuade the duke to accept. He insisted Richelieu take the presidency of the council for only under that circumstance would Russia become the friend of France and help mitigate the demands of the allied ultimatum. He released Richelieu from his commitments to Russia so he could serve France and Louis XVIII, and asked him to "Be the tie of sincere cooperation between our two countries. This I require in the name of the salvation of France."[24] After such pressure, the duke hesitated no longer and placed himself at his monarch's disposal. The king's choice turned out to be an excellent one indeed.

Knowing that Richelieu was not sufficiently acquainted with the capable men needed to form a ministry, Louis exercised his rights under the French Charter and appointed all the ministers. The ministry represented all political factions. As a concession to the right, Dubouchage[25] was made minister of the navy and the Count of Vaublanc[26] received the portfolio of the interior. The Genoese Louis-Emmanuel Corvetto[27] was given finance. He was considered a good technician and had served the empire. Count de Barbe-Marbois,[28] also an imperial official, was made the minister of justice. The Duke of Feltre,[29] a former Napoleonic official, was named minister of war; he had strong connections with the king's brother, the Count of Artois, and his royalist friends. The Duke Decazes[30] was named minister of police.

The Duke of Richelieu began his ministry in the shadow of the allied ultimatum. He faced completing negotiations on a peace treaty not only which was unfavorable for France but also which had been virtually written. He had to work under the pressure of the newly assembled Chamber of Deputies which was royalist in its views and to keep close watch as to whether the new ministry would be effective in its discussions with the allies. Richelieu gave primary and immediate attention to the treaty since much of France was under allied military occupation with all its daily exigencies and problems. In resolving his problems, he could count on his friendship with the czar and upon the fairness of Castlereagh. He was disadvantaged in his task by the Talleyrand ministry's admission in principle of a number of points contained in the allied ultimatum of September 20. For example, Talleyrand acknowledged that Louis XVIII would consent to negotiate cessions of territory, some type of indemnity, and some form of occupation. Richelieu's task was thus reduced to moderating the extent of the allied demands, such as limiting the duration of the occupation and the size of the indemnity. The duke echoed Talleyrand's argument against any territorial losses. The allied demands were not sanctioned by international law since Louis XVIII had been an ally in the fight against Napoleon.

Negotiations moved swiftly during the last week of September, and on October 2 a protocol was signed which contained substantively the major provisions of the final treaty which was signed on November 20.[31] Richelieu obtained considerable success in moderating the allied demands. The duke enjoyed the support of Castlereagh, Czar Alexander, and Wellington in working for the Bourbon cause. Basing the arguments upon the thesis that the only way to insure the Bourbons was by guaranteeing the integrity of France,[32] their joint efforts were successful in setting aside Prussian demands for dismemberment of France's eastern provinces of Alsace and Lorraine, and the northern province of Flanders. Richelieu was also able to obtain the restoration of some communes demanded in the ultimatum of September 20.[33]

Richelieu conducted the negotiations on the basis of maintaining friendly relations between allies. He offered in response to each point contained in the allied demands a counter proposal less than that of the ultimatum. Instead of 800 million francs indemnity, Richelieu offered 600. Agreement was reached on 700.[34] In place of seven years of occupation, Richelieu offered five. The final agreement of November placed the maximum number of years occupation at five with a minimum possibility of three. The final treaty contained an article allowing for the possibility of a partial evacuation after the first year.[35] Richelieu stated that France would not endure the humiliation of loss of land, and declared that "Rectification of the frontier [as called for in the allied note] is but a word politely disguising the word conquest."[36] He fought every step of the way against any loss of territory. The allies abandoned their claims to the fort of Ecluse, of Joux, and of Charlemont. Richelieu continued discussions to try and recover Givet and Condé, but he was unable to get the allies to yield more.[37] These provisions appeared in the protocol of October

2. The details were worked out in the form of four conventions which were attached to the protocol and made up the final act of November 20.

The allied powers continued their occupation of Paris and northern France while negotiations proceeded on the treaty and related conventions. The second *Treaty of Paris*, signed on November 20, 1815,[38] should be considered an integral part of the overall peace-making process of 1814–1815, though it stands outside of the final act of the Congress of Vienna. Article V of the definitive treaty between the allies and France clearly stated the two basic intentions of the victorious powers, the establishment of an equilibrium among themselves, and the prevention of further French aggression. In addition, that same day the allies renewed their alliance against the possibility of future French aggression.[39] A major step towards the achievement of these objectives was the allied decision to create a multinational military force and to station it along France's northern and northeastern frontiers. The military convention appended to the second *Treaty of Paris* announced that the allied sovereigns reserved for themselves the naming of the commander of an army corps consisting of 150 thousand men.[40]

The peace treaty placed the financial obligations for maintaining the corps squarely upon the French government. The French were made responsible for providing lodging and provisions for the allied troops and forage for horses. On a daily basis, 200 thousand rations were to be provided to assure that sufficient food was available for the army. France was required to provide sufficient forage for fifty thousand horses per day. In addition, France had to remunerate fifty million francs annually to pay, equip, and clothe allied troops. This sum was to be paid quarterly. These direct costs burdened France for the entire occupation, and would lead Richelieu to seek continually methods to reduce the payments. Moreover, these provisions do not include the various other burdens placed upon the populations of the occupied departments.[41]

The allies restricted the size of the zone of occupation by limiting it to the northeast quadrant of France, that is, to her borders with the Kingdom of the Netherlands and the German Confederation. Viscount Castlereagh, after considering the size of the army, pronounced it capable of supporting the French king from this position, and stated that the army "would dwindle to nothing if spread over the interior of France."[42] Military forces were to be deployed from Calais to the Swiss border. In order to obviate incidents between the occupying forces and the French army, the military convention to the peace treaty created a demilitarized zone between the departments occupied and the areas permitted for use by the French army.[43] By reducing the possibilities of confrontation between the troops of the occupiers and the occupied, the treaty designers planned to prevent situations from occurring which might embarrass the allied forces. No army command can long endure the embarrassment and humiliation such as the French suffered when the Imperial Guard broke and disintegrated at Waterloo. French army units might wish to annoy allied forces in some way to restore the honor lost at Waterloo.

By the treaty, Louis XVIII actually sanctioned the occupation of his own country until an army loyal to him was rebuilt. Success depended upon keeping the French and allied armies separated. The demilitarized zone which was created ran parallel to the zones occupied by the allies from the English Channel to Switzerland. The zone ran southeast from the Department of the Somme through the cities of Amiens, Reims, and Nancy. It turned south at the city of Sarrebourg into the Departments of the Vôsges and Upper Saône. The French army was given the authority to establish twenty-four small garrisons within the allied occupied sector in major urban centers. The French garrisons varied in size from one hundred to three thousand men and were located in such cities as Calais, Boulogne, Metz, and Strasbourg.[44] Though small, this concession to the French army proved dangerous as the placement of these garrisons posed potential problems for allied troops operating in these areas. For the most part, however, the creation of a demilitarized zone proved an effective deterrent for problems between allied and French soldiers.

It was not the intention of the allies to allow use of the army of occupation by French authorities for policing internal problems, nor was the occupying army to perform civil administrative duties.[45] It was also agreed that the army would not interfere with the authority of the French monarch. The treaty duly noted that Louis XVIII would gain the confidence of his subjects only through a wise and conciliatory leadership. Without restoration of this confidence it would be difficult for the allies to depart. As stated, the treaty of November 20 stipulated that the allies could remain for a period of five years. The allies also agreed that they would review the entire situation after three years, including reparations and internal events, and then determine the fate of the army.[46]

The allied powers, in a note to the Duke of Richelieu naming Wellington as commander-in-chief of the occupation army, noted that, "The Allied sovereigns trust the known prudence and discretion of the Duke of Wellington in full confidence he will not act without previously notifying the French king," and expressed confidence that Wellington would be guided by motives leading to the safety and welfare of French citizens. The powers promised to maintain contact with Wellington through the Council of Ambassadors in Paris, and to use him as a conduit between their governments and the French.[47] The allies recognized, in light of the return of Napoleon from Elba, that the revolutionary spirit of the French people was not dead and might reappear suddenly at any time. Since their need to react quickly was imperative, the allies left the power of decision concerning the deployment of the army entirely to Wellington.[48]

The allied army created by the treaty consisted of thirty thousand men from each of the four powers: Great Britain, Austria, Prussia, and Russia. Each ally maintained a blend of military power by including infantry, cavalry, and artillery units in their contingents. To provide rapid mobility for the army, each power contributed cavalry units numbering between three and five thousand men. This mobile force would allow Wellington flexibility with his rather small army.[49]

The allies involved the smaller states of Europe in the army of occupation by allocating a combined total of thirty thousand men to five countries. Bavaria, the largest German state other than Prussia, provided ten thousand men for Wellington, while Denmark, Saxony, Hanover, and Würtemberg each contributed five thousand soldiers to the peacekeeping effort. This action made the peace a European responsibility, not one limited to the major powers.

The allies gave Wellington broad discretionary authority to employ his forces consistent with the objectives of the occupation. This was a unique advance in the annals of military command, for the allies, in their battles against Napoleon, had never fully integrated their forces.[50] In the occupation, each country maintained administrative control and discipline over its own troops, but its commanders were placed under the orders of Wellington. Corps commanders reported to Wellington and obeyed his decisions on troop dispositions. The duke served as the point of contact between his army and the French authorities. By integrating allied forces, Wellington had command of all units should he need to employ the occupation army.

The second *Treaty of Paris* stated that, with the exception of the forces selected to remain with the allied command, all other foreign troops were required to depart France within twenty-one days of the treaty's ratification. Wellington was entrusted with this responsibility, and he arranged for the transfer of all troops out of the capital and into their cantonments. The movement of forces was accomplished by the end of January, 1816, and history's first joint multinational peacekeeping army commenced operations.[51]

The allied contingents assigned to the occupation moved eastward to their sectors along the French frontier. Wellington placed the Austrian troops, under the command of Baron Frimont,[52] in the farthest eastern point of the occupation with their headquarters at Colmar. The duke placed the Prussians, commanded by Count Zeiten,[53] in the vicinity of the city of Sedan. Baron Woronzoff[54] and the Russian forces were headquartered at Maubeuge. Cambrai served as both Wellington's and the British contingent's headquarters.[55] Wellington interspersed the smaller allied commands throughout the occupation zone. The Danish forces were placed at Bouchain, the Saxons at Tourcoing, and the Würtemburgers were located in Weissembourg. Wellington ordered the Hanoverians to Condé, while the ten thousand Bavarians were assigned to Pont-à-Mousson.[56]

When faced with the treaty and its military conventions, Richelieu became distraught at having failed to obtain more significant concessions from the allies. At first he refused to sign the treaty and threatened to resign. Louis XVIII met with him personally and implored him not to leave office; the king asked him to make a personal sacrifice and to sign the treaty.[57] Faced with a direct plea from his sovereign, the minister complied. It remained only for the duke to convey the treaty to the French chambers.

Richelieu had to present to his countrymen the rather unpleasant provisions of the treaty, such as the occupation, and the sacrifices they would now have to make without giving them a false idea of the situation which might cause a loss in confidence of the king and the ministry. The duke went before the chambers and reminded the deputies that France, with her invading armies, had created the mood of revenge that existed in the allies. The return of Napoleon had succeeded in striking fear into the heart of Europe. While Richelieu agreed that the obligations placed upon France were difficult and that the allies viewed her with mistrust, he reminded the chambers that France had violated "promises, good faith, and loyalty" during the previous twenty-five years of war. It was Napoleon's actions that caused the suffering Frenchmen were now enduring. Unfortunately for France, her enemies held the power "to impose their wills upon us." The allies held France answerable for Napoleon's deeds. He ended his speech, saying:

> In spite of the evil that the usurper has done to all nations,
> let us give reason to them to now grieve those wrongs that
> they now do to us. Let us give these nations and their
> peoples reason to rely upon us, to know us better, so that
> they will reconcile themselves freely and forever with us.[58]

Richelieu's words were met with silence, but the two chambers returned to their own halls where they approved the arrangements.[59] Richelieu believed that he had brought disgrace upon the honor of France with the treaty; from that moment, he dedicated himself and his government to freeing France from the treaty's provisions and to restoring her to her former dignity among the European powers.[60]

Louis XVIII also spoke to the French Chamber of Deputies concerning the convention, which had been signed while under an occupation enforced by allied arms. He stated, "You well know, Gentlemen, and all France will know, the profound grief I must have felt, but the very safety of my kingdom rendered this great determination necessary." The monarch offered to contribute part of his salary, along with that of his family and servants, to share the sacrifice of his nation.[61] The king drew attention to the fact that:

> The allied sovereigns promise to His Most Christian Majesty
> to support him with their arms against every revolutionary
> convulsion which might tend to overthrow by force the order
> of things at present established and to menace also again
> the general tranquillity of Europe.[62]

Napoleon's return to France had been brief but expensive. She lost important fortresses along her borders and some sixty thousand men on the field of battle. Her army was disbanded; she was occupied by foreign troops. France was called upon to pay about 1.5 billion francs in indemnities and occupation costs. As a final humiliation, she was to remain under the political surveillance of the Allied Council of Ambassadors throughout the occupation. Politically, internal France was divided into two camps, the royalists of various degrees, and the factions of the left, that is, republicans, Bonapartists, and supporters of the revolution.[63] France was to pay this debt for years.

OCCUPIED FRANCE 1816–1818
(Major Power Locations)

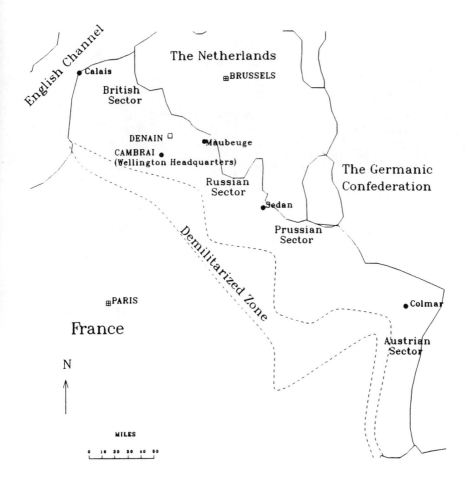

English Channel

The Netherlands

⊞BRUSSELS

• Calais

British
Sector

DENAIN ▢

CAMBRAI •
(Wellington Headquarters)

• Maubeuge

Russian
Sector

The Germanic
Confederation

• Sedan

Prussian
Sector

Demilitarized Zone

⊞PARIS

France

• Colmar

Austrian
Sector

N

↑

MILES

0 10 20 30 40 50

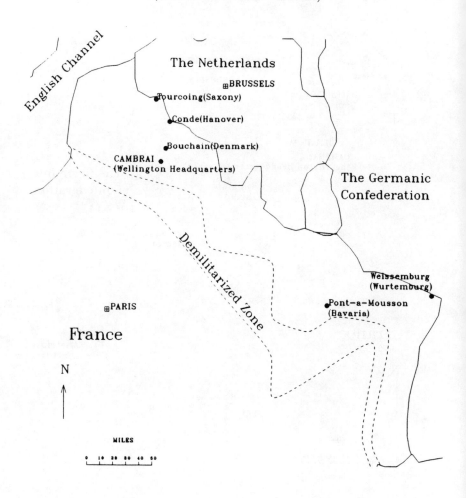

OCCUPIED FRANCE 1816–1818
(Minor Power Locations)

English Channel

The Netherlands

⊞BRUSSELS

Tourcoing(Saxony)

Conde(Hanover)

Bouchain(Denmark)

CAMBRAI
(Wellington Headquarters)

The Germanic
Confederation

Demilitarized Zone

Weissemburg
(Wurtemburg)

Pont–a–Mousson
(Bavaria)

⊞PARIS

France

N

MILES

0 10 20 30 40 50

NOTES

1. Robert Banks Jenkinson (1770–1828), second Earl of Liverpool, prime minister 1812–1822. He was a staunch ally of Wellington, and as secretary for war he had greatly expanded the size of the British army, including Wellington's Peninsular army.

2. Liverpool to Castlereagh, July 15, 1815, Wellington Papers 1/473, University of Southampton, Southampton, United Kingdom.

3. Charles William Vane, editor, *Correspondence, Despatches, and other Papers of Viscount Castlereagh, Second Marquess of Londonderry*, 12 volumes (London: William Shoberl, 1852), 10:423, Liverpool to Castlereagh, July 10, 1815 [hereafter *Correspondence of Castlereagh*].

4. Ibid., 10:432–33, Liverpool to Castlereagh, July 15, 1815.

5. Ibid. The Dutch barrier system would be the suitable replacement. See chapter 7.

6. Ibid., 10:432–33, Liverpool to Castlereagh, July 15, 1815.

7. Ibid., 10:454–55, Liverpool to Castlereagh, August 3, 1815.

8. Castlereagh to Bathurst, July 14, 1815, Papers of Lord Liverpool, Add MSS 37573, British Library, London, United Kingdom. Robert Stewart (1760–1822), Viscount Castlereagh, later Marquess of Londonderry, first entered Parliament in 1794. In 1805 was named to the war and colonial offices and helped plan Wellington's Peninsula expedition. He served as foreign minister from 1812 to 1822 under Liverpool. He was the senior British official at the Congress of Vienna. Castlereagh committed suicide in 1822.

9. Wellington to Castlereagh, August 11, 1815, Wellington Papers 1/478, contains the duke's proposal.

10. Charles Maurice de Talleyrand-Perigord (1754–1838) served many positions in various French governments but is best known as minister for foreign affairs under Bonaparte. He supported the first abdication of Napoleon, acted as head of the provisional government in 1814, and was France's representative at the Congress of Vienna, where he gained several concessions for Louis XVIII. After resigning his office in 1815, he spent fifteen years in retirement before returning to active political life. Along with Lafayette, he urged Louis-Philippe to accept the position of king of the French after the revolution of 1830. He accepted the ambassadorship to Britain under Louis-Philippe and became a close advisor to the king.

11. Joseph Fouché (1759–1820), Duke of Otranto and imperial minister of police, played an important role in the Hundred Days and the Second Restoration. As a member of the National Convention in 1792, he voted to execute Louis XVI. He became Minister of Police

under the Directory and kept that job under Napoleon until 1810 when he was dismissed for conducting secret talks with the British. He was refused a post with the First Restoration as a regicide, but he stayed in Paris upon Napoleon's return from Elba and was chosen to head the police again, though privately he did not believe that the emperor could hold his throne. After the debacle at Waterloo, Fouché worked to ensure the return of Louis XVIII in hopes of a high position. He directed the French Chambers into permanent session and a call for abdication by Napoleon. He also helped to create a provisional government with himself as head. He convinced Napoleon to leave France, and he negotiated with Wellington the retirement of the French Army to the Loire River. By maintaining a wide diversity of contacts with the allies, Fouché was able to remain as the head of the police for the moment. With the election of the *chambre introuvable*, Fouché was ousted and named minister to Dresden, a post he held until dumped by the Amnesty Law of January, 1816, which exiled the regicides who served under the Hundred Days.

12. Talleyrand, *Mémoires du Prince de Talleyrand*, 5 volumes (Paris: Calmann Levy, 1891), 3:270, reproduces the text of this ultimatum.

13. Ibid., 3:288–90.

14. G. Lacour-Gayet, *Talleyrand*, 3 volumes (Paris: Payot, 1931), 3:38–44. Talleyrand did insist that France not be force to cede any pre-revolutionary lands.

15. Talleyrand, *Mémoires*, 3:272–74.

16. Ibid., 3:494–95 reproduces the text of the allied note.

17. Ibid.

18. Lacour-Gayet, *Talleyrand*, 3:44; Louis de Viel-Castel, *Histoire de la Restauration*, 20 volumes (Paris: Michel Lévy, 1860–1878), 4:76–77. In his *Mémoires*, Talleyrand said he resigned so he would not have to sign a treaty so adverse to France (3:495), but Lacour-Gayet disputes this by emphasizing the opposition from the ultra-royalists and the Russian czar.

19. Armand-Emmanuel du Plessis, Count of Chinon, Duke of Richelieu (1766–1822) was first Lord of the Chamber under Louis XVI, emigrated 1789, served the Russian czar as governor-general in the Crimea. He was named a Peer of France in 1814 by Louis XVIII, and he became president of the council and minister of foreign affairs in September, 1815. He resigned his offices almost immediately after the conference at Aix-la-Chapelle and the allied withdrawal from France. After the assassination of the Duke of Berri in 1821, he returned to office, resigning in 1821.

20. Guillaume de Bertier de Sauvigny, *The Bourbon Restoration*, translated by Lynn M. Case (Philadelphia: The University of

Pennsylvania Press, 1966), 125.

21. Vane, *Correspondence of Castlereagh*, Castlereagh to Liverpool, 11:31–32, September 25, 1815. *The Morning Chronicle* called Richelieu "decidedly Russian" and considered his selection a demonstration of the czar's power over the other allied sovereigns. *The Morning Chronicle*, September 28, 1815.

22. Talleyrand, *Mémoires*, 3:240–41.

23. Bertier de Sauvigny, *Bourbon Restoration*, 125.

24. Louis Victor Léon Rouchechouart, *Memoirs of the Count of Rouchechouart*, translated by Frances Jackson (New York: E.P. Dutton and Company, 1920), 413; Marquis de Noailles, *Le Comte Molé, Sa Vie Ses Mémoires*, 4 volumes (Librairie Ancienne Adouard Champion, 1923), 3:131. The Count of Molé quoting Richelieu confirms the czar's insistence. In his letter of resignation in 1818, Richelieu reminded the king that he had accepted the ministry upon the insistence of Alexander, cited in Viel-Castel, *Histoire de la Restauration*, 4:95–97.

25. Francois-Joseph Dubouchage (1749–1821), an ultra-royalist, had a long career with the navy and became minister of the navy in 1792. He emigrated after the death of Louis XVI but returned under the Directory. He refused to serve Napoleon. He became minister of the navy again under Richelieu. Dubouchage opposed Decazes' electoral reforms and was removed from his post June 22, 1817.

26. Vincent-Marie Vienot, Count of Vaublanc (1756–1845), an ultra-royalist, was elected to the Legislative Assembly in 1791 and quickly was voted its president. He was forced into hiding during the "Reign of Terror" and was sentenced to death in absentia. He fled the country and returned under Napoleon. He served as prefect of Moselle and rallied to the Bourbons in 1814. Vaublanc fled to Ghent during the Hundred Days. He was given the ministry of the interior under Richelieu and was loyal to the king's brother, Artois. Vaublanc reorganized the National Guard under Artois' leadership. He resigned May 8, 1816, after Richelieu demanded the king fire him. He later served for many years in the Chamber of Deputies. His political career ended with the 1830 revolution.

27. Louis-Emmanuel Corvetto (1756–1821), Count, of Italian origin was named President of the Executive Directory of the Ligurian Republic when it was created by Napoleon. He served as counselor of state under the empire. Served as Richelieu's finance minister from 1815 to 1818.

28. Count Francois de Barbe-Marbois (1745–1837) was deported for his royalist sympathies in 1797 but returned under Napoleon, serving as a senator and president of the *Cour de Comptes*. He helped author Napoleon's first abdication and was on the commis-

sion that drafted the *Charte*. Under the Second Restoration he was named Keeper of the Seals and Minister of Justice. Barbe-Marbois was dropped from the ministry in May, 1816 and returned to serve on the *Cour des Comptes* until 1834.

29. Marshal Henri Jacques Guillaume Clarke, the Duke of Feltre (1765–1818) first served Napoleon during the Italian campaign of 1796. He held several diplomatic posts under the empire, and served as minister of war from 1807 to 1814; named duke in 1809. He joined with the Bourbons and remained loyal during the Hundred Days. He held the war ministry under the Second Restoration until 1817. He earned the title "Ink Marshal" because his only battlefield was at a ministerial desk.

30. Elie Decazes (1780–1860), duke, served under the empire but refused to rejoin Napoleon for the Hundred Days. When Louis returned under the Second Restoration, Decazes became prefect of the Parisian police which led to his appointment replacing Joseph Fouché as minister of police. Decazes became the special favorite of the king. The monarch, who wrote Decazes daily, referred to him as *mon fils*—"my son." Decazes continually fought the ultra-right by siding with the liberals. He later became president of the council but fell from power when the Duke of Berri was assassinated. He remained in the Chamber of Peers as as member of the center left, and rallied to Louis-Philippe in 1830.

31. Jacques Cretineau-Joly, *Histoire des Traités de 1815* (Paris: Colomb de Batines, 1842), 195; Etienne Denis Pasquier, *Mémoires du Chancelier Pasquier*, 4 volumes (Plon, Nourrit et Cie, 1896), 4:3.

32. Viel-Castel, *Histoire de la Restauration*, 4:55–56.

33. Alphonse Marie de Lamartine, *Histoire de la Restauration*, 8 volumes (Paris: Fagnerre, Lecou, Fourne et Cie, 1852), 3:231; Pierre Rain, *L'Europe et la Restauration des Bourbons, 1814–1818* (Paris: Perrin et Cie, 1908), 204; Viel-Castel, *Histoire de la Restauration*, 4:36.

34. See Article IV of the *Treaty of Paris* of November 20, 1815. The allies charged no interest on the indemnity. Of the 700 million francs, Russia and the United Kingdom were to receive 130 million francs each, Prussia and Austria 110 million each, Bavaria fifty-five million, Baden thirty-five million, and other states would receive 130 million francs. Rouchechouart, *Memoirs*, 314–15.

35. Eugene Francois Auguste d'Armand Vitrolles, *Mémoires et relations politiques*, edited by Eugene Forques, 3 volumes (Paris: G. Charpentier et Cie, 1884), 3:242–43. The peace treaty of November 20 and its military convention covered evacuation procedures.

36. Pierre de la Gorce, *Louis XVIII* (Paris: Librairie Plon, 1926), 26.

37. Louis Madelin, *Deux Relèvements Français, 1815–1818, 1871–1878* (Paris: Flammarion, 1951), 60; Pasquier, *Mémoires*, 4:3.

38. *Archives Parlementaires de 1787 à 1860, Deuxième Série 1800 à 1860*, 95 volumes (Paris: Librairie Administrative De Paul DuPont, 1869), November 25, 1815, 15:308–10 [hereafter *Archives Parlementaires*]; United Kingdom, Foreign Office, *British and Foreign State Papers* (London: James Ridgway, 1841–1977), compiled by Sir Edward Hertslet, 3:280–92 [hereafter *BFSP*].

39. By the *Treaty of Alliance and Friendship between Great Britain, Austria, Prussia, and Russia* [the Quadruple Alliance], of November 20, 1815, the allied powers renewed the *Treaty of Chaumont* of March 1, 1814 and the Vienna alliance of March 25, 1815. They agreed to use force to insure Europe's tranquillity. The powers promised to place sixty thousand men in the field immediately in addition to the forces assigned to the occupation army, and they promised to take whatever measures were necessary to protect themselves and bring peace to Europe. *BFSP*, 3:273–80.

40. "Convention concluded in conformity to Article V of the Principal Treaty relative to the Occupation of a Military Line in France by an Allied Army," *Archives Parlementaires*, November 25, 1815, 15:313–14; *BFSP*, 3:298–305.

41. "Tariff Annex to the Convention relative to the Occupation of a Military Line in France by an Allied Army," *Archives Parlementaires*, 15:314–15.

42. Vane, *Correspondence of Castlereagh*, 11:16, Castlereagh to Liverpool, September 14, 1815.

43. Article IV of the Military Convention, *Archives Parlementaires*, November 25, 1815, 15:313; *BFSP*, 3:300–01. See appendix B for the Military Convention.

44. *The Times* (London), November 25, 1815. See Article IV of the Military Convention (appendix B) for the towns that France could garrison.

45. Vane, *Correspondence of Castlereagh*, 11:16, Castlereagh to Liverpool, September 14, 1815. Castlereagh claimed that the allied army was in place to support Louis XVIII, but if another "convulsion" took place, the army would not help him.

46. *Treaty of Paris* of November 20, 1815, *Archives Parlementaires*, 15:308–10; Allied note to Richelieu, November 20, 1815, giving notice of Wellington's authority, *Examiner*, November 26, 1815; Eugene François Auguste d'Armand Vitrolles, *Mémoires et Relations Politiques*, 3 volumes (Paris: G. Charpentier et Cie, 1884), 3:242–43.

47. Allied note to Richelieu, November 20, 1815, giving notice of Wellington's authority, *Examiner*, November 26, 1815. The ambassadors serving on the council included Charles Stuart for Great

Britain, Baron de Vincent for Austria, Count de Goltz for Prussia, and Pozzo di Borgo representing Russia.

48. Lieutenant-Colonel John Gurwood, editor, *The General Orders of Field Marshal the Duke of Wellington in the Campaigns of 1809 to 1818* (London: W. Clowes and Sons, 1837), November 20, 1815, allied ministers to Richelieu.

49. Walter Alison Phillips, *The Confederation of Europe: A Study of the European Alliance, 1813–1823* (New York: Howard Fertig, 1966), 633.

50. Napoleon gained great advantage during the fighting in northeastern France in the spring of 1814 due to the lack of a unified allied command. He repeatedly attacked separate forces in hopes of inflicting a defeat on some nation that would cause them to drop out of the allied coalition. Napoleon also came dangerously close to victory in 1815 in his attempt to split Wellington and Blücher at Quatre-Bras and Ligny two days prior to Waterloo. Blücher, however, marched to the sound of the guns and helped carry the field of battle for the allies at Waterloo.

51. Wellington to Bathurst, January 22, 1816, War Office Report 1/209/11, Public Record Office, Kew, United Kingdom.

52. General Johann, Count of Frimont (1759–1831) served as a corps commander against Napoleon in 1813 and 1814. After service with the army of occupation, Frimont commanded Austrian forces in the 1820's suppressing revolts in Italy.

53. Field Marshal Hans Ernst Karl, Graf von Zeiten (1770–1848) commanded a brigade against Napoleon in 1813 and 1814 and distinguished himself at the Battle of Nations at Leipzig. He commanded a Prussian Corps at Waterloo before commanding his nation's forces during the occupation. He made field marshal in 1835.

54. General Michael Woronzoff (1782–1856), soldier and diplomat, fought against the French from 1812 to 1814. He attended the conference at Aix-la-Chapelle as a minister for the czar. He later built the formidable Russian defenses around the city of Sebastopol.

55. See maps of occupied France, pages 23–24.

56. WO 37/12/94, George Scovell Papers, State of the Allied Army, June–July, 1816. See appendix E for a list of allied commanders.

57. Lamartine, *Histoire de la Restauration*, 3:231–32.

58. Speech cited in *The Morning Chronicle*, November 29, 1815; Also by J. Fouques-DuParc, *Le Troisième Richelieu* (Lyon: H. Lardanchet, 1952), 215–16; and by Viel-Castel, *Histoire de la Restauration*, 4:237.

59. Fouques-DuParc, *Le Troisième Richelieu*, 123; Viel-Castel, *Histoire de la Restauration*, 4:237.

60. In contrast to Richelieu's personal feelings, *Cobbett's Register* welcomed Castlereagh home and congratulated him for his work. *Cobbett's* also noted the just treaty, stating, "Justice demanded that punishment should be inflicted on the guilty nation; but even in punishment we remembered mercy." *Cobbett's Weekly Political Register*, November 4, 1815.

61. Speech of His Most Christian Majesty, October 7, 1815, cited in *Archives Parlementaires*, 15:36–37; and in *Cobbett's Weekly Political Register*, October 14, 1815.

62. *The Examiner*, November 26, 1815.

63. Lamartine, *Histoire de la Restauration*, 3:233.

3

The British Army in France:

Order of Battle and Training

The British Army Order of Battle

With the decision to occupy France made, the Duke of Wellington began preparations for deployment of the British army in France. When he formed the British contingent for duty with the army of occupation, Wellington wanted his old Spanish peninsula veterans included in the command. He stated: "My opinion is that the best troops we have, probably the best in the world, are the British infantry, particularly the old infantry that has served in Spain. This is what we ought to keep up; and what I wish above all others to retain."[1] The duke believed that his old army "could go anywhere and do anything."[2] These are also the same troops that Wellington had once called the "scum of the earth" when they went on a looting rampage after the Battle of Vitoria.[3] The British war office honored the field marshal's request for his old veterans. London assigned twenty-one infantry battalions that had seen combat in the Iberian campaign to the contingent in France, which contained a total of twenty-five. Of the six cavalry squadrons assigned to occupation duty, five had seen action in Spain.[4] In addition, Wellington knew all his major subordinate commanders well and had seen combat with them. All of the British division and brigade commanders assigned to occupation duty had fought in Spain under the duke. Thus Wellington knew on which of his subordinates he could rely.

Wellington organized his British forces into a cavalry corps and an infantry corps, again similar to the army organization used in Spain.[5] The duke placed his field headquarters in the city of Cambrai, while maintaining a command headquarters in Paris. The British contingent took up deployments in many cities and villages in its assigned sector in the departments of Pas-de-Calais and the Nord.[6] The army placed its largest troop concentrations in Cambrai and

Valenciennes, but also assigned small units, down to platoon size, in many small villages throughout the British zone, due to the urgent need for shelter, for strategic military reasons, and to render visible the allied occupation army to the French citizenry.

The British cavalry corps, commanded by Lord Combermere,[7] consisted of three brigades of two squadrons each.[8] The first brigade, under the command of Lord Somerset,[9] consisted of the 2^d Dragoon Guards and the 3^d Dragoons. Sir Richard Hussay Vivian[10] commanded the second brigade with the 12th Light Dragoons and the 18th Hussars. General Colquhoun Grant[11] led the third brigade with its two squadrons, the 7th Hussars and the 11th Light Dragoons. Wellington assigned one troop of the Royal Horse Artillery to each cavalry brigade.[12]

Lord Rowland Hill[13] commanded Wellington's infantry corps, consisting of three divisions of three brigades each. Wellington augmented each division with one brigade of Royal Horse Artillery, and another artillery brigade was assigned as overall reserve to the infantry corps.[14] Seven brigades of infantry were organized with three battalions of foot infantry, the remaining two with two battalions, which gave the British contingent a total of twenty-five combat infantry battalions available.

The British army command assigned the first infantry division to Sir Lowry Cole[15] and located it at Wellington's headquarters at Cambrai. The 1st Brigade under Sir Peregrine Maitland[16] consisted of two battalions of the king's the Household Troops, which were the 3^d Battalion, Grenadier Guards, and the 2^d Battalion, Coldstream Guards. The 7th Brigade, under the command of Sir James Kempt,[17] controlled the 1st Battalion, 7th Regiment of Foot, the 1st Battalion, 23^d Regiment of Foot, and the 1st Battalion, 43^d Regiment of Foot. The 8th Brigade, under Sir John Lambert,[18] commanded the 1st Battalion, 27th Regiment of Foot, the 1st Battalion, 40th Regiment of Foot, and the 1st Battalion, the Rifle Brigade.[19]

The British army headquartered the second division at St. Pol, Sir Henry Clinton[20] commanding. The 3^d Brigade, under Sir Robert O'Callaghan,[21] administered the 1st Battalion, 3^d Regiment of Foot, the 1st Battalion, 39th Regiment of Foot, and the 1st Battalion, 91st Regiment of Foot. Sir Denis Pack [22] commanded the 4th Brigade which was comprised of the 1st Battalion, 4th Regiment of Foot, the 1st Battalion, 52^d Regiment of Foot and the 1st Battalion, 79th Regiment of Foot. The 6th Brigade, under Sir Thomas Bradford, [23] embodied the 1st Battalion, 6th Regiment of Foot, the 1st Battalion, 29th Regiment of Foot and the 1st Battalion, 71st Regiment of Foot.[24]

Sir Charles Colville[25] commanded the third infantry division which was headquartered in Valenciennes, the city with the second largest concentration of British soldiers. Sir Manley Power[26] commanded the 2[d] Brigade which included the 3[d] Battalion, the Royal Scots, the 1st Battalion, 57th Regiment of Foot, and the 2[d] Battalion, the Rifle Brigade. The 1st Battalion, 5th Regiment of Foot, the 1st Battalion, 9th Regiment of Foot, and the 1st Battalion, 21st Regiment of Foot comprised the fifth brigade of Sir Thomas Brisbane.[27] The ninth brigade, commanded by John Keane,[28] consisted of two battalions, the 1st Battalion, 81st Regiment of Foot, and the 1st Battalion, 88th Regiment of Foot.[29]

The British Army Training Program

Thus organized and into its cantonments by early 1816, the British army settled into the drudgery of occupation duty. Any peacetime army trains its soldiers in order to prepare for war. A successful training program relates directly to how well units perform in wartime. Habits developed by soldiers in training are used when units enter combat. If the Duke of Wellington were to encounter a situation requiring him to order the army of occupation into military action inside France, he could plan the employment of his command on the basis of its training programs. Within his multinational command, Wellington had to insure that all units of the army remained ready for deployment. One poorly trained contingent could ruin the reputation of the army with a single irresponsible act; likewise it could hinder Wellington's mission. Even the best disciplined troops can lose control in combat. Wellington had watched his British soldiers act irresponsibly in Spain. In some of the better known incidents, the duke's infantry had plundered Ciudad Rodrigo,[30] and they had elected to loot Vitoria[31] rather than to pursue the escaping French army. Wellington endeavored to prevent similar activity during the occupation through a vigorous exercise program.

Peacetime training requires officer responsibility in issuing practice instructions and insuring that they are carried out. The best assessment of the status of the British command in France comes from an evaluation of its training program. Wellington received the twice annual inspection reports of each of his infantry battalions and cavalry squadrons which provided him with an accurate expression of the status of his army.[32]

Overall, the British army found it difficult to conduct exercises because it lacked training areas. The army of occupation thus used small unit training (company level or smaller) on a wide scale. The cultivation of fields and bad weather limited the conduct of training.[33] Marching indiscriminately across plowed or freshly planted fields would have earned the enmity of the local inhabitants and damaged the reputation of the army. The British contingent found that it could freely conduct local training only during the winter months when damage to fields was minimal.[34] The British discovered that getting their soldiers outside to train in poor weather was a difficult undertaking. The posting of units on a dispersed scale whereby companies or platoons were scattered in local villages presented another problem.[35] Where officers were not present on a full-time basis, the British command found it difficult to insure that its units conducted meaningful training.

The Duke of Wellington set the standards he expected from lower level training and, from time to time, issued instructions on the direction that he wanted such training to take. He established an important philosophy in the army by insisting that troop training was a command responsibility, thereby making his officers responsible for its success or failure. Whatever restrictions might hinder training, Wellington wanted his units out of their barracks several days per week. He emphasized combat fundamentals such as riding and march formations. The duke insisted that officers take charge of training, putting themselves where they could be seen and followed. Wellington issued orders to his command listing the maneuvers he wanted pursued during exercises. These maneuvers do not represent any deviation from accepted tactical theory but rather were directly tied to the general maneuvers used in contemporary combat. The duke sought further improvement in maneuvers such as 1) marching in full, half, or quarter distance columns, 2) deploying close columns into line, 3) wheeling from columns to the flanks, 4) forming lines from columns by the march of companies in echelon, 5) forming squares, and 6) marching in line.[36]

General Sir Richard Hussay Vivian, commander of the second brigade of cavalry, stayed abreast of training problems in his brigade. Vivian refused to accept local problems as an excuse to avoid all exercises. In a written order to his command, Vivian announced that he would "be ready to make allowances for all the inconveniences arising from the circumstances under which the Regiments are placed, but he [Vivian] will not make allowances for any neglect of those means which are still within the power of commanding and troop officers." Vivian reminded his commanders that while they might make adjustments to compensate for training limitations, he wanted them to insure their units conducted training with the same spirit and precision as normally required. Vivian considered training that lacked spirit and precision to be useless.[37]

General Vivian issued guidelines for training adjustments to meet the needs of the greatly dispersed companies. Vivian circulated orders stating that not only should officers issue instructions about training requirements, but they should make on-the-spot corrections of any deficiencies they observed.[38] Vivian demanded high standards for his officers. He required them to master the fundamentals of cavalry movements or he would not consider them qualified to observe and correct mistakes. The officers instructed their enlisted men to maintain silence during their training exercises so that they could hear the orders the officers issued. With the poor winter weather of 1816–1817, Vivian gave instructions for training to be restarted at the lowest levels of fundamentals. His cavalry regiments began their practice of formations and movements at the lowest level so that by springtime they were ready for large unit training. The brigade commander ordered that any officer deemed unsatisfactory in his duties was not to go on leave until Wellington's multinational autumn exercises were completed.[39] Vivian ordered his cavalrymen out of their barracks to conduct training at least three days per week. Local commanders conducted practice at a walk pace until each and every officer and soldier knew his job. Vivian required any cavalryman who proved incapable of handling a horse to go to riding school.[40] Vivian's brigade established riding schools at squadron level, and created them at lower levels if the squadron was dispersed.[41]

The Annual Autumn Review

Wellington's command did not enjoy the use of large training areas reserved exclusively for military requirements. Despite the lack of a designated major training area, Wellington desired that the entire British contingent hold a training exercise and troop review each year. Just as local units planned training around the French growing season, the British contingent scheduled these major exercises for the autumn, usually in September or October. The army held the fall review on the plains of Denain, located halfway between the two largest concentrations of British units at Cambrai and Valenciennes.[42] Since local training prepared small unit readiness, Wellington designed the autumn review as a test of how well larger sized commands conducted themselves. The duke invited the other allied contingents to participate in the fall exercise, surely the first time any national armies conducted joint military training exercises. The autumn review provided Wellington with an excellent chance to see how well both the British and non-British units had prepared during the previous year, and how well allied troops could cooperate in training. The exercise presented Wellington's multinational command with the opportunity to work together, build confidence in each other, and create trust in allied commanders.

Wellington's headquarters controlled the autumn reviews, and prepared for each one by issuing the necessary information for movement to the exercise area. The duke's officers designed a training program built around whatever tactical and strategic goals the duke desired. Maneuver plans described in explicit detail to each command what movement it was expected to perform when it participated in the exercise.[43] Maneuvers that Wellington required of regimental units included skirmishing, cavalry screening, river crossings, cavalry charges, passage of lines, and retirement of forces. Passage of lines and retirement of units are especially difficult to perform in combat, and Wellington's multinational command trained hard to demonstrate their ability to conduct these movements successfully. The training plan included instructions for ammunition supply trains and pontoons units for river crossings, while other units were assigned to act as opposition to the major troop elements.[44]

Wellington's Royal Staff Corps normally functioned as the opposing force. Unassigned sapper and mine companies along with reserve artillery units aided the Staff Corps.[45] Pre-operational planning assigned the opposing force its initial positions. A detailed script informed all units of the maneuvers they were expected to follow.[46] As the attacking force moved forward, the opposition fell back or reinforced, depending on the actions of the offense. Maps showed the units the direction in which they were to move and the positions they were to occupy. When the program achieved the desired results, the autumn review ended with a ceremony for honored visitors during which the participating contingents assembled in parade formation and passed in review of the guests.[47]

For safety reasons, the troops prepared for the review by having their ammunition removed by their regimental quartermaster. Blank ammunition replaced ball cartridges. The opposing cavalry units did the same.[48] Even with these measures, injuries occurred. In 1817, three men died and numerous others were injured during the review, especially cavalrymen hurt in falls. Doctors amputated the arm of one seriously injured cavalryman.[49]

While the British command recognized the importance of the review, the line soldiers apparently failed to see the value of the exercise. The men abandoned their equipment, tossed their rifles into the mud. The training exercise exhausted the soldiers. One soldier later described the training on the plains of Denain:

> At last we waded down to Denain's plain,
> Where the Duke of Marlborough fought like blazes:
> We were told to fight Waterloo o'er again—
> We could not be water loosers in the hazes

That thickened around us in descending rain:
It quite my power of memory crazes,
To think how the heavens constant poured
And rusted my stirrups and broad sword.
The Duke of Kent was to see a sham fight
So early as a quarter before five
In the morning before it was light—
Many hours before the Duke did arrive—
We were in the field in watery plight,
Resembling drown'd rats more than men alive:
If the water under us had been salted,
We might have pass'd for sea-horses when halted.
This sham-fighting, without prize or glory
Was to the poor soldiers not exciting:
They droop'd, and fell as fast I can assure ye,
As if they had been really fighting.[50]

The British soldier of the line did not perceive the same value in the autumn exercises as the high command did.

Wellington designed the review in 1817 around the actual circumstances of the Battle of Waterloo. That year's review concluded with a charge of cavalry against infantry squares similar to the charges led by Marshal Ney at mid-day of the great battle. The British performance impressed the French citizens who observed the exercise. They wondered how the British forces had done so well during the real battle under such tremendous pressure from Napoleon's army.[51] Perhaps Wellington did not exaggerate when he described Waterloo as "the nearest run thing you ever saw in your life," an indication that the battle could easily have gone in favor of Napoleon.[52]

Unfortunately, Wellington lost a real opportunity to test the integration of allied forces as a result of the lack of participation on the part of the major allies. Had all the major contingents attended the autumn reviews, the duke would have seen first hand the ability of the occupation forces to operate together under a joint command. Participation by the allied powers would also have demonstrated further strength of commitment to the maintenance of European peace. Only the smaller national contingents normally attended the autumn review, though it served as a chance for important dignitaries such as Czar Alexander I of Russia, King Frederick William III of Prussia, and the Duke of Kent to see the troops.[53] In 1817, the Danes, Saxons, and Hanoverians attended. In 1818, with the occupation coming to an end, the Russians participated along with the smaller commands, probably due to the presence of the czar. Alexander I attended the Aix-la-Chapelle diplomatic conference, organized to bring an end to the occupation of France, and he probably desired to see his men in action before the breakup of the army. The King of Prussia also attended, yet the Prussian forces did not join in with the exercise. The review lacked all of the major contingents due to the costs involved, the suitability of the training area, and the distance to the site. Denain's distant location, situated near the northern end of the British zone, placed it a long way from the Prussian and Austrian zones, while the Russian sector was adjacent to the British zone. With the allied departure from France already planned in 1818, in order for the Prussians and Austrians to have participated, those contingents would have had to march westward for the review and then east again, pack their equipment, and depart for home, all between the October conference and the scheduled November evacuation date.[54]

Training Doctrine

In addition to training preparedness, national armies must remain up to date in training philosophy and doctrine. In the aftermath of a war and its demonstrated successful technology, an army adapts itself in order to prepare for the next conflict. The Napoleonic Wars, through the success of the Polish Lancers, demonstrated the added value of cavalry units equipped with a lance weapon.[55] The British army decided to adopt the lance for a number of its light cavalry regiments. The program represented a major change for the British cavalry which had long used the saber. Now the light cavalry would trained in the use of a thrust weapon rather than a cutting weapon. The lance equipped unit became a long serving standard in the British cavalry through the century.[56] The army established the length of the lance initially at fifteen feet, but when this proved unwieldy, a gradual reduction took place until 1840 when the length was set at nine feet.[57]

The adoption of the lance affected one cavalry regiment serving in France, the 12th Light Dragoons. The war office directed that the 12th Dragoons send a detachment to England in June, 1816 for training in the use of the lance. General Vivian, commanding the 2[d] cavalry brigade which controlled the 12th, instructed each troop of the regiment to send either a sergeant or an enlisted man to receive the training and return to assist the others in its use. The designated soldiers trained under the direction of Major R. H. de Montmorency, an officer assigned to the 9th Dragoons, a unit changing to the lance. Major Montmorency had earlier published a manual on the use of the lance based on his observations of the Polish Lancers. The French captured Montmorency during the Peninsular War and paroled him to Paris for three years. The major used this time to study the

training methods employed by the Polish Lancers, thereafter apply-
ing those lessons to the conversions of British cavalry squadrons.[58]

The British army formally created the 12th Royal Lancers in
March, 1817. Since it represented the latest tactics in weaponry,
heads of Europe, such as the Russian czar and Prussian king, closely
observed the regiment during the autumn reviews of 1817 and 1818.[59]
During the unit's first semi-annual inspection in April, 1817, after refitting with the lance, General Vivian questioned the ability of least
one hundred of the privates to become successful lancers. He based
his opinion on the men's lack of the size and strength required to
operate the weapon, though he admitted they had conducted themselves well. Vivian questioned whether there was enough practice
time available to perform the drills required on the new weapon while
also practicing standard cavalry movements. The soldiers walked
when they first attempted lance exercises, and only after sufficient
practice did they ride their mounts with the new weapon. Vivian
expressed his opinion that it would take another six months for the
lancers to complete their training and claim readiness. He also questioned whether the 12th Lancers could train while assigned to occupation duty because the squadron still had to prepare for the autumn
review.[60] By the next inspection, in October, 1817, Vivian considered
the regiment still deficient in the use of the lance, but he proclaimed
the unit ready for service.[61]

Evaluating the British Army Training Program

Training is vital to all military units and, in the case of the army
of occupation, it was also important because of the latter's limited
size and multinational composition. Had any threat similar to the
return of Napoleon in 1815 arisen, Wellington would have found his
army hard pressed to survive, much less to obtain victory on the
battlefield. The fear of renewed war placed a premium on effective
training. Multinational training was unknown prior to the allied
occupation of France. The autumn reviews were simple exercises but
they served as a fair beginning for the development of allied military
training operations. The reviews also demonstrated to the French
government and other observers what forces the Duke of Wellington
had available for military action should any French uprising occur,
though this may not have been the field marshal's intention.

On the small unit level, the British army in France worked hard
to circumvent limitations to good training, especially the lack of
training areas and the dispersed unit structure. Brigade and regimental commanders, under Wellington's directions, refused to allow
limitations to retard unit development; they correctly placed the re-

sponsibility for effective instruction on unit officers. Officers insured that quality practice took place in the absence of higher commanders. Training began at individual level, moved to small unit level, and finally reached the large unit training that took place in the fall review. The adoption of the lance for the 12th Light Dragoons demonstrates the adaptability of the British army to the latest tactical developments. The lance program also indicates that Wellington commanded an army prepared to improve its capabilities. The effective training program, ordered by Wellington and carried by commanders such as General Vivian, demonstrates the importance attached to having a well prepared command. With only a 150 thousand man army, Wellington could not afford anything less without jeopardizing his assigned mission.

Since Wellington never ordered the army of occupation into military operations against France during its three-year tenure, it becomes impossible to validate the effectiveness of the training program. Wellington could only review training effectiveness through the semi-annual inspections conducted by his subordinate commanders on the regiments assigned to France. Among a multitude of inspected areas, these reports provided the duke with a synopsis of how well his ranking British officers rated the readiness of their own units and noted what deficiencies training needed to correct.[62]

NOTES

1. Wellington to Lord Bathurst, October 23, 1815, Wellington Papers 1/482, University of Southampton, Southampton, United Kingdom.

2. Sir Charles Oman, *Wellington's Army, 1809–1814* (London: Greenhill Books, reprint, 1986, originally published 1913), 1.

3. This is probably the Duke of Wellington's most famous remark about his soldiers, and he wrote it to Lord Bathurst, Secretary for War and the Colonies, in response to the plundering of his men after the victory at Vitoria, June 21, 1813. Godfrey Davies, *Wellington and His Army* (Oxford: Basil Blackwell, 1954), 18.

4. Oman, *Wellington's Army*, 343–73 gives the British order of battle for Spain. Many of his units, especially cavalry commands, were rotated home occasionally for refitting after combat. In addition, twelve of Wellington's occupation battalions saw action at Waterloo along with five of the cavalry squadrons.

5. Ibid.

6. The British army was given the occupation sector nearest

the English Channel.

7. Sir Stapleton Cotton, Viscount Combermere (1773–1865) served with Wellington in Iberia where he commanded cavalry. He was sent home for wounds but returned to cross into France in 1814. After three years of service with the army of occupation, he saw extensive service abroad, including a tour as commander in chief in India.

8. The cavalry command originally totaled three brigades of three squadrons each. The British contingent numbered over thirty-seven thousand under this arrangement and thus had to be reduced. Three squadrons, the 1st Dragoon Guards, the 15th Hussars, and the 13th Light Dragoons were shipped home in May, 1816, reducing the British command to the authorized thirty thousand man figure.

9. General Lord Robert Edward Henry Somerset (1776–1842) served in the Peninsular War and commanded a cavalry brigade at Waterloo. He achieved the rank of full general in 1841.

10. Lieutenant General Sir Richard Hussay Vivian (1775–1842), Baron, commissioned in 1793, saw service under Sir John Moore and Wellington in Spain. He was knighted for service at Waterloo and served the entire three year occupation period. He made Lieutenant General in 1827 and became Master General of the Ordnance in 1835. He began a long parliamentary career in 1820.

11. Lieutenant General Sir Colquhoun Grant (1764–1835) fought in India and South Africa before he saw service in Spain. He commanded a hussar brigade at Waterloo, and served with the occupation army. He was promoted to lieutenant general in 1830 and later served as a member of Parliament.

12. *The Times* (London), October 27, 1815; Weekly Returns of the State of the Forces, April 1, 1816–October 11, 1818, Wellington Papers 9/7/2.

13. General Sir Rowland Hill (1772–1842) served in Egypt in 1801. He served under Wellington in the Peninsula and saw extensive combat, and received a division command. Hill was created a baron in 1814. He commanded a brigade at Waterloo, and served in France with the army of occupation for the full three-year tour. He earned his viscountcy in 1842. Sir Charles Oman, in his book *Wellington's Army, 1809–1814*, described Hill as Wellington's trusted and most responsible officer (115).

14. Weekly Returns of the State of the Forces, April 1, 1816–October 11, 1818, Wellington Papers 9/7/2.

15. Sir Galbraith Lowry Cole (1772–1842), lieutenant general, joined the army in 1787 and served in Egypt and in the Peninsula campaign where he commanded a division. After service with the army of occupation, he later became governor of Mauritius and of

the Cape Colony.

16. Sir Peregrine Maitland (1777–1854), colonial governor and general, fought in the aborted Walcheren expedition of 1809, and joined Wellington in the Peninsula in 1812. He commanded a brigade of the Guards at Waterloo. After service with the army of occupation he went on to become governor in the Cape of Good Hope.

17. General Sir James Kempt (1764–1854) was a brigade commander in the Peninsular campaign and took over the 3^d Division during the Battle of Waterloo. After service with the army of occupation he later became Governor of Nova Scotia, Governor-General of Canada, and Master General of the Ordnance.

18. General Sir John Lambert (1772–1847) served in Spain and also took part in the British military failures at Walcheren (1809) and New Orleans (1815). He fought at Waterloo, and was knighted the same year. He was promoted to full general in 1841.

19. Weekly Returns of the State of the Forces, April 1, 1816–October 11, 1818, Wellington Papers 9/7/2.

20. Lieutenant General Sir Henry Clinton (1771–1829) was commissioned in 1787. He served as an aide-de-camp to the Duke of York during fighting against France, and was captured in 1796. He saw service in Spain as a division commander under Wellington. Clinton fought at Waterloo before serving with the army of occupation.

21. Sir Robert O'Callaghan (1777–1840), general, joined Wellington in the Peninsula in 1811 where he commanded a brigade and was twice mentioned by Wellington in his dispatches. He continued his military service after his occupation command in France, rising to become commander of all troops in India.

22. Sir Denis Pack (1772–1823), major general, original joined the cavalry. He took a regiment to Spain with Wellington in 1808 and was involved in the Walcheren expedition in 1809. He served as a brigade commander in the Peninsula in the Portuguese army under Marshal Beresford. Pack later commanded a British division in Spain and was wounded eight times. He was a brigade commander at Waterloo. He last saw foreign service with the occupation army.

23. Sir Thomas Bradford (1773–1853), general, accompanied Wellington to Spain in 1808. He commanded both a brigade and division in the Portuguese army under Marshal Beresford. Badly wounded at Bayonne, Bradford missed Waterloo. After service with the occupation army, he later became commander-in-chief at Bombay.

24. Weekly Returns of the State of the Forces, April 1, 1816–October 11, 1818, Wellington Papers 9/7/2.

25. Sir Charles Colville (1770–1843), general, fought in Egypt in 1800–1801. Colville made major general in 1810 and was given

command of a brigade under Wellington in Spain. He was considered a favorite of Wellington and commanded divisions at different times in the Peninsula. Colville commanded a division at Waterloo. After service with the occupation army, he was commander-in-chief at Bombay and then governor of Mauritius.

26. Sir Manley Power (1773–1826), lieutenant general, was first commissioned as an ensign at the age of nine. He saw service in Egypt in 1800 and served under Wellington in the Peninsula until 1813 when he took a command in the Portuguese army. After service in France, Power became lieutenant governor in Malta.

27. Sir Thomas Brisbane (1773–1860), general, governor, and astronomer, served in Ireland in the 1790s where he struck up a friendship with Arthur Wellesley, then aide-de-camp to the Irish lord lieutenant. Bad health led him away from the military and into astronomy but Wellington asked for his active service in 1812 in the Peninsula. Wellington recommended him for service in North America which caused him to miss Waterloo. After service with the French occupation he became governor of New South Wales in Australia, and the city of Brisbane is named for him. His rule was considered a failure and he again took up his astronomical studies in 1825.

28. John Keane (1781–1844), lieutenant general, served in Egypt in 1800. Keane joined Wellington in Spain in 1813, and crossed with him into France. He made major general in 1814 and gained a command in North America. Severe wounds received at New Orleans caused him to miss Waterloo. After service in France he spent most of his military service in Jamaica and India.

29. Weekly Returns of the State of the Forces, April 1, 1816–October 11, 1818, Wellington Papers 9/7/2. See appendix F for a list of the squadron and battalion commanders assigned to occupation duty.

30. Ciudad Rodrigo, a fortress in the west of Spain near the Portuguese border between the Tagus and Douro Rivers, was plundered by victorious British soldiers after a short siege during the poor weather of January, 1812.

31. The Battle of Vitoria, in north central Spain, was fought June 21, 1813 and was part of Wellington's successful advance to the Pyrenees and the clearing of French forces from the Iberian Peninsula.

32. In accordance with standing army regulations for the time, each individual battalion and squadron was inspected twice each calendar year. The British army in France normally held its inspections in April and in October, the latter as part of the autumn review. See chapter 4 for the inspection reports.

33. Sir Richard Hussay Vivian Papers, General Orders Book, 7–10, April 1, 1817, National Army Museum, London, United Kingdom.

34. Vivian Brigade Order Book, 108–110, April 5, 1817.

35. The Papers of Sir Lowry Cole, PRO 30/43/1–3, Public Record Office, United Kingdom, provides an indication of the dispersion of an infantry division. The 1*ˢᵗ* division of infantry presented a good demonstration of how widespread the command was and to what size level units were dispersed. The division was headquartered at Cambrai along with the 1*ˢᵗ* brigade encompassing the Grenadier Guards and a portion of the Coldstream Guards, along with the assigned brigade of artillery. The Coldstreams also were cantoned in six other locations. The 7*ᵗʰ* brigade of three battalions was headquartered in St. Leger and had troops located in thirty-nine villages, the largest troop concentration having 372 men, the smallest having twenty-five men. The 8*ᵗʰ* brigade, headquartered in Beaumez with three battalions, placed in forty locales. The general division disposition was within the triangular area running from Cambrai west to Bapaume, north to Arras, then southeast back to Cambrai.

36. Lietenant-Colonel John Gurwood, editor, *The General Orders of Field Marshal the Duke of Wellington in the Campaigns of 1809 to 1818* (London: W. Clowes and Sons, 1837), June 28, 1816, 514.

37. Vivian Letter Book, 2*ᵈ* Brigade Cavalry, May 8, 1816, and June 26, 1816.

38. Vivian General Cavalry Orders, June 17, 1817.

39. Ibid., April 1, 1817.

40. Ibid., April 1, 1817 and June 17, 1817; Vivian Brigade Order Book, April 5, 1817 and April 10, 1817.

41. Vivian General Cavalry Orders, June 17, 1816.

42. The British army conducted the fall review in each of the three years it was in France.

43. "Sketch of the Movements for the Review of the British, Hanoverian, Saxon, and Danish Contingents between Valenciennes and Bouchain," October 22, 1816, Wellington Papers 15/3, shows the detail of the planning; See also Lord Rowland Hill Additional MSS, 35060/453, British Library, London, United Kingdom, which contains the "Memorandum of the maneuvers proposed to take place in the neighborhood of Denain on the 22*ᵈ* of October 1816" signed by Sir George Murray, Wellington's Chief of Staff.

44. The George Scovill Papers, War Office Report 37/12/96, Public Record Office, United Kingdom. Scovill commanded the opposing forces during the 1816 and 1817 reviews.

45. Rowland Hill Additional MSS, Military Correspondence, 35060/458–460, October 15, 1817.

46. "Maps, Plans and Drawings Relative to the Review of October 22, 1816." Wellington Papers 15/3. See appendix G for the training plan written for the October 22, 1816 review.

47. Scovill Papers, WO 37/12/96.

48. Gurwood, *General Orders of Wellington*, October 18, 1816, 475–76.

49. W.B. Whitman Papers, 120, file 8408–37, National Army Museum, London, United Kingdom.

50. Colonel Harold Malet, editor, *The Historical Memoirs of the XVIII (Princess of Wales's Own) Hussars* (London: Simpkin and Company, 1907), 180. This is an excerpt from a long poem by Subaltern H. de la Parteur entitled "The Hussars in Occupation, or a Souvenir of the Old Eighteenth."

51. Transcript of a memorandum on his uncle's service as a conductor of stores in the Waterloo campaign and the army of occupation in France, Whitman Papers, 120; Scovill Papers, WO 37/12/96; Papers of Sir Lowry Cole, PRO 30/43/3.

52. Richard Aldington, *The Duke* (New York: The Viking Press, 1943), 228.

53. The *Examiner* mocked the review attended by the czar and Prussian king. The paper claimed they amused themselves with the sham fight, stating, "They played at soldiers, the game which kings are said to be so fond of." November 1, 1818.

54. See chapter 10 concerning the allied departure.

55. Napoleon raised the Polish Lancers to serve in the French army after the campaign of 1806. The lancers were part of the French light cavalry along with hussars and *chasseurs à cheval*. Napoleon equipped his lancers with a shorter lance (nine foot) than used by other armies. The British apparently were impressed with lancer success in the Peninsular campaign, though their value was questioned. No foreign troops fought harder for France than the Polish Lancers, and Napoleon took a squadron with him into exile at Elba in 1814. See Gunther E. Rothenberg, *The Art of Warfare in the Age of Napoleon*, (Bloomington, Indiana: Indiana University Press, 1980), 71–74, for a synopsis of the use of the lance during the Napoleonic Wars.

56. Rothenberg, *Art of Warfare*, 73.

57. Captain P. F. Stewart, *The History of the XII Royal Lancers (Prince of Wales's)* (London: Oxford University Press, 1950), 103.

58. Vivian Brigade Memo, June 9, 1816; Stewart, *History of XII Royal Lancers*, 100–03.

59. Stewart, *History of XII Royal Lancers*, 102.

60. Vivian inspection report of 12th Regiment of Lancers, April 30, 1817, WO 27/141.

61. Vivian inspection report of 12th Regiment of Lancers, October 27, 1817, WO 27/142.

62. See chapter 4.

4

The British Army in France:

Inspection Reports

In accordance with established army procedures, the British army conducted general inspections of each of its battalions and squadrons stationed in France twice a year. The commander of the parent brigade or his designated representative normally conducted the inspection of each battalion sized unit and forwarded the inspection records to his next higher headquarters, providing Wellington and his command with a sense of the combat readiness of the inspected units and their leadership. This inspection was supposed to reveal how well unit commands had improved since the previous inspection, when an inspector had scrutinized areas which needed improvement and had ordered changes made. The inspection reports also revealed the attitudes of brigade commanders towards particular battalion and squadron commanders. These semiannual reports serve as the best analysis of the combat readiness of Wellington's British contingent assigned to occupation duty. The examples listed here make no claim to be exhaustive, but only indicate various problem areas which perhaps are no different from those of any army under normal conditions.

Commanders conducted their inspections according to a standardized format which revealed the unit status in numerous categories. The inspector rated all the personnel in the unit starting with the commander, his officers, the non-commissioned officers, the privates, the musicians, the chaplain, the paymaster, and the adjutant. The inspector probed functional areas such as the unit messing, forage for horses, interior economy (barracks readiness), regimental hospital and school, and the unit record books. The reviewing officer and his staff also perused such areas as ammunition and weapons, clothing and equipment, sword exercises, and field exercises and movements. Finally, the inspector investigated court-martial records to insure that they were conducted in accordance with regulations,and that the punishments rendered were not excessive.

Oftentimes, the inspection reports did not delve very deeply into the real status of a regiment and they failed to disclose fundamental weaknesses. Instead, many reports merely repeated previous evaluations of the same unit or echoed another battalion's summary verbatim. The Duke of Wellington found such reports "highly irregular" and wrote to Sir George Murray, his chief of staff and adjutant general throughout the occupation, to that effect. The field marshal complained to Murray that most of the confidential reports he received for signature appeared to be copies of other reviews.[1] Othertimes, a battalion received a passing rating in most inspected areas, but the inspector had concentrated his comments on one or two unsatisfactory areas. Thus, units that were otherwise considered good commands appeared to be poor battalions because of the substandard performance of one person or one inspected area. Too often, inspectors failed to highlight qualified commands because of a weakness they noted in their reports.

In spite of these limitations, the reports provided both revealing statistics and, on occasion, some cogent comments about the readiness of British officers. Wellington placed great responsibility on his officers for the vital functions of army training and for improvement of relations between his soldiers and the French population. The field marshal expected well trained soldiers, under the watchful eye of good officers, to behave properly in all aspects of occupation life. Failure to train officers properly opened possibilities for problems to arise between poorly trained men and the French citizenry. He also made his officers responsible for development of unit training programs and development of junior officers.[2] Negative comments in the summarized reports reflected a lack of trust and confidence by the command element in their officer corps. The inspection reports alerted Wellington as to where weaknesses in British leadership lay.

Negative Aspects

The semi-annual inspections broke the review of battalion officers into three groupings; the commander, the field grade officers (majors), and the company grade officers (captains, lieutenants, cornets and subalterns). The reports often innocuously remarked that the officers were capable, that they knew their jobs, or that the subalterns needed additional training. But if an officer stood out due to rank incompetence, the inspector made appropriate remarks to alert the army command of deficient leadership.

Ineptness among officers threatened the accomplishment of the occupation army's assigned mission. General Sir Richard Hussay Vivian, Second Brigade Commander in the Cavalry Corps, made pointed remarks about the officers with whom he was familiar during his reports. General Vivian frequently attacked Lieutenant Colonel Henry Murray of the 18th Hussars, a unit assigned to his brigade. For the three occupation years, Vivian's inspections of the squadron found Murray wanting in leadership skills. Vivian determined that Murray did not exert himself when things went wrong, though Vivian described the 18th Hussars as a good unit.[3] Later in 1816, Vivian wrote that Murray was a poor commander, but in Murray's recent absence, acting commander Lieutenant Colonel Philip Hay performed even worse. In spite of any former reports he might have submitted concerning Murray, Vivian wrote of Hay, "I never again wish to see him in command of the Regiment."[4] At that moment Vivian might have thought he wanted Murray back. In 1817, the brigade commander noted that while Murray had many excellent qualities, he claimed it "totally out of the question" that Murray could ever make a good regimental commander.[5] While Vivian vilified Murray, the general maligned another squadron officer, Lieutenant Colonel James Hughes. Though Hughes had health problems, Vivian called him as "bad an officer as I ever saw at the head of a regiment, and if I have before now spoken favorably of him, I have been wrong in doing so." From these inspections, Vivian's conclusions led him to state that while the 18th Hussars showed improvement in its standards, he desired a new commanding officer for the squadron.[6] Vivian continued his attacks on Murray in 1818, questioning Murray's knowledge of field maneuvers. He wrote that Murray would never hold a higher command and no unit could possibly perform well under him. Meanwhile, Colonel Hay deserted the unit, leading Vivian to write in his inspection of his wish that Hay never return.[7]

Infantry inspectors found similar targets. Lieutenant Colonel William Spring and the senior officers of the 1st Battalion, 57th Regiment of Foot serve as an excellent example. Before the formation of the army of occupation, the semi-annual inspections of the battalion challenged the abilities of the officers in charge. Lieutenant Colonel John Cameron spoke of the battalion's "lamentable situation," when he reviewed the field grade officers of the 57th, Colonel Spring, Major McGibbon and Major Thadford.[8] General Sir Manley Power, commanding the 2[d] Brigade during the occupation and a regular inspector of the 57th, described Spring as without intelligence, though he was attentive and exerted himself to the utmost. Power proclaimed Major McGibbon "indolent and inactive" and "totally useless to the Corps" because of bad health which constantly left him on the sick list.[9] Power remarked that Major Thadford, suffering badly from wounds inflicted in Spain and quite deaf, was anxious to do his duty. Power declared Thadford virtually useless in the field.[10] General James Kempt's independent report on the 57th reached the same conclusions about the battalion's leadership.[11] In spite of the apparent failure of the unit's leadership, General Manley Power considered the 57th Regiment acceptable in the conduct of field maneuvers.[12]

General O'Callaghan blamed the commander of the 39th Regiment of Foot, Lieutenant Colonel Cavendish Sturt, for that unit's problems. The general found Colonel Sturt lacking the action and ability to keep discipline in his command. The battalion conducted its field maneuvers in a "slovenly and incorrect manner."[13] General Thomas Brisbane, in a separate inspection, found Colonel Sturt "without the slightest claim to intelligence."[14] The British army eventually removed Sturt from his battalion command, but in early 1817, Sturt appealed to the commander-in-chief, the Duke of York, for reinstatement based on his long years of service.[15] The duke restored Sturt to his command rather than force him to sell his commission or retire on half-pay.[16] Apparently Sturt changed little. In a subsequent inspection, General Brisbane gave Sturt only the credit to know enough to accept advice from his subordinates.[17]

Throughout the British occupation contingent, many other senior officers received similar comments, all of which reflected badly on the state of the British leadership. In the 2[d] Battalion, the Rifle Brigade, General Thomas Brisbane defamed Lieutenant Colonel D. L. Gilmour for his lack of devotion to duty and his apparent lack of tactical knowledge. Gilmour demonstrated no aptitude for any possible improvement. Brisbane commented that the best thing for the battalion occurred when Colonel Norcott commanded during the long leave absence of Colonel Gilmour.[18] In spite of Gilmour's leadership deficiencies, Brisbane regarded the soldiers of the Rifle Brigade as excellent troops.[19] In another unit, the 3[d] Regiment of Foot, General Brisbane asserted that its commander, Colonel William Stewart, was without intelligence.[20] Brisbane wrote that Stewart could never command a larger unit "nor has he improved over the two years he has been under my command."[21] The general also commented that Stewart's field grade subordinates served the regiment poorly.[22] In the 21st Regiment, General Brisbane called Colonel Robert Henry "quite unfit," which resulted in Henry's retirement. He made positive recommendations for the regiment's two majors and described the unit as "a very good regiment, fit for any service" in spite of its commander.[23] In the 23[d] Regiment, General James Kempt remarked that he was thankful that the unit commander, Colonel Palmer, went on half pay which allowed Colonel Pearson to take command and attempt to solve the unit's discipline problems.[24] The next year Kempt reported the regiment much improved under Pearson's leadership.[25] General John Lambert wrote that Lieutenant Colonel Henry Thornton of the 40th Regiment did not have the talent to command in the field.[26]

Even with the arrival of new officers, the situations in some units did not improve. Lord Somerset complained about Major H. W. Davenport's transfer to the 3^d Dragoons since Davenport was an infantry officer and quite unfit for cavalry service.[27] When Major James Walsh transferred to the 91st Regiment, Sir Manley Power found him attentive but unintelligent.[28]

The absence of selected officers often caused problems for units. While General Vivian spoke harshly of the 12th Lancers and its acting commander, Colonel Bridger, Vivian consistently lamented that the squadron's regular commander, Lieutenant Colonel Frederick Ponsonby, was too often absent performing as a member of Parliament.[29] With the return of Colonel Ponsonby in 1818, Vivian's last report on the squadron was more than satisfactory. The squadrons "whole appearance does this officer [Ponsonby] the highest possible credit."[30] When Colonel James Sleigh of the 11th Light Dragoons went on leave, General Colquhoun Grant noted that his absence caused the dragoons to perform field exercises poorly. Grant rebuked the unit's officers for the decayed performance because they secretly opposed Sleigh and his disciplinary measures. Grant blamed the squadron's problems on two of its majors, Diggens and Mony. The general wrote that he considered Diggens incapable of maneuvering cavalry, and Mony unable to command.[31]

Wellington and the British command received numerous negative comments of poor leadership among junior officers in the inspection reports. These lapses threatened the success of the occupation just as much as shortcomings among senior officers. General Vivian wrote that the officers of the 18th Hussars rode badly and that improvement was essential.[32] Colonel Blakeney noted that many senior officers of the 23^d Regiment took furlough too frequently, leaving the junior officers in charge. These junior officers performed movement procedures incorrectly.[33] General Denis Pack complained that the captains of the dispersed 79th Regiment did not inspect their distant units often enough, and this allowed those units to falter in their readiness.[34] Pack found that the 4th Regiment lost too many promising young officers when its ranks were reduced after the wars against Napoleon ended.[35] Sir Manley Power discovered in his inspection of the 2^d Battalion, the Rifle Brigade, that the officers failed to insure the correct payment of their men,[36] a failure certain to lead to poor performance levels. Power also wrote that the lieutenants of the 1st Battalion, 57th Regiment were not very intelligent,[37] which presented a real problem considering the distrust Power held for the battalion's senior leaders.

General Colquhoun Grant blamed some deficiencies in the 11th Light Dragoons on the junior leadership whom he determined needed more practice in the field. The general defamed a young officer, Cornet Stewart, for his inability to ride and his lack of the exertion required of a cavalry officer.[38] Most importantly, Grant reported that secret opposition existed among the officers against the commanding officer. He wrote, "There is cause to suppose that unanimity and good understanding so desirable in a Regiment and essential to its reputation do not prevail in this Corps."[39] It was not until the last inspection of the regiment in 1818, prior to the breakup of the army, that Grant could advise that the officers had shown a great deal of improvement.[40]

A few medically unfit junior officers were assigned to France. One of these officers, Lieutenant Anderson of the 52^d Regiment, remained on active duty for most of the occupation in spite of an amputated thigh. This obviously rendered him unfit for service, and Wellington finally removed Anderson from active duty and recommended him for half pay.[41] The commander-in-chief of the British army, the Duke of York, did not review the case until 1818.[42] The medical officer of the 71st Regiment declared one officer, Lieutenant Lind, unfit for duty due to a shoulder wound suffered at Waterloo. Lind simply could not exert himself and perform his duties. The unit dispatched him home to Britain for duty at the regimental depot.[43] General Thomas Bradford recommended Lieutenant Young of the 29th Regiment for half pay due to illness.[44] Ensign Issac Bee of the 4th Regiment was long absent from his command because of tuberculosis.[45] General Bradford recommended Lieutenant D. Stewart of the 2^d Battalion, the Rifle Brigade, for assignment to garrison duty because of Stewart's long years of combat service, his multiple wounds, and because he had lost a brother in battle.[46]

Other officers assigned to occupation duty in France were unsuitable for a variety of reasons. Lord Somerset declared the assistant surgeon of the 2^d Dragoon Guards unfit for duty because, though he could treat patients adequately, he was unable to ride a horse and thus was of no use to the regiment.[47] Somerset maligned the paymaster of the 3^d Dragoons when the paymaster failed to perform his duties because of habitual intoxication.[48] The commander of the 79th Regiment reported that Ensign Carton of the regiment unfit because he was too young (age seventeen). General Pack ordered the ensign sent to a French military school with hopes that someday he would develop into a better officer.[49]

These type of comments reflected badly on the quality of leadership in the officer ranks of the British contingent. It must be remembered that inspectors often overlooked satisfactory officer performance by substandard leaders. Poor leadership indicated the possibility of weaknesses on the part of the individual soldier.

General John Keane found the problems of the 1st Battalion, 88th Regiment of Foot, an all-Irish unit, lay with its enlisted personnel. The battalion's leadership worked hard to overcome weaknesses in training and in observing authority. Keane wrote, "This Regiment is composed of a description of men who require the greatest and most constant attention and management on the part of the commanding officer." The general called regimental non-commissioned officers untrained and unintelligent. He wrote of the privates, "They are not very well drilled, nor very sober, and when well looked after, are tolerably well behaved." Keane later credited the commander for improved discipline.[50]

Wellington expected a great deal from his officer corps. Their abilities affected the entire contingent. When they failed to do their jobs, they threatened the army's mission. Where they did their jobs, inspecting officers reported quality organizations. When Denis Pack found numerous problems in the 79th Regiment, he offered a simple solution for the unit, a solution any unit could use to resolve its weaknesses. He desired more knowledgeable young officers available for duty and better training programs for them. He also demanded that all officers visit and inspect their distant unit elements in order that dispersed units were more closely observed. Officer responsibility demanded nothing less.[51]

The semiannual inspections identified a series of other important problems faced by the British contingent which went beyond the question of officer ability. Cavalry mounts, of vital importance to Wellington's military power, remained a problem throughout the occupation. The Napoleonic wars demonstrated the conclusive role of cavalry. Napoleon suffered from weak cavalry after the debacle in Russia, while Wellington's cavalry proved decisive at Waterloo.[52] Inspectors examined closely the horses assigned to cavalry squadrons during their reviews and they never found the condition of the horses very good. The French repeatedly provided forage of an inferior quality. During his inspection of the 7th Hussars, General Colquhoun Grant complained that the unit's horses were too small and their forage was of the "worst description."[53] General Vivian remarked that the 18th Hussars' horses were a poor lot and their forage was bad.[54] The following year, the condition of the horses of the Hussars improved as Vivian was able to report his pleasure with their cleanliness and their condition.[55] Vivian found deficiencies in the conditions of the 12[56] Light Dragoon's mounts because of their ages.[56] When the 12[56] refitted as a lancer squadron, Vivian complained that the horses were unfit to carry the heavier equipped cavalrymen.[57] At least one squadron had mounts in good condition. General Grant declared the horses of the 11[56] Light Dragoons to be in good shape in each of his inspections.[58]

All cavalry squadrons faced severe shortages of mounts. By 1816, only one squadron, the 7[56] Hussars, was at full strength. Each squadron required five hundred and eighty-one mounts. The 11[56] Dragoons was short ninety-seven horses, the 18[56] Hussars twenty-five, and the 2[56] Dragoon Guards deficient by one hundred and fifty.[59] The situation degenerated through the end of the occupation in 1818 as the number of horses ordered expelled exceeded the number of remounts accepted by the cavalry. By the second inspection of that year, each cavalry squadron, including the 7[56] Hussars, were short over one hundred mounts, except the 12[56] Lancers who were short fifty-two.[60] The horses ordered removed were often only those which were completely incapable of service. For example, after he instructed the 12[56] Lancers to dismiss twenty-three old mounts, General Vivian observed many others which he deemed would soon become unacceptable for use.[61]

When the British army allocated horses for their cavalry units in France, the squadrons competed vigorously to obtain them. The British Adjutant General's Office in London settled the issue by allocating the number of horses each squadron would gain. Each squadron selected an officer to ride to Calais to pick up his unit's horses. In Calais, the officers drew lots so that each squadron had a fair chance to choose reliable mounts, and parades were held to view the horses before selection.[62]

The shortage of mounts during the occupation placed the British army in a precarious situation. At any given time during the occupation, if Wellington had deemed military action necessary, the army would have lost up to fifteen percent of the cavalry due to lack of mounts, thus vastly restricting its operations.[63] Even those horses present were in questionable shape, while the forage provided by the French did nothing to strengthen the cavalry. The status of mounts did not enhance the readiness of the British army in France and plagued the contingent for three years.

Positive Aspects

While the negative inspection comments appear to present an army unable to perform its mission, positive inspection reports prove otherwise. Many battalions/squadrons were considered fit for military service, and many quality officers at both the senior and junior level served with the army of occupation. Finally, Wellington and his commanders refused to ignore questions of incompetence. Instead, the British contingent sought solutions to its problems.

Amongst all the incompetent leadership, the British army enjoyed the presence of good officers among its battalion and squadron commanders, officers who strove to insure that the junior leaders were also trained properly. The 2^d Battalion, Coldstream Guards, an elite unit,[64] expected to receive excellent comments about its leadership during any inspection. Colonel Alexander Woodford never relaxed on good unit discipline, which was expected of the Coldstreams, and General Peregrine Maitland, the Guards' brigade commander, considered Woodford outstanding in field maneuvers. Maitland could report with satisfaction the support the field officers gave Woodford along with the instruction they provided the new subalterns. The Coldstreams also received high evaluations for its well trained lieutenants and captains. General Maitland consistently reported improvements in the lieutenants of the Coldstream.[65] He reported that they were intelligent, active, and knew their duties. Maitland commended the senior leadership for excellence in training their junior officers. He considered all company commanders fit to command.[66] The 3^d Battalion, Grenadier Guards, also had excellent officers. The officers kept rigid discipline, taught their subalterns very well, and ran an excellent training exercise program. General Maitland stated that the battalion, "is in a most efficient state for any service it may be called upon to perform."[67]

The 1st Battalion, 79th Regiment of Foot, needed the help of a strong commander. General Sir Denis Pack, at the start of the occupation, blamed the unit's poor performance on changes in leadership over the prior six months. The regiment's shoddy appearance demonstrated the need for a "capable and unremitting" commander. The field officers did not help the situation with their "slovenly" habits.[68] With the return of Lieutenant Colonel Neil Douglas from leave due to wounds, General Pack wrote that the unit would surely do better.[69] General Bradford found that Douglas had done very well and "no officer could have taken more pain with the Regiment" in improving its discipline and appearance. However, Bradford did not trust the second-in-command, brevet Lieutenant Colonel Duncan Cameron, with control of the battalion.[70] General Pack later observed that while Lieutenant Colonels Brown and Cameron had demonstrated their ability in combat, they were not good leaders, stating, "I would be very sorry to see either of them in command for any length of time."[71] Pack concluded his last inspection of the 79th Regiment by reporting that the unit had improved greatly since

1816 under the excellent leadership of Colonel Douglas.[72]

The 11th Light Dragoons received top ratings in its reviews, and General Colquhoun Grant gave the credit to the squadron commander, Lieutenant Colonel Sleigh. The general stated that "Perhaps no corps in the services is in a higher state of efficiency" than the 11th Dragoons.[73] Grant gave credit to the commander, writing that Colonel Sleigh "makes his duty his beliefs, and he is unremitting in the conscientious discharge of it."[74]

Many units received excellent ratings from the inspectors. General O'Callaghan called the 3[d] Regiment very good marksmen.[75] General Brisbane said of the same unit, "This is a fine regiment with an excellent system established in it, and fit for any service."[76] General Lambert stated that the 5th Regiment, "is in every respect in a very efficient state for any service."[77] The 21st Regiment, which had been described as "losing ground" in 1816 by General Brisbane, improved to the point where Brisbane could say later that year that the "unit is a very good regiment, fit for any service."[78] The 23[d] Regiment rated very poorly under Colonel Palmer in 1817, but under the new leadership of Colonel Pearson, General Kempt considered the battalion much improved.[79] The 52[d] Regiment was described as "independently minded" where most soldiers did things without regard to regulations, but at the same time was called one of the finest regiments in the British army.[80] The 71st Regiment, while not in the highest state of discipline, was a unit which "can be counted on" with the reputation as a hard working group.[81]

An excellent indicator of unit training and morale is the desertion rate. The British army successfully reduced its desertion rate throughout the occupation. With only officers allowed to take leave, the British command should have expected that their privates and sergeants would take unauthorized absences. Officers set a poor example when they often overstayed their permitted leave time in England, but the army carried the officers on the unit rolls as absent without leave rather than as deserters. The situation was not excessive, and most units recorded only one officer in that status each six months.[82] But excessive absences could get out of control. For example, the 52[d] Regiment reported thirteen absent officers in 1817.[83] The British army command notified the Duke of Wellington of the repeated absence of any single officer.[84]

Though desertion remained a problem during the course of occupation, the total number of desertions dropped between 1816 and 1818. To meet the danger occasioned by Napoleon's unexpected return from Elba, the army had inducted many men who failed to meet military standards and were potential deserters.[85] Once the army settled into a routine and the problem soldiers departed, the desertion rate dropped. In the second inspection of 1816, the average desertion total per battalion was six, but by the second inspection of 1818, just prior to the dissolution of the army, the total was less than four per battalion.[86] The 7th Regiment suffered forty-five desertions in 1816, but reduced this to nine for the year 1818.[87] Elite units such as the Grenadier Guards rarely suffered from desertion. The unit had zero desertions in 1816 and only one in 1818.[88] Cavalry units enjoyed below average desertion rates.[89] Other regiments of the line did not fare as well. The 3[d] Regiment had sixteen desertions in the second inspection of 1816, and twelve in the second inspection of 1818.[90] The 3[d] Battalion, the Royal Scots, lost fourteen men to desertion in 1816, well above the battalion average.[91]

Another indicator of the condition of the British battalions in France is the death rate incurred while engaged in peacekeeping operations. A peacekeeping force should suffer no casualties as a result of its mission. Deaths would occur for other reasons, normally disease. From 1815 to 1818, the death rate of the British army in occupation fell. In the second inspection of 1815, the number of deaths over the previous six months included those who had been killed at the Battle of Waterloo. The first real figures which relate directly to the army of occupation are those from the initial inspection of 1816. The average number of deaths per battalion sized unit over the previous six months was over ten.[92] Units that fought at Waterloo still skew these figures, since deaths from wounds were still occurring.[93] The figures dropped to a rate of four per battalion per six months by the end of 1816. The 1817 average remained steady at four per battalion, but the 1818 rate dropped to three per battalion by the second inspection.[94] General Vivian involved himself in the quest for better health, and ordered his officers to inspect hygienic conditions. The general wrote that "cleanliness, exercise, and good diet are indispensable" for better health.[95]

The inspection reports reveal that the British command in France recognized the need to educate its soldiers and their dependents while on assignment overseas. Education can only improve the capabilities of a unit. The inspection reports included a segment concerning the regimental school, if one was established. Once settled in France, most battalions sought to open schools. Those units which did not have schools normally did not do so because of the unit's dispersion (such as the 3[d] Dragoons), the inability to hire a satisfactory school master (the 43[d] and 91st Regiments), or the school's location with the regimental recruiting depot back in England (including the 52[d] and 4th Regiments).[96]

The British army designed its schools along the ideas of Dr. Andrew Bell.[97] The regimental commander normally served as the school superintendent, while the regimental chaplain acted as the school master and supervised the school's day-to-day operations. The soldiers were entitled to attend school, but most students were children of soldiers who had their families with them. Regiments often opened their schools in the afternoon for commissioned officers for a two hour period, while enlisted men attended for two hours in the early evening.[98] The daily standard school enrollment stood at between twenty to thirty students.[99] The 2^d Dragoon Guards, a widely dispersed unit, could only muster four children for school.[100] The commander of the 29th Regiment, another widely dispersed unit, ordered his married men moved closer to regimental headquarters in order to improve school attendance.[101]

General Conclusions

The inspection records contribute valuable conclusions about the British contingent in occupation. The army compiled all of the inspection reports into a readable synopsis that was forwarded to the Duke of Wellington. This digest provided the field marshal with an overall view of the army in occupation which was highly favorable to virtually every battalion. It cited problems of individual units and normally mentioned the weak officers by name. The digest made the duke aware of dispersion problems, excessive absences, and field training weaknesses. However, Wellington received an outline that generally gave a positive report to each separate regiment under his command. Rarely did an entire regiment receive an unsatisfactory rating. Only the 1st Battalion, 88th Regiment of Foot, failed to meet army standards as a whole. Its division commander, General Sir Charles Colville, informed Wellington that the 88th was the "worst unit" in his division. The British army in France initially totaled thirty-one squadron/battalion sized units. In the first consolidated report of 1816, twenty-four of these units received a favorable rating. In the second report that year, twenty-eight units were rated favorably. The troop reduction of 1817 left the army with twenty-five battalions.[102] The second consolidated report of 1817 gave twenty-one battalions a favorable inspection. By 1818, the number rose to twenty-four.[103]

Weaknesses in senior officer ability at the battalion and squadron level threatened the eventual success of the British contingent in France, but at least the command identified problems and worked to circumvent them. Every battalion and squadron experienced weak leadership at some level. However, the future of the British army, no matter where deployed, lay with effective training of junior officers. Wellington placed great importance on the training of subalterns.

Comments in the inspection reports reveal the capabilities of the junior officers assigned to the various battalions. Unfortunately, the favorable comments made by inspecting officers did not delve very deeply into the qualifications of company grade officers. Such comments often pointed out that the officers were capable, knew their jobs, were attentive to their work, were united behind the commanding officer, or worked hard to develop the subalterns. Only when discrepancies existed did the inspector have anything other than a favorable general comment about the status of junior officers. It must be remembered that inspectors tend to focus on what is wrong, not on what is right.

By conducting the inspections, the command demonstrated its determination to improve the British army assigned to France. The Duke of Wellington desired the highest standards possible for his occupation contingent. Higher standards resulted in better relations with Frenchmen. The British contingent in France, along with the rest of the army, suffered from recruiting methods. Officers who had purchased their commissions and their position remained in Wellington's ranks, and the army suffered for it. Wellington successfully placed officers at division and brigade level that he was familiar with and whom he trusted, but he had little to do with regimental assignments. Officers within the regimental structure abused their privileges and proved deficient in their jobs. The British army often recruited foot soldiers through bounty and drink in time of crisis, such as at the time of Napoleon's return from Elba, and these soldiers performed poorly.[104] The deficiencies in cavalry mounts, however, threatened the overall performance level of the army in France. Fortunately for Wellington, this weakness was never exposed in a crisis situation.

The occupation army continued to improve itself. The British army in France did not settle in garrisons and wait out the end of the occupation. Wellington and his commanders made their units train to standards set by the field marshal. Wellington held his officers responsible for insuring that the army trained well. By training hard and inspecting units regularly, regimental performance demonstrated improvement. Health conditions improved and the desertion rate dropped. The command sought higher education for the soldier. Better performance in these vital areas improved the army. More and more regiments received satisfactory ratings in spite of the presence of one or two incompetent officers. Failure to solve the problems of the British contingent in France jeopardized the supporting role that the peacekeeping army contributed to the overall diplomatic peacemaking undertaking of the Napoleonic post-war era. Wellington was spared exposing any of his army's weaknesses because he never had to order it into action. At the same time he and his command strove to overcome the problems that existed.

NOTES

1. Wellington to the Adjutant General of the Forces, March 9, 1818, War Office Report 27/142, Public Record Office, Kew, United Kingdom [hereafter WO with file number].

2. Lieutenant-Colonel John Gurwood, editor, *The General Orders of Field Marshal the Duke of Wellington in the Campaigns of 1809 to 1818* (London: W. Clowes and Sons, 1837), June 28, 1816, 514; Michael Glover, *Wellington as Military Commander* (London: B. T. Batsford, 1968), 245.

3. 18th Hussars, May 22, 1816, WO 27/137.

4. 18th Hussars, October 29, 1816, WO 27/138.

5. 18th Hussars, April 21, 1817, WO 27/141.

6. 18th Hussars, October 24, 1817, WO 27/142.

7. 18th Hussars, April 14, 1818, WO 27/144.

8. 1/57, October 28, 1815, WO 27/136.

9. 1/57, May 15, 1817, WO 27/141.

10. 1/57, October 15, 1818, WO 27/145.

11. 1/57, April 20, 1818, WO 27/144.

12. 1/57, October 15, 1818, WO 27/145.

13. 1/39, May 31, 1816, WO 27/137.

14. 1/39, October 8, 1817, WO 27/142.

15. Torrens to Wellington, March 14, 1817, Wellington Papers 1/537, University of Southampton, Southampton, United Kingdom.

16. Sturt to Torrens, February 22, 1817, and Torrens to Sturt, March 6, 1817, Wellington Papers 1/537. The Duke of York was aware of Sturt's laxity of command but was willing to allow him to attempt to vindicate himself by restoring his command.

17. 1/39, October 10, 1818, WO 27/145.

18. 2^{d}/Rifle Brigade, May 7, 1818, WO 27/144.

19. 2^{d}/Rifle Brigade, October 8, 1817, WO 27/412.

20. 1/3, October 7, 1817, WO 27/142.

21. 1/3, October 10, 1818, WO 27/145.

22. 1/3, May 4, 1818, WO 27/144.

23. 1/21, October 25, 1816, WO 27/138.

24. 1/23, October 22, 1817, WO 27/142.

25. 1/23, October 12, 1818, WO 27/145.

26. 1/40, June 3, 1816, WO 27/137.

27. 3^{d} Dragoons, October 16, 1818, WO 27/145.

28. 1/91, October 16, 1818, WO 27/145.

29. 12th Lancers, April 30, 1817, WO 27/141.

30. 12th Lancers, October 26, 1818, WO 27/145.

31. 11th Dragoons, October, 1816, WO 27/138.

32. 18th Hussars, April 14, 1818, WO 27/144.

33. 1/23, May 20, 1818, WO 27/144.

34. 1/79, May 31, 1816, WO 27/137.

35. 1/4, May 10, 1817, WO 27/141.

36. 2[d]/Rifle Brigade, May 27, 1816, WO 27/137.

37. 1/57, October 28, 1816, WO 27/139.

38. 11th Light Dragoons, October, 1818, WO 27/145.

39. 11th Light Dragoons, October, 1817, WO 27/142.

40. 11th Light Dragoons, October, 1818, WO 27/145.

41. 1/52, October 10, 1817, WO 27/142.

42. 1/52 Regiment, May 11, 1818, WO 27/144.

43. 1/71, May 16, 1816, WO 27/137.

44. 1/29, October 30, 1816, WO 27/138.

45. 1/4, May 17, 1818, WO 27/144.

46. 2[d]/Rifle Brigade, May 8, 1817, WO 27/141.

47. 2[d] Dragoon Guards, November 14, 1816, WO 27/138.

48. 3[d] Dragoons, November 4, 1817, WO 27/142.

49. 1/79, October 10, 1817, WO 27/142.

50. 1/88, October 20, 1815, WO 27/135; 1/88, May 25, 1816, WO 27/137; and 1/88, October 27, 1816, WO 27/139. Undoubtedly anti-Irish sentiment showed in Keane's reports. The regiment departed France as part of the troop reduction of 1817.

51. 1/79, May 31, 1816, WO 27/137.

52. Napoleon suffered tremendous cavalry losses in Russia which affected his future campaigns. French soldiers ate their horses to avoid starvation in the retreat from Moscow, nor could they supply forage for their mounts. Though Napoleon was able to field an army for the 1813 campaign in Germany, he could not exploit victories at Lutzen and Bautzen for lack of cavalry. See Gunther E. Rothenberg, *The Art of Warfare in the Age of Napoleon* (Bloomington, Indiana: Indiana University Press, 1980), 55–56. Count Phillippe-Paul de Segur in his eyewitness account, *Napoleon's Russian Campaign*, translated by J. David Townsend (New York: Time Incorporated, 1958), recounts the same destruction of the French cavalry throughout his book. At Waterloo, Ponsonby's Union Brigade and Somerset's cavalry repulsed Ney's first major thrust against Wellington's center. Later, Ney's unsupported cavalry attacks retreated under the weight of Lord Uxbridge's cavalry counterattacks. See David G. Chandler, *The Campaigns of Napoleon* (London: Weidenfeld and Nicolson, 1966), 1064–95.

53. 7th Hussars, May, 1817, WO 27/141.

54. 18th Hussars, April 21, 1817, WO 27/142.

55. 18th Hussars, April 14, 1818, WO 27/144.

56. 12th Lancers, October 27, 1817, WO 27/142.

57. 12th Lancers, October 26, 1818, WO 27/145.

58. 11th Light Dragoons, April 1816, WO 27/137; October 1816, WO 27/138; October 1817, WO 27/142; May 1818, WO 27/144; and October 1818, WO 27/145. Some horses required removal, however.

59. April–May, 1816 for the six cavalry squadrons, WO 27/137.

60. October, 1818, for the six cavalry squadrons, WO 27/145.

61. 12th Lancers, October 27, 1817, WO 27/142.

62. Letters from Adjutant General and Military Secretary to Calais Assistant Quartermaster, July 8, 1817; August 2, 1817; September 22, 1817; April 12, 1818; May 8, 1818; and July 10, 1818; all WO 28/22.

63. Based on WO 27/138 to WO 27/145 for the six cavalry squadrons.

64. The two guard battalions assigned to France, the 3^d Battalion, Grenadier Guards, and the 2^d Battalion, Coldstream Guards, were normally assigned to the crown's Household Troops.

65. 2^d/Coldstreams, October 18, 1816, WO 27/138.

66. 2^d/Coldstreams, May, 1817, WO 27/140.

67. 3^d/Grenadiers, May 6, 1818, WO 27/137.

68. 1/79, May 31, 1816, WO 27/137.

69. 1/79, October 30, 1816, WO 27/139.

70. 1/79, May 8, 1817, WO 27/141.

71. 1/79, May 6, 1818, WO 27/144.

72. 1/79, October 12, 1818, WO 27/145.

73. 11th Dragoons, October, 1816, WO 27/138.

74. 11th Dragoons, May, 1817, WO 27/141.

75. 1/3, October 16, 1816, WO 27/138.

76. 1/3, October 10, 1818, WO 27/145.

77. 1/5, April 13, 1818, WO 27/144.

78. 1/21, May 21, 1816, WO 27/137; and 1/21, October 25, 1816, WO 27/138.

79. 1/23, October 12, 1818, WO 27/145.

80. 1/52, October 19, 1815, WO 27/135.

81. 1/71, October 24, 1815, WO 27/135.

82. WO 27/137 through WO 27/145 for all units assigned to France.

83. 1/52, October 10, 1817, WO 27/142.

84. In the digest report submitted to the field marshal biannually, WO 27/136 (1816), WO 27/143 (1817), and WO 27/146 (1818).

85. 1/3, May 9, 1817, WO 27/141.

86. Compiled from WO 27/137 through 27/145 for all squadrons and battalions that served the entire occupation period in France.

87. 1/7, May 22, 1816, WO 27/137; November 8, 1816, WO 27/138; April 23, 1818, WO 27/144; and October 10, 1818, WO 27/145.

88. 3^d/Grenadier, June 13, 1816, WO 27/137; October 18, 1816, WO 27/138; May 6, 1818, WO 27/144; and October 9, 1818, WO 27/145.

89. WO 27/137 through 27/145 for the six cavalry squadrons for years 1816 to 1818.

90. 1/3, October 30, 1816, WO 27/138; and October 10, 1818, WO 27/145.

91. 3^d Royal Scots, May 25, 1816, WO 27/137; and October 26, 1816, WO 27/138. High officer absenteeism existed at the same time. Seven officers were on leave and another was absent without leave.

92. Compiled from WO 27/137 for the battalions and squadrons serving in France.

93. Among the units who fought at Waterloo and served with the occupation army, the 40th Regiment had eleven deaths, the 23^d had nineteen, the 71st twenty-two, the 79th twenty-five, and the two battalions of the Rifle Brigade had thirty deaths between the fall 1815 inspection and the first inspection of 1816. See WO 27/137 (spring 1816) for these six battalions.

94. Compiled from WO 27/138 to 27/145 for the battalions and squadrons serving in France.

95. Sir Richard Hussay Vivian Papers, General Cavalry Orders, December 20, 1815, National Army Museum, London, United Kingdom.

96. See WO 27/144 (spring 1818) for the mentioned units.

97. Reverend Dr. Andrew Bell (1753–1832) is credited with developing the "Madras" system of education, a form of mutual instruction whereby students teach each other and act as both the master and the scholar. The system was designed to reduce school costs, foster the idea of self help, and end corporal punishment. His education program was considered a failure. See Sir Leslie Stephen and Sir Sidney Lee, editors, *The Dictionary of National Biography*, 21 volumes and supplement (London: Oxford University Press reprint, 1959–1960), 2:149–52.

98. 11th Dragoons, October, 1816, WO 27/138.

99. Complied from WO 27/138 to WO 27/145 for all units in France.

100. 2^d Dragoon Guards, May 25, 1818, WO 27/144.

101. 1/29, May 7, 1818, WO 27/144.

102. See chapter 8 for the 1817 troop reduction.

103. The outlines which reached Wellington are found in WO 27/136 (1816), WO 27/143 (1817), and WO 27/146 (1818), "Consolidated Reports of Regiments Abroad." The 1/88 comment is located in WO 27/136.

104. General Brisbane, in his inspection of the 1st Battalion, 3^d Regiment, lamented the many courts-martial of the battalion and blamed it on "a number of sailors, old marines, and other bad characters" improperly recruited. May 1817, WO 27/141. Colonel Stewart of the 4th Regiment noted that the reduced court martial totals in his battalion came about from the discharge of a "number of bad characters." October 1815, WO 27/135.

5

The British Army in France:

Troop Relations with French Inhabitants

Anytime an army fights in, marches through, or occupies foreign territory, be it friend or foe, confrontations and disputes between the soldiers and civilians occur. Regardless of the state of discipline, there are serious violations of the commands issued to preserve order and good relations. Mischief by soldiers, often with criminal implications, flood the reports recorded in the passage of armies. Sometimes this is the result of a thirst for revenge, whereas sometimes it is the simple result of those who cannot control their desire for pillage, rape, or loot.

The generation-long French Revolutionary and Napoleonic Wars created a desire for revenge among the European nations. The allies avoided political retaliation in 1814 and granted a lenient peace settlement, but the events following Napoleon's return from Elba in March, 1815 provoked a different allied response. After Waterloo, the allies planned to extract much more from an ungrateful France. The feelings of the occupying armies reflected the frustration of their respective nations. However, in terms of long range European peace-making objectives, of which Wellington's peacekeeping force was a powerful expression, the commander required that his occupational forces maintain a polite and courteous posture. Failure to maintain correct relations between the occupier and the occupied presented potential internal unrest that would threaten the ultimate peace-keeping mission of the allied forces in France. Wellington, recognizing this threat, feared that "if one shot is fired in Paris, the whole country will rise against us" which would lead to the resumption of military operations.[1] Any allied revenge-seeking also threatened the Bourbon rule, since the French king, Louis XVIII, had sanctioned the occupation of his own country by those very troops. Though the allies occupied only the northeastern departments, the entire nation experienced the weight of the occupation for all France was required to supply the provisions needed by the army through the the exaction of reparations. Relations between the allied army and Frenchmen were felt nationwide. Therefore, if the occupation army acted improperly, the repercussions would threaten the European peace settlement.

Common occupation problems such as excessive drinking, assaults, robbery, and desertions plagued Wellington's army. Even with such obstacles to good behavior, the British contingent worked very hard to maintain correct relations. The British shunned the vengeance that afflicted the other allies. For example, the Prussians expected to avenge all that had been lost at the catastrophe of Jena.[2] The Austrians had been humiliated by Napoleon three times.[3] The 1812 French invasion caused the Russians to conduct "scorched earth" tactics and to lay waste their own land to prevent the *Grande Armée* from obtaining badly needed supplies. Great Britain, however, had never faced a French force on its home soil and thus never suffered from the French extortions. By establishing a standard for behavior, however, the British contingent attempted to create an attitude of moderation that the other allies should follow. Wellington recognized that the troops of all the armies must avoid plunder and "useless destruction of houses and property."[4]

Wellington did not enjoy full authority over all allied contingents in his role as commander-in-chief, and his actions could only influence the other allied units. But because of Wellington's prestige amongst the allied leadership, the subordinate commanders followed the field marshal's lead on most issues. The duke expected his British units to set the example for the other contingents. Had Wellington enjoyed total jurisdiction over his command, the results might have been different.[5] National authorities, while prepared to operate their forces under Wellington's leadership, were unwilling to submit their contingents to the duke's complete authority. With an ever-continuing desire for revenge on their minds, the other allies demanded extractions from France over which Wellington had no controlling jurisdiction.

Wellington had a documented history of moderation. He had observed uncontrolled soldiers in Spain and he knew what his own troops were capable of after battle.[6] The guerrilla war in the Peninsula, nearly total war, had created deep animosity between Spanish and French soldiers. French troops pillaged Spain for six long years. If Spanish soldiers were allowed to loot and plunder upon reaching France, Wellington's army would face a French population more determined than ever to defend itself against invasion. The other alternative to the duke was to command a civilized army passing through the French countryside to fight the next battle. When the duke's army marched into France in 1814, he observed the presence of vengeful Spanish troops. Shortly after crossing the French frontier, Spanish soldiers pillaged the village of Ascain. Wellington decided to send most of his Spanish forces home, though his decision left him inferior in numbers to the forces of Marshal Soult.[7] The Spanish corps he retained was placed under direct control of British officers. The duke also issued an order against plundering. His policy rendered success. The French peasantry in the south met Wellington's army favorably, since his army had behaved better than French troops fighting the British in the region. One British colonel stated that no conquering force had ever acted better than this invading army, and gave full credit to the duke's regulations.[8]

As the allied armies marched on Paris after the Battle of Waterloo, Wellington issued orders for his British army to respect the French countryside, then at the height of its growing season. Wellington's army remained a model of conduct for all of the allied armies. This action contrasted sharply with the plundering of the Prussians, Bavarians, and Austrians on their way to Paris.[9] Wellington knew that Prussian soldiers lived off Frenchmen by forced requisitions because of the poor logistical system of the Prussian army. The duke issued a reminder to all troops under his command that only Napoleon was the enemy, that the allied sovereigns were friends with the French monarch, and France was considered a friendly country. He ordered all army requisitions to be accompanied by payment. Wellington expressly forbade extortions of any type. He issued orders which instructed commissary officials to provide receipts for any procurements. The duke held his officials responsible for any demands they placed on the French. Wellington proclaimed to all Frenchmen that though he entered their country at the head of a victorious army, he was not their enemy but rather the enemy of Bonaparte. He desired only to help Frenchmen overthrow the vestiges of Bonapartist rule.[10]

Wellington had managed to prevent some planned Prussian acts of violence in Paris in 1815. He kept the Prussians from destroying two bridges, the Pont de Austerlitz and the Pont D'Iena.[11] The duke placed a British sentinel on Pont D'Iena when he received word that Marshal Blücher had ordered the bridge's destruction. By doing so, the field marshal prevented an act that would surely inflame the passions of Frenchmen. Wellington implored Blücher not to sanction such acts without the support of the allied sovereigns, for these actions would infuriate the French king and cause civilian disturbances in Paris.[12] The Prussians defended their actions by claiming they had suffered when overrun by Napoleonic troops, but Wellington rejected the validity of these actions. Interestingly, the poor conduct of the Prussians rallied support around the French king and his government.[13]

Wellington placed responsibility for the control of troop behavior with his officers, just as he held them accountable for training.[14] Officers receive credit for victory or defeat on the battlefield, regardless of their personal role. If a battle plan succeeds, the leader receives commendation. If the troops break and run, the leader has failed. When soldiers loot and pillage, their officers receive the blame. Commissioned and non-commissioned officers must set an example that their men will follow. Corrupt leadership begets corruption in the ranks. If the officers are negligent, the men will take advantage. Well trained troops will not rampage unless provoked to an unmanageable extent. Wellington thus gave his officers an important role which insured their participation in the preservation of discipline.

Unfortunately, many British army officers lacked the leadership qualities sought by Wellington. Most British army officers had purchased their commissions just as Wellington had. It was the officer who was often on leave from the occupation army, not the enlisted men. Continued absenteeism of officers set a poor example.[15] Some officers were unhappy to be assigned to occupation duty in France, as Subaltern Pasteur wrote:

> Now, alas! to the troop's vexation
> There came an order from the Horse Guards
> That caus'd an end to their relaxation
> And sent them away soon afterwards to the Army of Occupation
> In the land of brewers, tho' not of bards
> Quartered in the mud villages in French Flanders
> Where the men caught cold, the horses glanders.[16]

Regardless of the quality of leadership, Wellington reminded his officers of their role in keeping good contact with the French. The duke ordered that they visit their men on an irregular basis. Wellington issued this order to insure that the men be present for duty and conduct themselves in an orderly fashion. The dispersion of British units, oftentimes broken down to company level, made the order difficult to implement. In many locations, no officer was assigned. In these units the field marshal expected his non-commissioned officers to demonstrate the same leadership that an officer would have provided. Unfortunately, many sergeants and corporals failed to meet the standards required to maintain discipline. Sergeants often were involved in robberies or they failed to prevent crimes of which they had knowledge. This failure in supervision required the British contingent to place officers where they could maintain proper discipline and prevent incidents between soldier and citizen.

In order to establish an officer presence in outlying areas, Wellington ordered his officers out to inspect training. Through this visitation system, officers could insure that correct discipline was maintained. By showing up unannounced, officers could keep their men fully alert and ready for inspection at any time. Wellington requested that his officers wear sidearms whenever out of quarters to prevent the troops from fighting.[17] The duke ordered his squadron and battalion commanders to submit daily reports to their brigade commanders concerning any incidents or complaints which had taken place in the troop cantonments.[18] British officers also sought assistance from French civil authorities as an added means of maintaining orderliness. To gain French assistance, the field marshal instructed his officers to visit village and city mayors, and to request that they close public houses and clubs during the workday hours of British servicemen.[19]

Confrontation was likely between occupying troops and French soldiers where French garrisons were located in the allied sector.[20] Wellington issued orders to prevent problems from occurring. His instructions required allied troops not to stop inside French occupied villages without the consent of the French commandant. Orders also required soldiers traveling individually in these villages to show their passports. When allied officers, whether on business or pleasure, decided to remain in one of these villages, they had to present themselves to the local commandant and were under the jurisdiction of French police. Wellington's orders held for any French military personnel who passed through allied occupied villages and cities.[21]

Wellington involved himself in cases regarding incidents between British soldiers and French citizens. His actions clearly demonstrate the sense of fairness he hoped to establish with the French. The duke turned several of his own soldiers over to French civil authorities because they had spoken seditious words about the French government and Louis XVIII.[22] When allied troops occupied French ground for an encampment, they told Frenchmen to make their claims for the occupation of that ground to their own government which would make good the claims. However, it was made clear to the troops that they would be held accountable for damages that they committed.[23] Wellington also recommended the payment of rewards for the return of deserters to military authorities if the soldiers involved were convicted.[24] The duke dictated that drunks, deserters, criminals, and other problem soldiers be returned to England as soon as possible to prevent repeated incidents. During the three-year occupation period, the British army on occupation duty returned home to England over two hundred soldiers under sentence of court-martial or under commutation of punishment.[25] The field marshal also recognized that unfamiliar faces caused unwanted trouble. The duke ordered that any stranger arriving in Cambrai, regardless of rank, who decided to remain there for more than twenty-four hours, must hand his passport over to the French police and keep them posted of his whereabouts.[26]

Wellington also intervened in army courts-martial to create an environment of fair play between occupier and occupied. In one case involving arson, an army court-martial acquitted a deserter of charges that he had started the fire in question. The soldier allegedly started the fire to distract the townspeople while he committed robbery. Wellington studied the case and arrived at the conclusion that the soldier was guilty, in spite of the lack of evidence which led to the acquittal. Having made his own decision in the case, Wellington obtained restitution of one hundred pounds sterling for the French citizens who suffered from the fire. In another arson case, the duke agreed that a British soldier had started a fire, though he had done so inadvertently. But Wellington was not convinced that the town residents had done enough to minimize the damages once the fire started. Having decided this, the duke sought no payments to offset damages incurred by the local inhabitants.[27]

In spite of all his efforts to establish and maintain the best possible relations with the French, Wellington still feared a civil uprising which could have been very dangerous. The duke wrote, "If troops of the several armies are not prevented from plundering we will have the whole country against us."[28] He told the Allied Council of Ambassadors that he had complete confidence in the discipline of his army and, that after seven years under his command, they would follow his instructions. The duke warned the ambassadors that he would assign responsibility for any allied troop casualties arising from violent acts to French inhabitants. In the event of a popular uprising against the allied forces, the field marshal ordered his corps commanders to assemble their commands in their cantonments. The troops would respond to any resistance offered by the French by firing on the leaders organizing the violence.[29] British ambassador Sir Charles Stuart[30] urged the Council of Ambassadors to act jointly, should Wellington be unable to force the Duke of Richelieu to curb disturbances, and "induce the French government to take measures to prevent an evil of which the consequences are most alarming."[31]

Wellington offered his subordinates his remedy to solve confrontational issues with the French. First, the commander should call upon local civil authorities to assist. British troops should not be called out to attack even if ill-treated. Wellington rejected the idea that his men should take the law into their own hands. Troops in the village in question should be placed in a military position with regularly mounted guards. The soldiers should establish an alarm post to alert others in case of attack. British soldiers should defend themselves, to include firing weapons against those in opposition. Finally, the duke recognized that most trouble occurred on Sundays or festival days. He wanted his officers present those days, and he ordered the troops kept away from the inhabitants.[32]

Lord Combermere, the British cavalry commander, issued his own set of orders which echoed Wellington's directives and leadership style and were intended to support the duke's goals. Combermere desired that his cavalry corps cultivate a better understanding with French inhabitants within the assigned occupation zone. Vigilance on the part of officers would set the example desired, and civility and discipline on the part of the men would fulfill the commander's desires. Combermere wanted all complaints of the local inhabitants investigated in a timely fashion but without haste, which might create a situation whereby the plaintiff would have no later redress. The general warned his investigating officers not to reach premature decisions. Rather he demanded that they be calm and dispassionate, while weighing both sides of the evidence. Combermere ordered his brigade commanders to adopt measures to maintain their regiments in a state of readiness with the correct equipment. Combermere reminded his officers that even though the war was over, "indolence must not be indulged in."[33]

General Sir Richard Hussay Vivian followed Wellington's directive that general officers set the example for obedience by issuing a similar directive calling for restraint by his subordinates. The general wisely reminded his soldiers that they were occupying a foreign country, and they should consider what their feelings might be should foreign troops occupy their own hometown.[34] Vivian promised to do all he could to relieve the suffering of those inhabitants forced to shoulder the burden of quartering his men. He also promised to use all of his available resources to insure discipline from his men.[35]

In order to control excessive drinking, Vivian ordered proprietors of cabarets located in his sector to close their doors to locally quartered soldiers no later than 9 P.M.[36] Proprietors were told to report any British soldier who failed to obey the order.[37] Concerning public drunkenness, the general believed that "nothing can be more prejudicial to the character of the British state—or the Regiment."[38] Vivian ordered his officers to separate their drunks from those soldiers who exhibited good conduct. The general suspected that drunks committed theft and other crimes detrimental to the army. To control the actions of drunks, Vivian wanted them performing menial labor allowing his disciplined troops more leisure time.[39]

General Vivian ordered his officers to visit their outlying companies and inspect troop quarters. His officers were to stay in towns in time of festivals. He instructed them to confine drunks to prevent development of further problems. The general required his officers to meet with mayors and other local officials to discuss any problems, real or imagined. Vivian directed them to investigate all complaints and correct the evils caused by British soldiers.[40] The general forbade his officers and men to live outside their assigned cantonments without prior authorization from their superiors. Vivian advised his troops that they would be responsible for paying for any damages they might commit because, "private property must be considered as sacred in this country as it is in England."[41]

Lord Vivian took decisive action when required. A hussar company assigned to the village of Longvilliers had a long series of confrontations with the local inhabitants which finally culminated in violence in 1818. Vivian blamed the French for the dilemma, stating that the populace of the entire area had an "evil disposition towards the British Troops." Those troops had earlier experienced trouble in the same village when Vivian sent three officers to investigate why the inhabitants fired upon locally quartered soldiers.[42] In 1818, thrown rocks caused injuries to eight cavalrymen while a Frenchman suffered a head injury, possibly caused by a thrown rock or by a blow from a sword. Three other disturbances in a nearby village occurred which Vivian believed were incited by the Longvilliers mayor, M. Mason. Vivian finally acted after an incident in the village on May 11, 1818, occurred when twenty soldiers of the squadron drew their sabers during a fight with local townsmen. The general blamed these incidents on the mayor and townspeople. In spite of this belief, the general ordered that the hussars assigned to the town be replaced immediately.[43] Vivian also ordered an additional fifty men placed in cantonments in the area because of the bad feelings, and ordered the subprefect to direct local mayors to provide additional quarters. The general instructed the squadron to occupy Longvilliers in strength.[44]

General Vivian undertook other changes to prevent further disputes. He required any cantonment with more than twenty personnel to maintain a regularly posted guard. The general expected posted guards to act properly at all times and prepared to defend themselves. Vivian stated he was still pleased with the general feeling of harmony between his men and local inhabitants, but he reminded his troops to assume a posture of improved military readiness to protect themselves because of recent bad feelings. Mounting numbers of insults concerned the general and he desired to "slow the audacity of the peasantry."[45] The general condemned Frenchmen for some of the incidents they reported. During an 1818 court-martial, some citizens refused to come forward and testify as requested by the acting British cavalry commander, Lord Somerset. Vivian assumed their reluctance to testify was an indicator that they were involved in the events which led to the court-martial.[46]

Vivian expected restraint from his men, and discipline failures led to punitive action by the general. In February, 1816, he ordered a sergeant and several cavalrymen to be held under guard and to work in stables for stealing chickens until it was discerned who had perpetrated the crime.[47] He ordered the investigation of a trooper who struck a Frenchman with his sword when the citizen protected his hay from confiscation. After these incidents, Vivian reminded his squadron commanders "in the strongest manner the necessity of enforcing the strictest discipline," especially in light of the dispersal of his cavalry units.[48]

Vivian recognized the danger of unknown personnel traveling into troubled villages. He issued instructions that no British officer, unknown to the French commandant of Montrieul, enter the town unless authorized by Vivian to do so. Vivian established a brigade passport system for the locally stationed officers, who were required to enter the town in uniform unless specifically exempted by their commander.[49] In a similar case, a cavalry squadron took the liberty of passing through St. Omer (Department of Pas-de-Calais), a French garrison town, without prior authorization and without weapons. The unit failed to make necessary arrangements for their movement. Vivian received the wrath of Lord Combermere, his corps commander, who called the actions of the squadron commander, Major Verner, "thoughtless" and "ridiculous."[50]

General Vivian's actions demonstrate him to be an officer who sought solutions to soldier-civilian incidents which would improve relations between occupier and occupied. On occasion Vivian believed he faced incidents in which French citizens deliberately attempted to embarrass his soldiers, yet he sought to soothe feelings. Vivian reminded local prefects that he planned to keep the tightest discipline, but insults and insolence against his men would not be tolerated. He wrote to a subprefect, "I trust, sir, you will immediately take such measures as will protect British officers from the insults of the disaffected and ill disposed."[51] Vivian urged that civil authorities punish those Frenchmen who sought confrontation with his soldiers. The general reminded his command that the best way to punish insults was to ignore them, especially those made by ignorant Frenchmen. He refused to accept insults as sufficient rationale for confrontations with the natives.[52] The general insisted that episodes which threatened harmony with local inhabitants be investigated by officers conversant in the French language in order to reduce any feelings of distrust on the part of Frenchmen.[53]

Like all general officers, Sir Charles Colville, commander of the Second Infantry Division, supported Wellington's policies. Because of the size of the British contingent in Valenciennes, which included his division, General Colville had difficulty locating sufficient living quarters for his men. The situation forced the quartering of some soldiers in French homes, thus creating uneasy feelings between soldiers and inhabitants. Colville, in an attempt to limit requisitions against the city, informed all British troops quartered inside the town that all they could expect or request was "fire and candle." Colville asked that the townspeople acquaint him with whatever discipline problems they might encounter from his men. Colville's intelligence reported the city satisfied with British orderliness.[54]

The requirement for training areas created the possibility of still further problems between Wellington's army and the local inhabitants. The British contingent had no formal training sites, and soldiers often trampled across farmland during training exercises. Bitterness was certain if a year's worth of labor was ruined. Later restitution, if forthcoming, did not promise to soothe feelings of anger. The situation threatened Wellington's army, for the French had to feed themselves along with the occupation forces. In an attempt to placate farmers, Wellington authorized his soldiers to assist in the harvesting of matured crops.[55]

Some officers, including Wellington, normally used local fields to hunt. The British command issued orders stating that the hunting season could not start prior to the end of the growing season. General Vivian likewise issued a followup order halting officer hunts until all Frenchmen harvested their wheat. His order required that regimental commanders "adopt such measures as will ensure a good understanding between the troops and the inhabitants" with regard to riding over unharvested fields.[56] The general promised to convene courts-martial against those who chose to ignore his orders concerning the hunting season. In 1816, Wellington ordered that the game season not start until September 20. When the subprefect of St. Omer pushed back the game season until October 1, Lord Combermere enforced his decision.[57] When the spring planting season arrived, the British command issued similar instructions ending the shooting season as requested by local authorities. Wellington involved himself again by publishing orders halting the hunting season to allow for the spring planting to commence.[58]

The occupation of France presented ample opportunity for ill feelings between the British army and local citizens. In the midst of the bitterness of occupation, personal relationships started to flourish between British soldiers and French women in ever-increasing numbers during the three years of occupation. A number of soldiers sought consent to marry French girls, though Wellington expressly restricted approval of such requests. In 1816, only one soldier obtained permission to marry a French woman. By the following year, seven men received authority to do the same. In 1818, the last year of the occupation, thirty-three soldiers received approval for matrimony.[59]

When the occupation ended in 1818, Wellington could express satisfaction with his British soldiers and their attitudes towards the French citizenry. War between Britain and France had lasted since the failure of the *Peace of Amiens* in 1803, but Wellington refused to excuse bad behavior in the name of revenge. Frenchmen may have instigated confrontations, but most of them remained isolated and did not lead to any major incidents. Relations between occupier and occupied were satisfactory. The British command fully investigated disputes and made restitution when appropriate.[60] The British army established better relations with the French than did those of the other allies. When the Duke of Wellington issued his last dispatch to his troops just prior to the end of the occupation, he congratulated his officers and men for their good conduct.[61] He could issue this commendation with full knowledge that it was true.[62]

NOTES

1. Philip Guedalla, *Wellington* (New York: The Literary Guild, 1931), 280.

2. Napoleon humiliated the Prussians at the Battle of Jena-Auerstädt, October 14, 1806, thanks to the movement by Marshal Davout around the Prussians to cut their lines of communications. Instead the Prussian army, withdrawing from Jena, fell on Davout's smaller French force at Auerstädt, attacked and was badly mauled. The French army then conducted pursuit operations towards Berlin, leading to Prussian capitulation.

3. The Italian campaign of 1800 which ended in defeat at Marengo, the 1805 campaign which saw Austrian losses at Ulm and Austerlitz and led to the *Peace of Pressburg*, and the abortive 1809 war which culminated at Wagram.

4. Wellington to Castlereagh, July 14, 1815, Wellington Papers 1/476, University of Southampton, Southampton, United Kingdom.

5. J. Garston, "Armies of Occupation, I: The British in France 1815–1818," *History Today*, 11 (July 1961), 396–404. Garston notes that Cambrai was a long way from the Austrian headquarters at

Colmar, and Wellington could hardly hope to influence behavior at such a distance.

6. The British soldiers plundered after the battles of Vitorio and Ciudad Rodrigo rather than pursue a beaten enemy.

7. Marshal Nicolas Jean Soult (1769–1851) earned his marshal's baton in 1804, and saw service in Spain for six long years, facing Wellington on several occasions, especially after the French effort began to crumble in 1813. Soult rallied to Napoleon for the Hundred Days, and went into exile after Waterloo. He served both as Minister of War and Minister of Foreign Affairs under Louis-Philippe.

8. Elizabeth Longford, *Wellington: The Years of the Sword* (London: Weidenfeld and Nicolson, 1969), 412–13.

9. Castlereagh to Lord Bathurst, July 14, 1815, Add MSS 37573, Papers of Lord Liverpool, British Library, London, United Kingdom. Castlereagh stated that restraining the other allied troops seemed impossible. See also Stuart to Castlereagh, August 24, 1815, Foreign Office Report 146/4/162, Public Record Office, Kew, United Kingdom.

10. Reverend G. N. Wright, *Life and Campaigns of the Duke of Wellington* 4 vols. (London: Fisher Son and Company, 1841), 11–12; Godfrey Davies, *Wellington and His Army* (Oxford: Basil Blackwell, 1954), 83.

11. Named in celebration of the 1805 Napoleonic victory over Russia and Austria, and the 1806 victory over Prussia.

12. Wright, *Life and Campaigns of Wellington*, 35.

13. Stuart to Castlereagh, August 21, 1815, FO 146/4/160.

14. See chapter 3 concerning training.

15. General Richard Hussay Vivian Papers, General Cavalry Orders, December 4, 1816, National Army Museum, London, United Kingdom notes the disgust of Wellington and Lord Combermere with officers overstaying their leaves; and the Vivian Brigade Order Book, April 1, 1817, notes that officers were abusing the liberal leave policy of Wellington.

16. Colonel Harold Malet, compiler, *The Historical Memoirs of the XVIII (Princess of Wales's Own) Hussars* (London: Simpkin and Company, Ltd., 1907), 159, has a poem by Subaltern de la Pasteur entitled "The Hussars in Occupation, or a Souvenir of the Old Eighteenth," a humorous verse describing life in France from 1815 to 1818. Glanders is a contagious and sometimes fatal respiratory horse disease.

17. Lieutenant-Colonel John Gurwood, editor, *The General Orders of Field Marshal the Duke of Wellington in the Campaigns of 1809 to 1818* (London: W. Clowes and Sons, 1837), September 27, 1817, 533.

18. Ibid., November 26, 1817, 497.

19. Ibid., November 26, 1817 and April 10, 1818, 488 and 497.

20. See chapter 2 and appendix A for a list of these garrisons.

21. Sir George Murray Papers, 46.7.20, October 25, 1816, National Library of Scotland, Edinburgh, United Kingdom.

22. Wellington to Stuart, February 14, 1816, FO 146/7/66; and Wellington to Bathurst, February 15, 1816, WO 1/209/17.

23. Murray to Rowland Hill, July 14, 1816, Murray Papers 46.6.20.

24. Bathurst to Wellington, December 30, 1815, Wellington Papers 1/485, allotted three pounds sterling reward for the apprehension of deserters.

25. Weekly Returns of the State of the Forces, Return of men sent to England under sentence of court martial or commutation of punishment, November, 1815 to November, 1818, Wellington Papers 9/7/2; and Vivian Papers, General Cavalry Orders, January 14, 1816.

26. Gurwood, *General Orders of Wellington*, Order of October 27, 1816, 486.

27. Wellington to Bathurst, September 5, 1818, WO 1/215; Wellington to Bathurst, May 5, 1816, WO 1/210/28. On at least three occasions Lord Bathurst wrote Wellington approving similar payments. He reminded the duke that the losses would have to be substantiated by the victims.

28. Wellington to Castlereagh, July 14, 1815, Liverpool Papers, Add MSS 37573.

29. Stuart to Castlereagh, June 24, 1816, FO 146/9/228; and Stuart to Castlereagh, June 27, 1816, FO 146/9/234.

30. Sir Charles Stuart (1779–1845), Baron Stuart de Rothsay, longtime diplomat, envoy to Portugal 1810, minister to the Hague 1815–1816, ambassador to Paris 1815–1830, and later ambassador to Russia.

31. Stuart to Castlereagh, July 1, 1816, FO 146/9/241.

32. Wellington to Sir Henry Fane, May 30, 1818, Wellington Papers 1/580.

33. Vivian General Cavalry Orders, December 20, 1815.

34. Vivian Brigade Order Book, June 2, 1816.

35. Vivian Brigade Cavalry Orders, February 14, 1816.

36. Vivian Brigade Order Book, April 22, 1817.

37. Ibid., Childers to the sous-prefect of Boulogne, July 1, 1816.

38. Ibid., July 1, 1816.

39. Vivian General Cavalry Orders, December 20, 1815.

40. Vivian Brigade Order Book, February 5, 1816.

41. Sir George Murray to Lord Rowland Hill, July 14, 1816, Murray Papers 46.6.20.

42. Vivian Brigade Order Book, September 5, 1816. These incidents all involved elements of the 18th Hussars.

43. Vivian Brigade Order Book, May 22, 1818.

44. Vivian General Cavalry Orders, June 2, 1818.

45. Vivian Brigade Order Book, September 5, 1816; Vivian Brigade Order Book May 22, 1818; Vivian General Cavalry Orders, June 2, 1818.

46. Vivian Brigade Order Book, February 14, 1818.

47. Ibid., Childers to Verner, February, 1816. This incident involved members of the 7th Hussars.

48. Ibid., Childers to Bridger, February, 1816.

49. Ibid., (September 23, 1815 to July 31, 1816), Order of February 26, 1816.

50. Vivian General Cavalry Orders, September 2, 1816. This case involved the 7th Hussars.

51. Vivian Brigade Cavalry Orders, February 20, 1816.

52. Vivian General Cavalry Orders, May 11, 1816.

53. Ibid., December 20, 1815.

54. *The Times* (London), April 13, 1816.

55. Ibid., September 6, 1817.

56. Vivian General Cavalry Orders, November 22, 1816.

57. Ibid., September 7, 1816.

58. Ibid., September 7, 1816, November 22, 1816, March 4, 1817, and March 10, 1818.

59. List of persons who have obtained permission to marry, November, 1816 to October, 1818, Wellington Papers 9/7/1. *The Morning Chronicle* later claimed that five thousand French women followed the departing British troops to Calais hoping to travel to England, but since most were unmarried, army authorities sent them back home. November 16, 1818.

60. Murray Papers 46.7.10, April 20, 1818. Reportedly an incident took place in St. Pol (Pas-de-Calais) when French troops passed through that town. In spite of the lack of evidence of any trouble, the British troops in the town were temporarily removed and housed elsewhere until the situation calmed down.

61. Murray Papers 46.7.14, Wellington to his army upon the breakup of the occupation command, November, 1818.

62. The Prefect of the Nord to Wellington, October 25, 1818, Wellington Papers 1/592. The prefect thanked Wellington for the good conduct of his forces in France which allowed for good relations between Frenchmen and British soldiers.

6

French Relations with their Occupiers

In his effort to reduce confrontation with the French, General Vivian had requested his men to put themselves in the place of the inhabitants and to ask themselves what their attitude would be if they were occupied by a foreign country.[1] This seems a sincere concern in light of the circumstances in which France found herself after Waterloo. The French had gone from the grandeur of empire to total catastrophe in a very short time. Just a few years earlier the French had defeated every enemy in battle and had gained control of most of Europe. French soldiers were deployed throughout the continent. In 1815, those formerly occupied countries controlled the destiny of France. She was occupied by soldiers of small nations that could never match the greatness of France. She was occupied by soldiers of nations that just a few years earlier had suffered repeated humiliating defeats at the hands of Napoleon. The average Frenchman must have been very apprehensive, at best, at the very thought of what occupation at the hands of their former victims could mean. With the terms of the peace treaty, France had to support an army that occupied her. This requirement to support the army would come out of the pocketbook of every French taxpayer. Even though most Frenchmen never saw an allied soldier because of the restricted zone of occupation, they were well aware of the humiliation of Waterloo, the occupation of Paris, and the resulting peace treaty. Furthermore, it was obvious to most that, after the easy return of Napoleon from Elba, the allied troops were in reality serving as a prop to the Bourbons. This could only have had an adverse effect on their perspective of their government. There can be little doubt that most Frenchmen were embarrassed by the occupation and wanted the allies out at the earliest possible moment.

All commanders are concerned with the relations between their troops and local citizens. Wellington made this a cardinal concern in general for the allied army and specifically for his British troops. The British contingent was concerned about its relations with the inhabitants of its sector of occupation. Poor behavior by British soldiers would leave bad feelings, and the message would be passed on to the rest of France that the allies were exacting revenge. No matter how hard the British strove to keep confrontations to a minimum, and regardless of Wellington's policies, he was sensitive to the fact that bad behavior on the part of any portion of the allied army would not bode well for relations between France and Europe. And there is little doubt that those who had suffered the worst at the hands of the French Empire, notably Prussia, planned to extract everything possible from their victory. Bearing this in mind, the French relations with their occupiers were never very good, nor should it have been expected that they would be. Association often became confrontational. Anytime French authorities were caught appearing to side with an allied soldier concerning an incident, the French government would emerge as an agent of the occupation forces. Since the government could not afford this viewpoint, it could be expected to side with its citizens. Thus, while it was in the allied interest to avoid confrontation, Frenchmen could seek incidents whenever possible to embarrass the allied soldiers, to gain restitution when possible, or even to embarrass the French monarchy. To those enduring the occupation, every victory, however small, was to be savored.

The picture that is drawn of British soldiers from the French viewpoint is far different from the British perception of themselves. The French government did not sit idly by and wait for the end of the occupation to report its concerns to the allied army. The government passed the complaints it received from its local communities about allied actions to the Duke of Wellington through the offices of the Duke of Richelieu. Richelieu followed up the complaints of his countrymen and sought relief from Wellington.[2] The French looked to Wellington for support of their claims against allied soldiers. Foreign Secretary Castlereagh believed that having Wellington in command of the army would render the plan of occupation "less unpopular" in France.[3] The French expected Wellington to take corrective actions against his own troops.[4] French communities expected the duke to curtail training maneuvers and hunting conducted on farm land.[5] Wellington agreed that British personnel accused of crimes against French citizens of property would receive a trial in French courts.[6] The Duke of Wellington demanded that his officers keep track of their men and thought that the former's presence would prevent crimes from taking place. The British did not want the reputation that the Prussians had with Frenchmen, for it would not serve the larger policy aims of the British government. In spite of these desires, British soldiers committed crimes with or without the presence of officers.

Richelieu received almost daily the reports from the occupied areas of French dissatisfaction, especially concerning the cost of occupation and the crimes committed by allied soldiers.[7] The complaints eventually became so numerous that Richelieu only forwarded to Wellington those which he considered the most legitimate.[8] The French foreign minister vowed to control two principal items: first, that the consumption of the allied troops be kept in line with the peace treaty allowances and the orders of Wellington; and secondly, that the rations of the allied officers be regulated.[9] In any case, with the huge costs involved in supporting the army of occupation, the French government could not sit idly by and fail to seek redress for the excesses committed by allied troops.

The French government informed its lower officials of their responsibilities in an effort to ease the pain of occupation. Count de Barbe-Marbois, the minister of justice, wrote to his district and municipal attorneys in the occupied eastern departments concerning his expectations of them. They were to maintain good relations and harmony with allied army officers. He ordered attorneys who arrested military personnel who had committed crimes to deliver them to allied authorities with the appropriate data concerning the nature of their crimes. Attorneys were to push for trial and punishment of these soldiers. Allied personnel would not appear before French tribunals, while Frenchmen would not appear before allied military courts. If allied soldiers were needed to testify in French courts, attorneys should make requests through the allied headquarters. Marbois ordered French citizens summoned to allied courts to appear. He concluded his instructions by requiring the lawyers to maintain all the rights of royal jurisdiction, as agreed to by both Richelieu and Wellington.[10]

France felt the weight of occupation immediately after the signing of the second *Treaty of Paris*. The British received vigorous complaints from the French government as the allies moved into their cantonments after the signing of the peace treaty. The movement caused distress upon the French as they observed foreign troops marching across their land. As the troops arrived, they issued new exactions. When a British cavalry unit put a lodgment demand on Le Havre for six hundred men enroute to its cantonment, the minister of war, the Duke of Feltre, refused to budge at all and provide the facilities, for no such agreements had been reached.[11] In December, Feltre complained to Richelieu about the damages committed by two British regiments. He accused the two units of pillaging and violence which caused considerable damage in merchandise.[12] The ration demands of the occupation army quickly became an issue, and it was unclear if France could supply the army and its own people. Feltre begged Wellington to insure that his men did not draw more rations than authorized for the army.[13]

Oftentimes, little could be done to remedy French complaints. As the allied army was being formed in 1815, Talleyrand expressed his displeasure with the ever increasing amount of provisions that had to be surrendered to allied troops. Wellington wrote Talleyrand stating that it was up to the French authorities to conciliate the minds of the inhabitants. The duke warned that often "there can be no remedy or redress." He also promised to speak with Louis XVIII concerning exaggerated complaints which were actively sought by French authorities from their citizens, and which would not be acknowledged by the allies.[14]

The British spent their time stamping out the vestiges of the Napoleonic empire. The commandant of the gendarmes in Arras (Department of Pas-de-Calais) wrote to the minister of war that the British were hunting down any rumors that Bonaparte was going to return or any indications that praise was still placed on the emperor. The British troops ripped down portraits or papers indicating support for Napoleon. They announced their belief to the population that the French king had returned to power and that he would be able to maintain his throne.[15] The casual observer might note that those "guaranteeing" the Bourbon throne were taking up residence in France, not departing.

At the same time as some British personnel appeared to be supporting the crown, other were doing the opposite. The prefect at Calais was concerned with English journals that embellished Napoleon's accomplishments and his life in exile at St. Helena's while appearing to threaten royalist officials. These writings gave him the impression that Great Britain wanted Napoleon back on the French throne.[16] Other British officers claimed that most Frenchmen supported the return of Napoleon.[17] In February, 1816, French officials arrested two British officers for defamation of the king's character when they made injurious comments about Louis XVIII.[18] The British officers who spoke these seditious words claimed that it was customary in England to speak one's mind, and they thought they should enjoy the same right while serving in France. The French government preferred not to hear such irreverent remarks about the king.[19]

The quartering requirements caused some citizens to lose their homes to British troops. Some could no longer work because of the presence of soldiers, while others were ordered to build new homes for British officers.[20] The British forced themselves on communities in an arbitrary manner.[21] A Calais newspaper expressed the initial impact of the British presence in the department. Peasants were forced out of their homes to make room for occupying troops. Even

British officers, with all their luggage, servants, and horses, exacted a great toll. With the increased demand for goods, the average Frenchmen could not afford many necessities. The paper concluded to its readers, "Hitherto we have had only roses, now we feel the thorns."[22]

The French government, amidst the complaints of their citizens, continued to insure that it upheld the provisions of the peace treaty. When the French failed to deliver some supplies to his troops, Wellington complained to Richelieu. Richelieu had to respond to Wellington or risk a British reaction. The minister wrote to the official involved in the issue for an answer for his actions. The gentleman excused his actions because of the overextension of his budget. There was simply no money with which to buy the supplies required to support the army of occupation.[23] Whatever the feelings of the French about the British soldier, the British prince regent expressed his satisfaction with the spirit of accommodation of the French government towards the British army in France.[24]

British reaction to complaints gave some satisfaction to the French officials. The interior minister informed Richelieu that even as the situation deteriorated, the British command supported his office with attempts to prevent further crimes. General Henry Clinton indicated his unhappiness with criminal acts and promised to make every effort to arrest those wanted by French authorities. Clinton promised efforts to stop inflammatory remarks directed against the French authorities, and he planned to remind his soldiers of the support of the British government for Louis XVIII. The prefect of Pas-de-Calais commented that he believed that the sentiments of Wellington and his generals indicated their disapproval of criminal behavior. He believed that Wellington desired the prosecution of British criminals to the full weight of French law, though he also commented that little success had been achieved.[25]

One particular case, involving a counterfeiting operation run by British soldiers, demonstrates how the British command sought to alleviate French dissatisfaction. French officials in Valenciennes captured four soldiers involved in the operation. The British army tried the men via court-martial and sentenced them to deportation to the Australian penal colony of Botany Bay. Wellington personally reviewed the case and confirmed the penalty.[26]

Some British crimes went beyond complaints to the French government. French citizens were outraged at the actions of one soldier of the 43^d Regiment, who stole a cross from a church and destroyed it. Police discovered fragments of the cross in his room. This sacrilegious act had a very bad effect on the local populace, and the interior minister sought reparations from the British command.[27]

In some cases, Frenchmen did not go out of their way to prevent problems with the occupying troops. Lieutenant John Machell
of the 18th Hussars related his complaints about housing to General
Vivian, and offered the French response to his objections. The mayor
stated that "stables were sufficiently good for English soldiers." This
episode required Vivian to approach the subprefect of Montrieul for
correction. Vivian wrote, "my men are staying in places hardly fit
for pigs while good housing goes unoccupied." The general promised
the subprefect that his men would only use the minimum housing required but for health reasons would only stay in acceptable
accommodations.[28] Drinking often brought on problems that might
have been avoided. The French tried to make profits by encourag-
ing young soldiers to frequent bars and nightclubs. Vivian warned
the subprefects of both Boulogne and Montrieul that cabaret owners
were welcome to give credit to his soldiers, but the British army was
not responsible for insuring repayment to proprietors.[29] The results
were predictable. Drunken British soldiers tried to reopen bars in
Valenciennes for more drink.[30] Soldiers of the 43^d Regiment broke
into a store in Bapaume (Pas-de-Calais) and drank themselves into
a stupor. Their actions resulted in a fight, followed by destruction
and injuries to the store owner. When these soldiers were arrested,
other regiments in the vicinity complained to French authorities.[31]

Relations with the other occupying contingents could not have
been expected to have been good. The British had never been invaded by Napoleon's forces and thus were not subject to the massive
pillaging of which French troops proved capable. The other powers
could use the occupation to deliver a message to the French. The
Prussians had never gotten over their defeat at Jena. Napoleon's
troops defeated the Austrians three times. The Russians had suffered dearly in the campaign of 1812. Even though they had emerged
victorious, their own "scorched earth" tactics that repulsed Napoleon
had ravaged Russia as well.

The French considered the Prussian contingent the most vin-
dictive. Even Wellington, when considering the command of the
occupation army, expressed doubts of whether he could manage the
Prussians.[32] Before the occupation was underway, the actions of the
Prussian forces had earned them no friends, and rallied the support
of Frenchmen for their king.[33] The Prussians demonstrated their feelings when they attempted to blow up the Jena Bridge (*Pont D'Iéna*)
in Paris. The bridge symbolized the ultimate Prussian disaster. Only
Wellington's intervention prevented the bridge's destruction. The
Prussians took actions which deliberately sought revenge and could
only have left the French citizenry of their sector embittered. The
Prussians issued a circular in their occupation zone in 1816 which

stated that former French military personnel who wished to reside in a village occupied by the Prussian army had to produce a certificate from the commune mayor where they elected to live granting his approval. In turn, only then would the Prussians issue a visa allowing the soldier to reside in the village.[34] In one particular case, Minister of War Feltre wrote to Richelieu seeking Wellington's assistance in overturning a Prussian move to deport a retired colonel from the city of Longwy (Department of Meurthe and Moselle). Feltre was concerned that if the Prussians got away with the move, they would expand similar measures to other communities.[35] The Prussians issued double requisitions on the citizens of Longwy and threatened the mayor if the city did not deliver the supplies.[36]

The Russians offered similar treatment and the French classified them in the same category with the Prussian soldiers. In January, 1816, the local gendarme lieutenant in Sedan (Ardennes) protested to the Duke of Feltre about a rape of a young girl in the village of Donchery (Ardennes) which had left the mayor in great terror.[37] Another report in that month complained of one robbery, one rape and four cases of bad treatment.[38] The Prefect of the Nord noted that though his department had only received one-third of its expected allied troops, the district of Avesnes had been crushed by increased charges. The residents complained that the Russians were worse than the Prussians. The Russians placed extra strain on the local inhabitants by refusing to put two men in a bed. Two other districts, Douai and Cambrai (Department of the Nord), had each received an unexpected regiment of Cossacks for a temporary period. The prefect claimed that a Cossack presence had been forbidden. Foreign occupation had paralyzed the collection of taxes, and had caused some communities to pay well beyond their fair share.[39] The municipal council of Landrecies (Nord) rated the Russians as equal to the Prussians for bad treatment.[40] The mayor of the village of Montigny complained that when the Russians arrived in their cantonments, they had helped themselves to whatever lodging and other requirements they needed, all without consideration of the community. The village was dissatisfied with the ill-treatment it had received.[41] The prefect of the department of Nord wrote to the Duke of Feltre that as the allies were entering their cantonments, they made exaggerated comments about their intentions to the inhabitants which only succeeded in raising the fears of Frenchmen. He urged that the Russians be held "scrupulously" to the treaty conventions so that excesses could be avoided.[42]

The Duke of Feltre pleaded with Richelieu about the bad situation in the department of the Ardennes caused by Prussian and Russian demands. He reported the destitution of Frenchmen, and the assistance that had to be supplied to the army of occupation was only increased by the exactions of the eastern powers. Feltre noted that the foreign troops respected nothing, and there had been over a dozen rapes, including one on a girl six years old. The only solace provided by the occupiers was to encourage the French authorities to do their own investigation.[43] Feltre requested that a liaison officer be placed near Wellington. He wanted this officer to have ties with the French gendarmes and to have the authority to intervene in cases of conflict between local police and allied soldiers.[44] If the Russians were as bad as the Prussians, the prefect of the Nord acknowledged that the English and the Hanoverians conducted themselves much better than the Russians.[45]

The situation in the Austrian sector appeared better. The Austrians arrived with good intentions. The governor-general sent by the Austrians issued a proclamation stating that he had been charged by his emperor to attend to French interests. The emperor desired that his troops abandon the role of enemy and protect all citizens from disorders and the excesses of war.[46]

Among the smaller contingents in France, the Bavarians caused ill feelings. As the Bavarians settled into their lodgings, the Prefect of the Meuse complained to Feltre of Bavarian actions as they departed temporary locales. In Lunéville (Department of Meurthe and Moselle), the Bavarians had left over one hundred fifty men behind to conduct surveillance of one hundred thrity-six sick soldiers unable to move. This had disheartened the inhabitants of the Department of the Meuse for the treatment they received had been poor, and this new action could be considered dangerous.[47] The Bavarians also interfered with French officials conducting the normal business of collecting customs.[48] Meanwhile, French authorities pronounced themselves satisfied with the conduct of Saxon troops.[49]

When the day of the allied departure finally came, cause for French celebration had arrived. The key aim of the French government was to insure there were no incidents so that the allies would have no reason to remain or strike out against Frenchmen. The commander of the gendarmes in Givet (Ardennes) wrote to the minister of war, Gouvion-Saint-Cyr, that when the Russians had departed, a great day had finally arrived. He assured the minister that he had taken measures to maintain harmony with the allies as they left, and passage of troops was being effected without incident.[50] The war minister was kept apprised of the exact date of allied movements and their units involved. These reports gave Saint-Cyr the ability to order French army units to move forward into the demilitarized zone and the allied sectors without confrontation.[51] Early movement of his forces into the evacuated zone was essential to energizing support for the French monarch, for their prompt arrival would give the army the appearance of having helped effect the allied departure.

The Duke of Castries wrote to the war minister that the allied departure caused problems in the city of Châlons. The departing Russian and Saxon units issued unusual demands for lodging on the city which led to an uneasiness among the populace. De Castries refused to meet the demand. He also wrote that the city of Verdun had refused to allow a sick Saxon remain in the city hospital though he was in the process of trying to reverse this sign of resistance.[52] De Castries understood the importance of not provoking the allies as they were in the process of withdrawing. Other areas reported no problems. Saint-Cyr sent a mission to Sedan to observe the Prussian departure of that sector. The report came back that there were no problems.[53]

The British regiments that departed from the port of Calais did not enter the city itself. Instead the soldiers remained billeted outside the city until such time as ships were available for embarkation. *The Morning Chronicle* reported some hissing from the French as the troops departed, but British officials reported not the slightest disturbance from the Calais residents as the withdrawal concluded.[54]

This catalog of incidents is normal and could be continued for the entire three years of occupation. These incidents are familiar to any commander in an occupied or friendly area. Troops will be troops, and their relations with the populace are not always good, in spite of the efforts of military authorities. Complaints are what are heard and entered into the official records. Good relations usually go without mention. What emerges from the documentation, however, is normalcy. Both the allied occupational command and French authorities made every possible effort to cooperate and to make a success of the situation. Wellington refused to tolerate exploitation of the French, violation of French law, or abuse of French subjects. Wellington and Richelieu cooperated to find solutions and punish culprits. They achieved cooperation through the structure designed to report and resolve incidents. French prefects reported to the minister of justice, and army officials reported to the minister of war. These two ministers in turn reported to Richelieu's office, which communicated French concerns to the Council of Ambassadors or directly to Wellington's headquarters. Wellington then used his military command structure. The tone of the letters between Richelieu and Wellington is one of cordiality. Everything considered, the incidents between occupied and occupier may be classified as normal for the situation, perhaps even minimal, as no stress arose between the government and the occupational command. Wellington often went beyond the expected, allowing British soldiers to be tried by

French courts and British officers to testify in those courts. Punishments of those proven guilty were carried out.

NOTES

1. Sir Richard Hussay Vivian Papers, Brigade Order Book, June 2, 1816, National Army Museum, London, United Kingdom.

2. Andre Vovard is highly critical of British officers and soldiers in his article "Les soldats anglais en France en 1814 et 1816," *Revue des Études Napoléoniennes*, July–December 1918, 14:240–43.

3. C. K. Webster, editor, *British Diplomacy 1813–1815. Select Documents Dealing with the Reconstruction of Europe* (London: G. Bell and Sons, Ltd., 1921), Castlereagh to Liverpool, August 12, 1815.

4. Minister of the Interior to Richelieu, January 25, 1816, Correspondence with Great Britain relative to occupation, 1815–1818, Mémoires et Documents, Fonds France 702, 1815–1818, Archives du Ministère des Affaires étrangères, Paris, France [hereafter MD].

5. Ibid., Minister of Interior to Richelieu, January 25, 1816; and Richelieu to Wellington, February 20, 1816.

6. Ibid., Richelieu to Decazes, February 20, 1816.

7. There are nine volumes of correspondence filled with these complaints at the French foreign ministry archives.

8. Pierre Rain, "La France at les armées d'occupation, 1815–1818" *Revue des Questions Historiques*, (1907), 81:233.

9. Feltre to Richelieu, January 15, 1816, Correspondence with Prussia relative to occupation, 1815–1818, MD, Fonds France 706.

10. Marbois instructions cited in *The Times* (London), March 4, 1816.

11. Feltre to Richelieu, October 26, 1815, MD, France 702.

12. Ibid., Feltre to Richelieu, December 22, 1815.

13. Duke of Feltre to Wellington, December 12, 1815, Wellington Papers 1/485, University of Southampton, Southampton, United Kingdom. Lord Bathurst gave Wellington total control over the ration question and authorized him to purchase army needs above allowable levels. Bathurst to Wellington, December 26, 1815, Wellington Papers 1/485.

14. Wellington to Talleyrand, August 24, 1815, MD, France 702.

15. Commandant, Arras gendarmes to Minister of War, January 2, 1816, General Military Correspondence of the Second Restoration, 1815–1830, *Archives de l'armée de terre*, D3-18, Château de Vincennes, France [hereafter War Ministry Archives].

16. Prefect of Pas-de-Calais to Minister of the Interior, January 6, 1816, MD, France 702.

17. Ibid., Prefect of the Nord to Richelieu, January 6, 1816.

18. Ibid., Minister of Police to Richelieu, February 17, 1816.

19. Ibid., Minister of Justice to Richelieu, March 27, 1816.

20. Ibid., Town council of Avesnes (Nord) to the Duke of Feltre, February 7, 1816.

21. Ibid., Minister of Interior to Richelieu, January 25, 1816.

22. Article cited in *The Times* (London), January 10, 1816.

23. Wellington to Richelieu, April 12, 1816, MD, France 702, includes a copy of the letter sent by Richelieu to M. Doudon.

24. Castlereagh to Stuart, February 7, 1816, Foreign Office Report 146/12/15, Public Record Office, Kew, United Kingdom.

25. Minister of the Interior to Richelieu, March 2, 1816, and March 9, 1816, including comment by M. Malouet, prefect of Pas-de-Calais, MD, France 702.

26. Ibid., Minister of Justice to Richelieu, March 27, 1816, April 9, 1816, and May 4, 1816.

27. Ibid., Minister of Interior to Richelieu, May 1, 1816.

28. Vivian Brigade Order Book, June 3, 1816, and June 5, 1816.

29. Ibid., Circular of August 23, 1817.

30. Minister of Justice to Richelieu, April 23, 1816, MD, France 702.

31. Ibid., Minister of Interior to Richelieu, February 16, 1816.

32. Webster, *British Diplomacy*, Castlereagh to Liverpool, August 12, 1815.

33. Stuart to Castlereagh, August 21, 1815, FO 146/4/160.

34. Order of Prussian military police, January 12, 1816, War Ministry Archives, D3-18.

35. Duke of Feltre to Richelieu, January 18, 1816, MD, France 706.

36. Ibid., Feltre to Richelieu, January 8, 1816, also includes a request to seek Wellington's assistance in the matter.

37. Report of gendarmes of Sedan to Minister of War, January 14, 1816, War Ministry Archives, D3-18.

38. Ibid., January 15, 1816.

39. Ibid., Prefect of the Nord to Minister of War, January 15, 1816.

40. Ibid., Municipal Council of Landrecies to Minister of War, January 18, 1816.

41. Ibid., Mayor of Montigny to subprefect of Cambrai, January 2, 1816.

42. Ibid., Prefect of the Nord to Minister of War, January 3, 1816.

43. Feltre to Richelieu, February 9, 1816, MD, France 706.

44. Ibid., Feltre to Richelieu, February 17, 1816.

45. Prefect of the Nord to Minister of War, January 15, 1816, War Ministry Archives, D3-18.

46. Proclamation of Charles Baron de Baden to the inhabitants of Haute Marne, Haute Saône and Cote D'Or, July 31, 1815, Correspondence with Austria relative to occupation, 1815–1818, MD, France 703

47. Prefect of the Meuse to Minister of War, January 4, 1816, War Ministry Archives, D3-18.

48. Minister of Finance to Richelieu, April 22, 1816, MD, France 702. Corvetto urged Richelieu to approach Wellington to take action. At the same time, British troops in Valenciennes also interfered with the collection of customs.

49. Prefect of Pas-de-Calais to Minister of War, January 21, 1816, War Ministry Archives, D3-18.

50. Colonel of gendarmes at Givet to Minister of War, November 2, 1818, War Ministry Archives, D3-57.

51. Ibid., Proteau reports from Calais to Minister of War, November 2, 1818; Murray report to Minister of War, November 7, 1818.

52. Ibid., Duke de Castries to Minister of War, November 18, 1818.

53. Ibid., November 22, 1818.

54. *The Morning Chronicle*, October 31, 1818, and November 16, 1818. The *Chronicle* stated that the hissing represented French hatred of British soldiers who were "the primary instruments of their downfall."

7

Wellington and the Barrier Fortresses

The Dutch Barrier Fortresses

The allies included the reconstruction of the Dutch barrier fortresses, running along the current Belgian-French border, in the 1815 peacemaking process. Britain had voiced its support for an adequate military barrier in the lowlands to the allies in 1814. After the first restoration of the Bourbons in 1814, the allies assigned the reconstruction of the fortresses jointly to Great Britain and the newly created Kingdom of the Netherlands.[1] Lord Liverpool considered the defense of the Low Countries a "distinct British interest" of great significance.[2] Castlereagh told Parliament "that to fortify the places in Belgium was not a Dutch object merely, but one which interested all Europe, and this country in particular."[3] *The Morning Chronicle* stated, "The fair interest of Great Britain extends no further than a secure frontier for the Netherlands, and if that can be obtained by the re-establishment of the Flemish fortresses, it is no more our policy ... to promote dismemberment [of France] by which we cannot profit."[4] Napoleon's 1815 military campaign in Flanders demonstrated that the guaranteeing of the defense of the southern border of the Netherlands belonged to all Europe. This new guarantee became a part of the overall European plan to establish and maintain order. Though the barrier forts were not the direct responsibility of the army of occupation, both devices were part of the peacemaking process and were designed to keep France within her borders. The continued stay of the allied army in France was subject for review after three years of occupation. The allies could not consider the subject of a withdrawal unless the Dutch barrier reconstruction program was completed. The barrier forts occupied territory parallel to that occupied by Wellington's army inside France on the other side of France's northern border. Lord Liverpool stated that the allies could not leave France until the barrier in the Netherlands was completed. He recognized that this was a process that could take up to seven years to fully complete, depending on what the Duke of Wellington deemed necessary.[5]

The allied powers gave responsibility of governing both projects to the Duke of Wellington.[6] By overseeing both programs, Wellington was in a better position to evaluate the progress of the reconstruction project against the continued presence of the allied army inside France. The allies expected the duke would insure that the fortress rebuilding program was completed and capable of performing its assigned mission. Wellington had learned the value of fortifications during the Peninsular War where siege warfare was an almost regular occurrence.[7] The field marshal relied largely on the Royal Engineers for expertise concerning the Dutch barrier system. During the three years that the army of occupation served in northern France, Wellington periodically inspected the fortifications and kept the allied sovereigns aware of construction progress of the barrier system. Whenever the allied powers asked their commander his views concerning the ultimate fate of the occupation army, he had to consider the military equivalents required to replace it. Wellington needed to have full knowledge of the status of the forts, for this knowledge would guide his final recommendation for the army. As occupation commander-in-chief and untitled military advisor to the allied courts, the duke could not recommend a removal of the army until a suitable replacement was available.

Historically, barrier fortresses had long protected the Low Countries from France. They stood astride part of the traditional invasion route into and out of France. In 1715, the Dutch had gained the right to garrison eight fortresses in the southern Netherlands, running from the North Sea towards Germany, after the War of the Spanish Succession by the *Peace of Utrecht*. Austria maintained administrative control of the area surrounding the fortresses. The Dutch planned to protect themselves from any further detachments by France, which had already annexed Artois and parts of Flanders. The British, in the interest of trade protection, joined in that settlement. Marshal Saxe of France captured the fortresses in 1745 during the War of the Austrian Succession, but their ownership reverted back to the Dutch in 1748 by the *Treaty of Aix-la-Chapelle*. The Austrian Emperor Joseph II began dismantling the fortress system after the marriage of his sister Marie Antoinette to Louis XVI of France.[8] During the era of the French Revolutionary and Napoleonic Wars, the Belgian regions of the Netherlands became joined to the French Empire.

By the Convention of August 13, 1814, Britain and the Kingdom of the Netherlands agreed to rebuild the fortresses under the direction of Wellington.[9] Both Britain and the Dutch agreed to contribute two million pounds sterling each toward improvement of the defense of the enlarged kingdom.[10] The nations created two committees, one of British engineers, one of Dutch, which would submit proposals for the restoration of destroyed forts and construction of new ones.[11] Wellington's memorandum of 1814 on the barrier system served as the basis for the committee proposals. The two committees of engineers aimed at making the forts operational at the earliest possible date. Guidelines called for fortifications to be constructed which would insure the garrisons holding out against siege, anywhere from seven to twenty days.[12] This period presumably would allow Dutch mobilization while the allies began preparations to place troops into the field. Planning also required the engineer committees to determine the size of the garrisons necessary to man the fortresses with respect to the desired defense time for each particular fort.

Wellington stated that no natural barrier in the Low Countries existed upon which a defensive plan could be oriented. He agreed with the diplomatic plans to increase the size of the Netherlands through the addition of provinces essential for a defense of the Netherlands and to assure the objectives of the powers. Wellington acknowledged that the events of the recent wars might have made the idea of defense by strongpoints outdated, and that the rebuilding of the barrier fortifications might not be worth the expense. He stated his awareness of the "general unpopularity attached to fortifications." Notwithstanding this, he planned to defend the Netherlands on the lines of the previous barrier forts. He added to his defensive proposal a requirement for a water inundation capability in the western sector of the defensive plan, from the River Scheldt to the English Channel. Defense in the eastern sector, encompassing the area from the Scheldt to the Meuse, also relied on flooding, but primary defense for the area belonged to the Dutch army and the fortress system.[13]

In 1814, upon his return to France from London, Wellington conducted his first inspection of the Netherlands-French frontier. Enroute to his post as ambassador to France, he made a cursory two-week inspection. Though he was unable to predict where the next battle, if any, would take place, Wellington found several positions that would be excellent for defensive operations. Among these positions was "the entrance of the *forêt de Soignies* by the high road which leads to Brussels from Binche, Charleroi, and Namur." At this time the field marshal had his first glimpse of the site of the future battlefield of Waterloo.[14]

Napoleon's 1815 invasion of the Low Countries clearly demonstrated the urgency of a restoration of the barrier fortifications. The Anglo-Dutch engineer committees quickly submitted reports, and Wellington investigated all proposals carefully before he accepted plans and dismissed the commissioners.[15] The senior British engineer commissioner wrote to Lord Bathurst that the Dutch did not have the engineering capability to complete the fortress rebuilding within the envisioned five-year period.[16] The engineer suggested that the British engineers join the Dutch in handling the contracting requirements. He also recommended that Bathurst appoint a senior British officer to direct the engineering effort and to report his findings to Wellington, King William I of the Netherlands, and the allied powers.[17]

In October, 1816, Great Britain and the Netherlands signed an agreement which gave Wellington full control over construction demands and expenses that he deemed necessary for the defense of the Netherlands. Wellington controlled six and one-half million pounds sterling for spending, which included two and one-half million from France's reparations to the Dutch.[18] He allocated these moneys based on his review of the engineer's recommendations. The field marshal also contributed to the overall rebuilding program by reviewing the engineering reports of the British and Dutch officers. The duke made the final decision on construction issues on which the engineers themselves failed to reach agreement. Technical aspects of each fortification, such as the construction of revetments or lunettes, normally caused differences of opinion between the British and Dutch engineers. In addition, the duke regularly exchanged letters over the next few years with General Kraijenhoff, chief engineer for the Netherlands, concerning his ideas for the defense of the Low Countries. Wellington based his plans on two principles: first, protection of the Netherlands-French frontier against a main attack in order to allow time to assemble troops for defense and secondly, protection of the lines of communication among the Netherlands, Germany, and England.[19]

Wellington discovered that his duties as commander of the occupation forces did not allow him to devote all his energies to overseeing the reconstruction program. He desired the right to appoint an officer to inspect the fortresses under the duke's auspices.[20] The duke named Colonel John Jones[21] of the Royal Engineers as his sole representative and inspector of the Dutch barrier. He gave Jones full authority to insure that the agreed plans were followed by the construction groups. Colonel Jones enjoyed the complete support of the field marshal.[22] When the British army later attempted to place Jones on half-pay (as part of an overall reduction in forces) and make him unavailable for military assignment, the duke requested that the army rescind the order.[23] Wellington informed the war office that if Jones was no longer available for inspection duty, the duke would relinquish his responsibility of overall supervision of rebuilding the barrier. The army promptly restored Colonel Jones to full duty.

Wellington retained his role as supervisor long after the dissolution of the army of occupation. He visited the fortresses once or twice each year until he became prime minister in 1828, always accompanied by Colonel Jones. During the occupation years, Jones remained attached to Wellington's headquarters at Cambrai. Each year he conducted two inspections and wrote two reports covering the progress of the fortifications.[24] Jones continued to inspect the barrier years after Wellington gave up his primary role supervising the fortress reconstruction.

The barrier fortresses stood on the soil of the southern Netherlands along the French frontier. On the English Channel, forts were located at Nieuport and Ostend. Moving eastward, engineers rebuilt forts at such cities as Ypres, Courtrai, Tournai, Ath, Mons, Charleroi, and Dinant. The eastern fortress sector existed along the Meuse River at Namur, Liège, and Maastricht. Forts located at Ghent, Louvain, Huy, and Dendermonde, as well as those further north at Antwerp, Fort Lillo, and Fort Lietkenshoek provided depth to the defensive system. These forts, located near water, had the capability to add to their defensive posture by flooding the countryside in case of an attack by the French.[25]

The British and Dutch engineers planned construction of each fort for a garrison of predetermined size which could withstand an assault for a prescribed number of days. The British engineers also recommended the number of artillery pieces and mortars required for a successful defense. For example, the engineers expected Nieuport to withstand successfully assaults for thirty days with a garrison of three thousand, sixty heavy guns, sixty flanking guns and howitzers, and eighteen mortars. The engineers designed Ypres also to hold out for thirty days with a garrison of five thousand, seventy-five heavy guns, eighty howitzers, and twenty- five mortars. The plans called for Menin to defend for seven days provided it received a garrison of three thousand and ten artillery pieces. Antwerp required a troop strength of eight thousand, one hundred and fifty heavy guns, one hundred and sixty flanking guns and howitzers, and forty mortars.[26]

Wellington had the option to improve Dutch defenses prior to completion of the reconstruction program by providing Dutch forces with excess British army supplies. He transferred to the Dutch forces guns, shells, and mortars not required or inappropriate for the army of occupation. Wellington received authority from the British prince regent to effect the transfer. From August, 1814 to June, 1816, the British army stationed in the Low Countries and in France contributed almost one-quarter of a million pounds sterling out of its own military chest in support of the fortification reconstruction.[27] In addition, the army ordnance department paid another ten thousand pounds for the engineering officers who were supervising the work.[28]

The anticipated completion date of the fortress system presented a problem when the allies determined that they would terminate the occupation in 1818 rather than remain for the allowable five years. Based on reports submitted in 1815, engineers programmed a few fortresses for completion by 1817, notably those at Ostend and Antwerp. They planned to finish Nieuport, Ath, Namur and Huy by the end of 1818. The reconstruction efforts at Charleroi, Liège, Ypres, Menin, and Grammont required four years for completion. By the end of the fifth year, 1820, the expected date of termination for the occupation army, engineers scheduled Dendermonde for completion, leaving only Courtrai and Mons unfinished.[29]

Unfortunately, the engineers were overly optimistic. They encountered delays which Colonel Jones reported in December, 1817. Delays arose from requirements to obtain possession of land for fort improvement and from negotiations of contracts for material supply. Colonel Jones remained optimistic, however, that work could still be finished by 1820 with the exception of Mons.[30] In his next report, from his June, 1818 inspection, the colonel sounded a troubling note that seasonal work had only commenced six weeks earlier, threatening the planned yearly work goals.[31] As for Wellington, the duke was pleased with the quality of work accomplished. He wrote that work was progressing to his satisfaction and he thought that the Dutch king "will have some of the finest fortresses of Europe."[32] Wellington remained concerned only with the completion of the reconstruction program. Supplies, armaments, and troops remained the responsibility of the Dutch government.[33] Jones reported in December, 1818, after the occupation army had departed, that all of the yearly work was completed. Workers achieved the scheduled work and the entire barrier neared completion.[34]

A continued slippage of planned completion dates threatened to affect the final departure of the occupation army. By using Wellington's role as arbiter of indemnity claims against France, the Prussians favored advancing the Dutch portions of moneys. The duke could settle claims and have the Dutch paid first before any changes in the attitude of the French government precluded easy settlement. The Prussians suggested that the Dutch government hire extra workers to complete the barrier work, aware of the potential for slippage in final completion and the threat it posed to the overall peace process.[35] It is obvious that the Prussians wanted to link the completion of the fortresses with total evacuation of France.

By his December, 1819 inspection, Colonel Jones seemed satisfied with the work accomplished on the barrier "as to leave no apprehension of any one."[36] He also added, "it may reasonably be expected that, at the conclusion of next season, the whole line of fortresses will be in a state to be armed."[37] The fortress at Mons remained in need of the most work, a fact to which the colonel had alerted Wellington in 1816. In 1820, Jones feared only the effects of weather on the new fortifications. Colonel Jones reported some renovation and rework throughout the decade of the twenties. One crisis arose in 1826. Jones was forced to conduct an investigation based on allegations coming out of Prime Minister George Canning's office that work had been accomplished in a haphazard way using inferior materials. The allegations went unsubstantiated.[38]

The security role of the forts changed with the Belgian revolt in 1830. The French army eventually intervened in support of the rebellion. The Netherlands divided and Belgium received its independence. Britain, which had long supported the construction of the barrier fortresses as a means of keeping the French out of the Low Countries and which had backed the creation of a stronger Netherlands in 1814, agreed to the division. The forts, constructed at great cost and effort to strengthen the Dutch government and help maintain European security, passed over to Belgium.[39] Agreement reached in London in April, 1831,[40] stated that, given French recognition of Belgian neutrality and Belgian inability to garrison all the forts, some forts would be demolished. Acknowledging that circumstances were different from those of 1815, another London convention, signed in November, 1831, agreed that five fortresses, Menin, Ath, Mons, Philippeville, and Marienbourg, would be demolished and their artillery and supplies transferred to the remaining forts. The convention ordered demobilizing work completed by the end of 1834, and required that remaining fortresses be kept in good order by the Belgian government.[41]

The French Fortresses

As work continued on the Dutch barrier, the allies also concerned themselves with the ongoing military position of the occupation army. The army had to have the ability to withstand any attack which might arise from a dissatisfied French army before Louis XVIII could finish the army rebuilding process.[42] Fortresses and citadels had long existed in the northeast quadrant of France, alongside the same invasion route partially guarded by the Dutch barrier. These fortresses were now under the control of the occupation army. The fortifications afforded the allies a means of protecting themselves in case of any future French attack, but they needed a fair amount of reconstruction because of the partial destruction resulting from the combats of 1814 and 1815.

The British cabinet rejected calls for the dismantling of the French fortresses. Prime Minister Liverpool feared that the French could restore the forts at little expense at a later date. He favored British occupation of the fortresses until the Dutch finished construction of their own forts. Upon the departure of the army, the allies should return them to the French to improve the crown's defensive position. This provided added insurance to the king's authority and to European security. Liverpool proclaimed that dismantling the fortresses would be "counterproductive."[43] Wellington preferred the temporary occupation of France to permanent control of strongpoints for the long range peace of Europe. He wrote, "These measures [the occupation] give us military security as if it were a permanent cession, but if carried into execution in the spirit in which they are conceived, they are in themselves the bond of peace."[44] Lord Liverpool demanded that the French agree to the occupation of their fortresses along with a portion of their territory. The allies would occupy those forts until another barrier protecting surrounding nations was completed.[45] Article V of the *Treaty of Paris* of November 20, 1815, thus gave the allied occupation army the right to occupy many French fortresses.[46]

British engineers kept Wellington posted about the improvement program for the French fortifications. The British inspectors conducted their first reviews in early 1816. The two most important French fortresses under British control were the main troop centers at Valenciennes and Cambrai.[47] Valenciennes and its citadel were located at the confluence of the Scheldt and the Rouelle; they acted as a first line of defense along with Maubeuge and Condé, which were situated on the far western edge of the allied locales. The royal engineer inspectors found the fortifications at Valenciennes had been largely ignored since the French Revolution and needed repair. Seven hundred men were housed in the citadel, which required about a thousand to conduct a valid defense. Soldiers billeted in the city served as the reinforcements needed for the defense. Water supplies were adequate but the army failed to stock sufficient provisions. Nearly one hundred and thirty guns and howitzers were serviceable and ready for defense, though gun platforms required additional work. Though the magazine had sufficient room for ammunition, ammunition shortages existed. Hospitals could handle five hundred casualties, with additional help coming from regimental hospitals. In the city itself, barracks were not bombproof and in need of repair. Available housing served sixty-six hundred men. The garrison needed some ninety-five hundred men to hold out against siege in combination with the citadel. The British army stationed two thousand men in the city and while the remainder of the third infantry division, another six thousand men, encamped outside Valenciennes. Engineer observations expressed confidence that sufficient defense around Valenciennes existed and maximum effectiveness was within reach with additional work.[48]

Cambrai, situated eighteen miles from Valenciennes, also had a citadel to assist in defense. The 1816 inspection reported the citadel in need of immediate attention. Its bastion walls were in general disrepair with a whole new wall needed in the west. Only one entrance to the citadel existed. Thirty-two guns were in place with platforms in satisfactory condition. The citadel required twelve hundred infantrymen and two hundred artillerymen to withstand siege, with one artillery company and five companies of the Coldstream Guards present for duty. The inspector reported that many underground caverns existed which, if improved, would allow for the establishment of magazines, hospitals, and barracks.[49]

The city of Cambrai also possessed an old surrounding wall. The revetments were leftovers from the famous French defensive expert, Vauban.[50] Weather had caused numerous large openings in the fortifications. No other gun ordnance, outside of unit artillery, was available. The two available ammunition magazines stocked no ammunition. Limited stocks of grain existed in storehouses. Available barracks could house up to three thousand men while the civilian hospital could monitor two thousand sick. The inspection concluded that sixty-five hundred men were needed to withstand a siege, along with fortress improvements and additional ordnance. The British deployed a brigade of artillery, some two hundred fifty soldiers from the Coldstream Guards, and the Third Battalion, Grenadier Guards inside Cambrai. With this elite garrison, the fortress and city of Cambrai were probably well defended against any possible assault by French forces.[51]

Outside of the two main fortresses of Valenciennes and Cambrai, the other allied contingents garrisoned the remaining French fortification sites. British engineers periodically inspected these locations, but since Britain allotted no money for their reconstruction, the officers limited their inspections to comments about the ability of the defenses to withstand a siege. Inspectors reported that artillery was available in sufficient quantities to withstand assaults. They also reported that most garrisons had available troops assigned to cover defense requirements. Exceptions noted included Grand Givet and Petit Givet, both of which had no ordnance or troops available. Le Quesnoy, whose full complement consisted of one hundred forty guns, had fifty-two artillery pieces available of which fifteen were mounted and ready. While the city needed four hundred infantrymen and two hundred cavalrymen for defense, it had a battalion of nine hundred Saxons available. Maubeuge had no ordnance and required five thousand men to hold its redoubt. The Russians stationed a regiment of three thousand infantry at Maubeuge along with five hundred Cossacks and two brigades of artillery. Landrecies demanded nearly two thousand men for a successful defense, and the Russians garrisoned twenty-two hundred men there, including two hundred Cossacks. The fort at Avesnes had no ordnance and needed considerable repair. The Russians assigned only eight hundred men of the required three thousand to withstand siege. The Russians placed twelve hundred men in Rocroy, where British engineers reported fifteen hundred soldiers necessary.[52]

The Prussian contingent also had limited ability to man their fortresses. Montmedy had fifty-four guns and needed a garrison of up to two thousand. The Prussians assigned a battalion of one thousand men there along with a company of artillery and a company of sappers. Thionville had fifty-five pieces of artillery and required sixty-five hundred troops to man its bastions. The Prussians could garrison only two battalions in the fort, totaling fifteen hundred men along with a brigade of artillery. Longwy had twenty guns in place and needed three thousand men to guard its six bastions. The Prussians garrisoned only two battalions with fifteen hundred men in the city.[53]

British inspectors also scrutinized fortresses under the control of the smaller contingents. They considered the fortress at Condé, guarded by the Hanoverians, important because it was located on canals leading into the Low Countries and was also tied into the defenses at Valenciennes. The fortress had available fifty-five guns, seven howitzers and twenty-two mortars of various sizes. The barracks housed fifteen hundred men and six hundred horses. The hospital could serve two hundred soldiers. The fortress stocked a three month supply of rations, and had an excellent water supply. The British engineer inspector reported that the garrison defense needed up to thirty-six hundred infantrymen, two hundred cavalrymen, four hundred artillerymen, and another two hundred sappers in order to resist siege. The Hanoverian command, with only a five thousand man contingent available in France, garrisoned three battalions of six hundred men each into Condé along with one hundred twenty-five artillerymen. The fort's exterior required inundation if threatened because flooding would limit the enemy attack to one side of the fort. The lack of overhead cover would make a bombardment difficult to withstand. The inspector concluded that a small force could successfully besiege Condé, but that type attack was preferable to a frontal assault.[54] In the Bavarian sector, the British inspection of the fortress at Bische revealed forty guns in place for defense and required a garrison of four hundred troops. The Bavarian command assigned seven hundred soldiers to the fortress.[55]

If allied military operations resumed on the European continent, it was essential that the occupation army, from the English Channel to the French-German border, successfully defend its positions until additional allied relief forces arrived on the battlefield. Considering the allied troop dispositions, failure to defend successfully assigned sectors would cause breaks in the line of defense, and would allow the enemy to swallow the occupation army in piecemeal fashion if it held the other fortress sites. At that point, only a general retreat would avoid defeat. The allied dispositions utilizing the French line of fortifications were in a precarious situation because they did not exist in great depth. Furthermore, the allied army numbered at its inception only 150 thousand. Failure to maintain the line of occupation inside France would throw open the invasion route into the Low Countries, where the Dutch barrier network remained incomplete. Though the French fortifications afforded a means of protection for the occupation army, they required costly improvements. Reconstruction improvements meant that at some future date the French army would replace the allies and take over fortifications which could conceivably be used in another war against the better interests of Europe. The traditional invasion route required a strong defense for no one could accurately assess whether the Bourbons would retain their hold on the French throne. The fortification system on both sides of the Belgian-French border, controlled for the time being by the allies, continued its historic role. Improvements for the French forts served Europe only until the time came that the allies departed France. When that day arrived, European security would depend on other instruments of peace such as the Dutch fortifications.

NOTES

1. Castlereagh to Liverpool, January 8, 1814, Additional MSS 38566, Papers of Lord Liverpool, British Library, London, United Kingdom. The Prince of Orange thanked the British government for demanding a suitable barrier when it appeared the other powers had no interest in the issue.

2. Charles Duke Yonge, *The Life and Administration of Robert Banks, Second Earl of Liverpool, K.G.*, 13 volumes (London: Macmillan and Company, 1868), 2:85, Liverpool to Castlereagh, December 23, 1814.

3. United Kingdom, *The Parliamentary Debates for the Year 1803 to the Present Time*, 1st series, 41 volumes (London: T.C. Hansard, 1812–1830), June 12, 1815, 31:751.

4. *The Morning Chronicle*, July 27, 1815.

5. C. Nelson, "The Duke of Wellington and the Barrier Fortresses after Waterloo," *The Journal of the Society for Army Historical Research*, volume 42 (1964), 37, the Convention of August 13, 1814.

6. Charles William Vane, editor, *Correspondence, Despatches, and Other Papers of Viscount Castlereagh, Second Marquess of Londonderry*, 12 volumes (London: William Shoberl, 1852), Liverpool to Castlereagh July 15, 1815, 10:432–33 [hereafter *Correspondence of Castlereagh*].

7. Sieges took place at such fortifications as Burgos (twice), Badajoz, Ciudad Rodrigo, and San Sebastian, amongst others.

8. Roderick Geikie and Isabel A. Montgomery, *The Dutch Barrier, 1705–1719* (Cambridge: Cambridge University Press, 1930), 334–70.

9. Convention between Great Britain and the Netherlands relative to the Dutch colonies, August 13, 1814, First Additional Article. *British and Foreign State Papers*, compiled by Sir Edward Hertslet, 170 volumes (London: Jones Ridgwey, 1841–1877), 2:370–78.

10. A long standing belief has held that Britain, in reality, agreed to the contribution as a payment for the cession of four Dutch colonies, including the Cape of Good Hope, to Britain. William H. Robson, in his article, "New Light on Lord Castlereagh's Diplomacy," *The Journal of Modern History*, 3 (1931), 198–218, claims that the payments were for the legitimate desires of Britain for Dutch defensive needs.

11. Lieutenant General Sir Harry D. Jones, editor, *Reports Relating to the Re-establishment of the Fortresses in the Netherlands from 1814 to 1830* (London: Spottiswood and Company, 1861), xi. This book compiles all the inspection reports conducted by Colonel John Jones from 1817 to 1828 under the direction of Wellington. It also contains Wellington's memorandum on the defense of the Netherlands frontier, and the report of British and Dutch engineers for fortifying the Netherlands barrier.

12. Nelson, "Wellington and the Barrier Fortresses," 38–41.

13. Jones, *Re-establishment of the Fortresses*, 2–9 contains Wellington's memorandum.

14. Philip Guedalla, *Wellington* (New York: The Literary Guild, 1931), 257.

15. Committee reports were submitted in August, 1815, and commissioners discharged the following March.

16. A date which presumably matched the expected departure of the occupation army.

17. General Alexander Bryce to Lord Bathurst, April 25, 1816, British Library MSS, War in Germany, France, and Belgium, 1813–1815, volume 2, f. 175, British Library, London, United Kingdom. General Bryce commanded the team which included Colonel John Jones and Colonel William Ford. This final recommendation indicates the importance that General Bryce placed on the barrier system for the defense of Europe.

18. Wellington Memorandum of Agreement on Dutch fortresses, October 1816, Wellington Papers 1/522, University of Southampton, Southampton, United Kingdom; Nelson, "Wellington and the Barrier Fortresses," 37–38.

19. Jones, *Re-establishment of the Fortresses*, Wellington Memorandum, 4–9.

20. Wellington Memorandum on the Fortresses in the Low Countries, July 22, 1816, Wellington Papers 1/514.

21. John Thomas Jones (1783–1843) was one of the three original members assigned to the British commission in 1814.

22. Jones, *Re-establishment of the Fortresses*, xiii.

23. Ibid., xv.

24. Ibid., xv.

25. See map of Dutch barrier fortresses, page 107.

26. Nelson, "Wellington and the Barrier Fortresses," 38–41.

27. United Kingdom, *House of Commons Sessional Papers*, H.M.S.O., volume XXVI, 1831–32, Costs of the Dutch Fortresses, gives this figure covering the period August 1814 to June 1816.

28. Ibid., volume XXVI, 1831–32.

29. Jones, *Re-establishment of the Fortresses*, 13–60, Report submitted by the Committee of British Engineers, 1815.

30. Ibid., 169, Inspection report of November–December 1817.

31. Ibid., 173, Inspection report of May–June 1818.

32. Wellington to Castlereagh, August 7, 1817, Wellington Papers 1/555.

33. Wellington memo to Liverpool added to Colonel Jones' semi-annual inspection report of June 1818, Liverpool Papers, Add MSS 38367.

34. Jones, *Re-establishment of the Fortresses*, 191, Inspection report of November–December 1818.

35. Stuart to Castlereagh, February 2, 1818, FO 146/24/42, Public Record Office, Kew, United Kingdom.

36. *Jones, Re-establishment of the Fortresses*, 212, Inspection report of November–December 1819.

37. Nelson, "Wellington and the Barrier Fortresses," 40.

38. Jones, *Re-establishment of the Fortresses*, xvi–xvii.

39. Ibid., xvii–xviii.

40. *House of Commons Sessional Papers*, 1831, volume XX, 1, Protocol of Conference held at the Foreign Office on April 17, 1831 and signed by Palmerston for Britain, Esterhazy for Austria, Bulow for Prussia, and Lieven for Russia.

41. Ibid., volume XLVIII, 1831–32, 27, Demolishment of the Dutch Barrier Fortresses.

42. See chapter 9 concerning the French army bill.

43. Liverpool to Castlereagh, July 28, 1815, Wellington Papers 1/474.

44. C. K. Webster, editor, *British Diplomacy, 1813–1815. Select Documents Dealing with the Reconstruction of Europe* (London, G. Bell and Sons, Ltd., 1921), Wellington to Castlereagh, August 11, 1815.

45. Vane, *Correspondence of Castlereagh*, Liverpool to Castlereagh, August 3, 1815, 10:456.

46. Including Cambrai, Valenciennes, Maubeuge, Sedan, and Longwy. See appendix A for a list of all occupied French fortresses.

47. See chapter 3 for the British troop dispositions.

48. State of the French Fortresses occupied by the Allied Army, August 28, 1816, WO 55-1554/2, Public Record Office, Kew, United Kingdom, based on inspections of Valenciennes conducted by Captain Walls, Royal Engineers.

49. Ibid., State of the French Fortresses occupied by the Allied Army, March 1, 1816, based on inspections conducted by Captain Harris, Royal Engineers.

50. Sebastien Le Prestre de Vauban (1633–1707), Marshal of France and engineering expert during the reign of Louis XIV. He designed many new innovations in the construction of urban fortifications.

51. State of the French Fortresses occupied by the Allied Army, WO Report 55-1554/2, based on the inspections of Captain Harris, Royal Engineers.

52. Ibid., compiled from State of the French Fortresses occupied by the Allied Army.

53. Ibid.

54. Ibid., May, 1816, based on inspections conducted by Captain Harding, Royal Engineers.

55. Ibid.

THE DUTCH BARRIER FORTRESSES

North
Sea

The
Netherlands

N

MILES
0 10 20 30 40 60

FT. LILLO
FT. LIETKENS
HOECK
OSTEND
NIEUPORT
GHENT
ANTWERP
DENDERMONDE
R.SCHELDT
R.MEUSE

YPRES
OUDENARDE
COURTRAI
GRAMMONT
LOUVAIN
MAASTRICHT

TOURNAI
ATH
HUY
LIEGE

CHARLEROI
MONS
BINCHE
R.SAMBRE
NAMUR
R.MEUSE
DINANT

Allied Army Zone of Occupation

France

OCCUPIED FRENCH FORTRESSES

8

The Troop Reduction of 1817

In order to build support for the monarchy and insure the survival of his ministry, Richelieu sought a reduction in the troop strength of the occupying army earlier than originally proposed by the allies. Richelieu broached the subject with the allies in the summer of 1816, barely a half-year into the occupation. The timing presented the duke with the opportunity to further strengthen his government while the Chamber of Deputies was in recess. Public order had been maintained, he argued to the occupying powers, and indemnity payments, at least for the time, were being made on the assigned dates. Based on the conditions inside France, Richelieu thought he could safely approach the allies and point out the positive good that would result from a diminution. A diminution would reduce France's occupation costs and would avoid the possibility of embarrassment if France failed to meet her reparations payment schedule. Additionally, a reduction would demonstrate the good intentions of the allies and would confirm their confidence in the French crown, the French people, and the Richelieu ministry.[1] Thus, the possibilities of an early diminution of the occupation forces presented a golden opportunity for the French government to rally support since it would enhance the legitimacy of Louis XVIII's rule if could be demonstrated that the reduction was a direct result of the government's actions.

Richelieu communicated his thoughts personally to the Duke of Wellington in a meeting on June 6, 1816. It was readily apparent to Richelieu that Wellington was the key to achieving a troop cut, and, if Wellington were convinced that a reduction was in order, the allied governments would surely accede to his decision. Wellington forwarded the message to his government, which convinced Richelieu that he had gained the field marshal's unqualified support.[2] Richelieu also wrote to his old benefactor, Czar Alexander I of Russia, expressing his hopes of a reduction. He decided not to make a formal request to Russia. Richelieu thought that the Prussians would not join with the Russians in supporting a reduction since they found it in their interests to maintain sizable military forces inside France.[3]

Wellington responded to Richelieu's informal inquiry reporting the British cabinet's response. The cabinet did not reject the idea completely, nor did it approach Richelieu's expectations. British foreign secretary Viscount Castlereagh expressed his regret that Britain could not form any opinion on such a major issue without consulting its allies.[4] Britain did express an interest in handling any financial arrangements required by the French government. The earliest that Britain would entertain any ideas about a withdrawal would come at the close of the next French parliamentary session. The British decision remained contingent upon the state of French internal affairs.[5] Thus it was essential that France demonstrate continued progress in achieving internal stability.

Richelieu experienced disappointment at this response, since he believed that he had gained Wellington's support. Wellington must have changed his mind since there exists no reason to suppose that the British cabinet held a position at variance with that of the duke.[6] In the meantime, Richelieu pursued the subject and sought out Austrian and Russian approval for a reduction. He won only their qualified support when both nations agreed to follow Wellington's lead. Richelieu realized he would have to redirect his efforts to gain Wellington's approval. In a meeting between the two dukes and the French king, Louis XVIII and Richelieu expressed to Wellington the importance they attached to the issue. The field marshal replied that he would not favor a diminution if pressed for an immediate decision. He urged that they not push the issue until they determined it absolutely essential that a reduction take place. He added that this should not occur before the end of 1816. Richelieu reminded the field marshal that France had made great strides since the summer of 1815. Wellington countered that the real consideration was the actual state of France and its future, and asked what effect a reduction would have on France's discontented political factions. Wellington argued with full knowledge that both Austria and Russia probably favored a reduction, and that Prussia had not yet been consulted. He knew that Richelieu would find it difficult to convince Prussia to agree to support any reduction whatsoever even if he, Wellington, recommended it.[7]

By dissolving the *Chambre Introuvable* on September 6, 1816, Richelieu placed additional pressure on Wellington for a troop reduction. The day after the dissolution, Richelieu wrote to the field marshal informing him that he was writing to Berlin requesting Prussian approval for the proposed reduction. The minister asked Wellington to put in a good word with Prince Hardenberg[8] concerning a diminution. If Louis XVIII announced a reduction in his opening speech to the new parliamentary session, the Richelieu ministry would rally a considerable amount of support.[9] Wellington replied that he did not think Hardenberg would defer to his judgment on the question. The field marshal clearly stated to Richelieu that no troop cut would be announced before the next legislature was seated.[10]

After the election in October, 1816, Richelieu again approached Wellington concerning the positive impact of a diminution in troop size, but the field marshal remained reluctant.[11] In the meantime, the French ambassador in Vienna spread the word that his country found it increasingly difficult to pay her indemnities. He did so as a ploy to gain Austrian support for a troop reduction. A reduction offered immediate financial relief to France since the continued occupation only drained his government's finances. A reduction of any size would reduce the strain of the occupation on the nation since France paid for the food and equipment needed by the allies. But Richelieu's call for the allies to cut back their forces was more than a mere monetary scheme. A reduction would bring on a sense of satisfaction for all Frenchmen.[12]

Wellington equivocated and replied to Richelieu that the powers could not evacuate France until they had ascertained the attitude of the newly elected chamber. The duke enjoyed the backing of the Austrians for this delay. He reminded the minister of the responsibility of the occupation army to insure Louis XVIII's security as well as that of Europe. Wellington was not yet convinced that belligerency had been successfully suppressed inside France to the level that would allow him to call for a troop cut.[13] Richelieu continued to pledge himself and his ministry toward obtaining an immediate diminution.[14]

Calls in support of a diminution arose from British sources. Many British anxiously awaited the return of their troops. They feared that potential agrarian and industrial unrest at home might require the presence of additional soldiers on the Isles.[15] Britain also struggled with its longtime fear of a large standing army. After so many years of war, with peace finally appearing a reality, those fears again surfaced. The British press remarked that a reduction presented an opportunity for economic growth, but their concern was not necessarily for the French. *The Times* of London editorialized that France could not expect to maintain normal commercial transactions if she were saddled with huge support payments. If a reduction were made, trade between Britain and France would increase.[16]

From the beginning of the discussion of the reduction until the final arrangement was made, the allies stood firmly behind the actions of Wellington. The duke remained the focal point for any allied decision on the subject and, if one was arranged, what shape and form it would take. One by one the allies agreed that the duke should guide their decision. Prince Metternich advised the Austrian ambassador to Paris, Baron Vincent, to follow the lead of Wellington. Czar Alexander I of Russia ordered his representative to the Council of Ambassadors, Pozzo di Borgo, to vote "according to the opinion of His Grace."[17] The British prince regent reminded his ambassador in Paris, Charles Stuart, that the reduction issue was a military question and he ordered him to seek Wellington's judgment and "be guided wholly by His Grace's opinion."[18] While the prince regent hoped that the army would not be removed prior to achieving its aims, the "general interests of Europe" was the guiding factor in any final decision. He urged caution before any decision was made, but he also realized that a reduction would encourage confidence in the French government and aid in the struggle for continental stability.[19] These allied attitudes demonstrate their total reliance on the Duke of Wellington for military matters as well as a statement of their respect for his judgments. On a major subject such as the diminution, the duke's expertise extended beyond purely military issues.

No commander, wherever he may be stationed or in what circumstances he may be placed, wants to lose any part of his assets. Commanders are assigned missions to be completed and, in most situations, a larger complement of troops makes accomplishment of the mission easier. Reductions threaten the successful completion of missions. Wellington, looking at the subject of a troop reduction from his position as commander-in-chief, reached the same conclusion. Reviewing the duke's position, occupying a small corner of France with a multinational force of only 150 thousand men whose national governments had their own self interests at stake, clearly demonstrates Wellington's precarious military situation.

When first queried on the possibilities of a loss in troop strength, Wellington had rejected the suggestion. As an alternative, Wellington sought a reduction in the French indemnity payment schedule. Alteration in payments did not appear to be a long-term solution for the problem. In December, 1816, after the dissolution of the *Chambre Introuvable* and subsequent elections had produced more moderate representation, the duke continued to express reservations about a reduction. In his opinion, the newly seated chamber still needed to formulate its position on French indemnities. A troop withdrawal might later render it impossible to force France to adhere to its financial obligations. From a military standpoint, Wellington correctly foresaw difficulties in enforcing future allied decisions on the French.

The situation began to change towards the end of 1816. In a meeting of the Allied Council of Ambassadors, the Austrians tried to go on record favoring a reduction in troop strength.[20] The deciding factor behind the changing attitude seems to have resulted from the deteriorating French financial situation. France paid quarterly installments of the indemnity totaling 140 million francs per annum. She paid another fifty million francs per year for the salaries of the army of occupation. The costs of providing the allied army with rations, forage, and lodging added another hundred million francs to her yearly bill. The annual 290 million francs charge placed huge deficits in the French budget. Increased taxation was out of the question, for it was believed taxes were as high as the country could stand in the current economic crisis. Corvetto, the finance minister, insisted that France meet all her financial obligations in spite of the reparations payments. Corvetto obtained a loan from the Baring and Labouchère financial houses to avoid defaulting on the indemnity and to get France beyond her immediate budget crisis. Government bonds were used as collateral for the cash received.[21]

Though France made her payments on time, Wellington continued to maintain that no reduction was possible until there was a definitive settlement of the financial questions. As France began to seek a rather huge loan from Hope-Baring, she was forced to suspend payments to the allies in November, 1816. Wellington recognized the seriousness of financial crisis and worried that if the problem persisted, "France will be aground this year, and our settlement of last year will be entirely destroyed."[22] The suspension threatened all of Richelieu's work, for if payments were not forthcoming, the allies would have to act to insure collection. The suspension of payments greatly disturbed Wellington since it presented his army with immediate supply problems. The lack of satisfactory forage had previously forced the army of occupation to cancel some of its autumn maneuvers. As the Hope-Baring transaction was being negotiated, the duke reviewed Richelieu's request for a twenty percent reduction in his army.

To provide France with interim relief from her financial problems, Wellington issued orders for the army contingents to adjust their assigned troop strengths back to the levels stated in the November, 1815 peace treaty. This meant the allied army was to cut back to its authorized level of 150 thousand men. The action would marginally reduce the French support requirements to the army because the contingents, due to transfers, illness and the like, often carried several hundred more men on their rolls. When the order was issued, the allied forces totaled 157 thousand men. The move offered some relief until the French could show their intention of maintaining internal order and allow the allies to withdraw more meaningful numbers. The French government saved approximately ten million francs per year from this adjustment. Wellington informed the French government that, while he was a friend of France, he remained opposed to a reduction. He wanted France to take strong monetary actions, not merely request a diminution from the allies, if she wished to see a larger reduction.[23] It appears that the field marshal's position resulted from a decision of the British cabinet, which reacted to the possible economic consequences of not according some type of relief. The cabinet proposed a reduction only when the French government demonstrated its intention of fulfilling its financial obligations.[24]

Suddenly and unexpectedly in January, 1817, Wellington reversed his position from that which he had held just one month earlier. The duke reviewed the issue from a statesman's point of view rather than from a commander's. Since European courts respected and normally accepted his position on most questions, the reduction was no exception. The duke began to sense the loss of favorable French public opinion for the occupation and the rise of hostility towards the allied troops welcomed one year before. Now he felt constant antagonism on the part of the government, the royalists, and Frenchmen in general. Wellington's change in attitude resulted from the reality of the state of near bankruptcy of the French treasury; it was not derived from military policy.

Financial negotiations leading towards a diminution began in Paris on January 9, 1817. Wellington wrote to the Russian czar on that day appealing for his support for a financial plan sponsored by the house of Hope-Baring. In the letter, Wellington stated that if the plan were not adopted, the allies might be required to resort to armed force to provide means for subsistence for the occupation army. Likewise, Wellington warned that the failure of the plan would mean bankruptcy for the French government and then the allies would receive none of the indemnity due.[25] The financial negotiations continued through January and into February. Austria and Russia gave their approval to the plan on January 13.[26] Richelieu and Baring agreed to the arranged loan on February 4, and the French government ratified it on February 7.[27]

Wellington submitted his plan for a major reduction in the army to the Council of Ambassadors on January 9. The duke prefaced his plan with a long discourse on why the allies had initially consented to occupy France. He reviewed the facts: The army served a need of the French king by offering him protection while preserving peace, order, and security. After the Battle of Waterloo and subsequent abdication of Napoleon, France did not possess an army to back up the decisions of its own government. Wellington's occupation army was primarily conceived as a European effort to help restore the order lost after 1792. It also provided additional assurances for the execution of

the *Treaty of Paris* of November 20, 1815. Considering the state of
continuing unrest in France and hostility towards the allied army,
some gesture directed towards eventual evacuation might improve
the French political and economic situation.[28]

Wellington stated that the occupation served the objectives of
both parties and thus should not be thought of as a condition imposed on the French by the allies in 1815. The field marshal accepted
the reality that the French political situation had changed following
the elections dissolving the *Chambre Introuvable*. The new chamber
had already demonstrated its loyalty to Louis XVIII. French internal order appeared to be re-established. Wellington realized that the
Richelieu government needed the popularity that any troop reduction would afford. In a recent trip to Paris, Wellington had found
that the allied diplomatic representatives favored a troop withdrawal.
The duke predicted that if the army were kept at 150 thousand men,
the French would find it increasingly difficult to provision the occupation forces. Considering the bad harvests of 1816, Wellington
foresaw the possibility that the occupation army might be forced into
military action to obtain its subsistence. Using such force to pro-
cure supplies was certain to raise resistance from Frenchmen. Public
opinion would turn against the occupation army and undermine its
peacekeeping mission.[29]

Wellington's proposal to the Council of Ambassadors on January
9 consisted of seven points. He recommended a troop withdrawal totaling thirty thousand men, one-fifth of his army. Each contingent
would be proportionally reduced by one-fifth. By cutting troops from
each contingent, the balance between the allied forces would remain.
The balance might prevent abuses which could exacerbate passions
between the inhabitants and the allied soldiers. Wellington settled
on the total of thirty thousand and he rejected a proposal to remove
twenty thousand men per year for two years. The field marshal believed that the financial relief for France would be the same under
either plan, but his plan left him an extra ten thousand men available
for peacekeeping. The French requirement to supply provisions was
also cut proportionally, from 200 thousand daily rations to 160 thousand. The duke ordered that the horse forage requirement, however,
remain sufficient to feed fifty thousand horses daily. He was well
aware that the unit inspections reports continually emphasized the
poor quality forage the French were supplying. If the forage supply
were reduced, the quality might deteriorate even further. Wellington
stated that once France concluded negotiations and arranged a loan
for the payment of indemnities, he would order the reduction. He
scheduled the troop reduction for April 1, 1817. The French ration
supply requirement was to be reduced that same day.[30]

Negotiations concluded with a protocol. Official notification of it was submitted to the Duke of Richelieu by the Council of Ambassadors on February 10. Richelieu, in turn, notified the Chamber of Deputies the same day.[31] The ambassadors acknowledged to Richelieu that since July, 1815, Louis XVIII had successfully diminished passions and rallied Frenchmen around his throne. The protocol reaffirmed that the purpose of the occupation was to assist in the consolidation of the monarchy.[32] The allied sovereigns wished to aid the French monarch, at a time when they regarded France's internal affairs sufficiently quiet to allow a reduction in forces. Wellington requested that the Richelieu ministry inform the French public of the allied diminution in the most favorable manner and help maintain public opinion in support of the allied presence. The Duke of Richelieu had accomplished a major objective of his government with the announcement of the reduction. The president of the council achieved his success thanks to the decision of Wellington, who saw the reality of all costs of the occupation to France, rather than limit his viewpoint to purely military issues. Increasingly Wellington rose above his military training and took on the role of statesman.

Following Wellington's order, the allied contingents began the process of withdrawing their designated forces in March in order to beat the April 1 deadline. As commander-in-chief of the British contingent, the field marshal was responsible for meeting his own order. Wellington wished to meet his requirement by reducing his strengths to six hundred men per infantry battalion which, when combined with the additional removal of unattached artillery companies, would fulfill the twenty percent cut.[33] However, the Duke of York, commander-in-chief of the British Army, rejected the idea.[34] York wanted instead to maintain unit integrity at current established levels. York ordered Wellington to remove six complete battalions of infantry.[35] In this way, the commander-in-chief met his own requirement to reduce manpower levels by demobilizing regimental second battalions deployed in Ireland and replaced them with the returning units. The Duke of York allowed Wellington to reduce the strength of his two foot guard battalions, 3^d Battalion, the Grenadier Guards and the 2^d Battalion, the Coldstream Guards, each by two hundred troops.[36] By direct order, the Duke of York commanded Wellington to return the 3^d Battalion, The Royal Scots, home to Britain.[37] All other decisions rested with Wellington. The other five battalions designated for return to England and ultimate assignment to Ireland were the 21st, the 27th, the 40th, the 81st, and the 88th Regiments of Foot.

With the deadline of April 1 rapidly approaching, preparations for withdrawal were made in order for units to depart France before the new French support requirements began. British soldiers began leaving France on March 17 when the 21st Regiment of Foot embarked. The withdrawal operation was a major exercise and, in the mind of General Sir George Murray, Wellington's Chief of Staff, could serve a model for the ultimate withdrawal of the occupation army. And in reality, the withdrawal served as the basis for the November, 1818 final allied departure. Planning was required for transport, routes, road movements, rations for men and horses while enroute, and encampments on the road to the French coast. In order to expedite the move, shipping tables were designed to transport those units whose travel distance to Calais were the shortest.[38] This would release ships more quickly for return to France and receive the next departing units. The Royal Scots were transported out of France on March 18 along with the 81st Regiment. The 88th Regiment departed the next day. The movement concluded on March 20 when the remaining two battalions, the 27th and 40th Regiments, boarded ship.[39]

With the reductions, the British reorganized their infantry command from three to two divisions. In Cambrai, Sir Lowry Cole commanded the First Division, which consisted of four brigades and ten battalions. The First Brigade, under General John Lambert, consisted of the 3^{d} Battalion, Grenadier Guards, and the 2^{d} Battalion, Coldstream Guards. Second Brigade, commanded by Sir Manley Power, controlled two battalions from the 57th and 91st Regiments of Foot. Sixth Brigade, under the command of General James Kempt, had three battalions, the 7th, 23^{d}, and 43^{d} Regiments of Foot. Seventh Brigade, with Sir Robert O'Callaghan commanding, consisted of the 1st Battalion, 5th Regiment, the 1st Battalion, 9th Regiment, and the 1st Battalion, the Rifle Brigade.

Sir Charles Colville took command of the Second Division, encompassing three brigades and ten battalions headquartered in Valenciennes. The Third Brigade, under General Thomas Brisbane, consisted of the First Battalion, 3^{d} Regiment, 1st Battalion, 39th Regiment, and the 2^{d} Battalion, the Rifle Brigade. General Denis Pack commanded the Fourth Brigade with three battalions from the 4th, 52^{d}, and 79th Regiments of Foot. General Thomas Bradford commanded the Fifth Brigade, also with three battalions from the 6th, 29th, and 71st Regiments.[40]

The Russians met their reduction requirement by withdrawing three of their regiments. From their cavalry division, the Courlande Cavalry Regiment, composed of six squadrons, was chosen to return home. From the Ninth Infantry Division, the command chose the 38th Regiment of Chasseurs (3^{d} Brigade) with two battalions and the Abcheronsk Regiment of Infantry (1st Brigade), also with two battalions, to return home to Russia. The contingent commander-in-chief, General Michael Woronzoff, reorganized his Ninth Division by disbanding the 3^d Brigade and shifting its remaining regiment, the 10th Chasseurs, to the 1st Brigade.[41]

The Austrian army retained its original three division organization. The Austrians ordered home a complete brigade of two infantry regiments (eight battalions), and reduced their 2^d Division to a one brigade division. The other two divisions had two infantry brigades.[42]

The smaller allied commands also had the option to remove whatever troops appropriate to meet Wellington's orders. The Saxons, for example, removed their 2^d Battalion of Light Infantry.[43] The Danes withdrew their Holstein Rifle Battalion. The Bavarians issued orders for the return home of the 12th Infantry Regiment, while Würtemberg withdrew its 3^d Infantry Regiment.[44] Only the Hanoverians kept their old command structure and met reduction requirements by a twenty percent drop in personnel strength in all units.[45]

The King of Würtemberg orchestrated a major challenge to the Wellington plan of a twenty percent reduction by all commands. The king proposed that he would withdraw his force in its entirely. The king gained the strong support of both the Duke of Richelieu and Czar Alexander I for his plan. Richelieu saw the proposal as an opportunity to get rid of all smaller elements completely,[46] which would still meet the overall one-fifth reduction requirement. Only the four powers would remain inside France under the scheme. If France wished to re-enter the European diplomatic system as a major player and act as a power broker, removal of the weaker European nations was essential. A nation under occupation by troops from the states of Saxony, Würtemberg, Bavaria, Denmark, and Hanover can hardly be called a major power. Russian General Woronzoff informed Wellington in mid-March that the czar hoped to avoid removing any of his troops. Woronzoff wanted Wellington to remove other forces, specifically the Würtembergers. The czar's reported concern the was the distance his men would have to travel to get home.[47] The Russian goal was to maintain its present troop strength in western Europe, and preserve the czar's influence in major allied decisions.

Wellington rejected the Würtemberg proposal. He recognized that if peace was a goal of all European nations, then all nations had to make an investment in security. Wellington perceived the important role of all of the allied contingents in the accomplishment of his army's mission of achieving tranquillity inside France. If the small nations were to benefit from the continued occupation of France, Wellington expected them to continue their contribution.

Had the duke endorsed the plan to remove the complete contingents
of the smaller powers, he would have opened up the possibility of a
long-term presence of unwanted Russian troops in western Europe.
This presented a situation which might cause breaks in the alliance.
Wellington assessed what was in the best interests of Europe, though
undoubtedly his military command would have been strengthened by
the removal of only the smaller contingents.

Western Europe had long feared that if the Russian military
gained a foothold in the west they would never leave. This fear
was heightened when the Russian forces failed to meet the departure
deadline of April 1. The delay was blamed on slowness in the issuance
of orders, due to distances involved which prevented their timely
delivery.[48] Based on the Woronzoff message to Wellington concerning the Würtemberg proposal, the delayed departure can be assigned
to the czar's reluctance to remove any of his troops. No other command experienced a problem in issuing orders. Orders did not reach
the Russian units until mid-April. The Russian cavalry was ordered
to march back home via Germany, while Russian vessels were assembled to sail for France and move the balance of departing troops.[49]
Over four thousand Russians remained in Calais for over a month
awaiting transport. Their departure did not occur until June.[50] Per
the reduction arrangements, France was not held accountable for
supplying provisions for the Russians since their obligations ended
on April 1. The delay must have caused much consternation and the
allies may have been as glad to see the troop removal completed as
the French were. The suggestion for a troop reduction stirred a vigorous debate over whether it was a good idea and, if so, what shape
it should take take. The European powers were willing to go along
with the idea if it was militarily feasible. To answer that question,
the allies went to Wellington, their commander-in-chief. Wellington
alone decided when and what size reduction would take place. The
ultimate decision for a diminution was the correct choice for both
France and Europe. Louis XVIII, in a speech to his Chamber of
Peers, announced an improvement in French attitude towards occupation arising from the allied troop reduction. The monarch noted
that, while the army was in place to maintain peace, all France felt
the presence of foreign troops. When the news of the impending departures spread, French cities celebrated, and Richelieu, in line with
Wellington's desire, passed along a favorable word to the public for
the allied move. Any nation would have celebrated the removal of
foreign soldiers. Richelieu's government enjoyed a major success at
a time when it was most needed.

On the allied side, Wellington promised that, if the troop removal failed to bring about a similar reduction in tensions, any fur-

ther drop in military strength before the specified end of the occupation period would be out of the question.[51] He feared the dangerous consequences of another cut since it would be impossible for his army to act with any strength. The duke proved adroit at assuming the role of statesman when he reached his decision on a troop withdrawal. Wellington was well aware that, considering the fresh memory of the Hundred Days, Louis XVIII and Richelieu were in a precarious position and needed the approval the troop withdrawal would provide. He was also able to view the situation as the military man, worried about future military intervention possibilities and what his requirements might be. The allies turned to Wellington for a crucial decision, and he based his judgment on the best interests of Europe.

The troop reduction, with the exception of the delayed Russian departure, took place on scheduled and caused no long-term ill effects on Wellington's army. As the 1st Battalion, 88th Regiment of Foot left France, the Third Division commander, General Sir Charles Colville wrote to the battalion commander, Colonel Alexander Wallace, thanking him and the regiment for their service during the occupation, saying,

allow me therefore to request you will do me the honour to express in my name my hearty wishes for the honour and well being of the Regiment in whatever situation or service it may be placed, and that the officers, NCO's, and Privates will accept my thanks for the ready attention paid to my recommendations during the period I had the honour to have the Regiment under my command.[52]

NOTES

1. J. Fouques-DuParc, *Le Troisième Richelieu* (Lyon: H. Lardanchat, 1952), 69, cites the letter of Pozzo di Borgo to Nesselrode.

2. Richelieu to Osmond June 6, 1816, Fonds Richelieu 147, *Bibliothèque de Victor Cousin*, Paris, France; Wellington to Richelieu, July 18, 1816. Wellington Papers 1/514, University of Southampton, Southampton, United Kingdom.

3. Richelieu to Osmond, June 17, 1816, Fonds Richelieu 147.

4. Castlereagh to Charles Stuart, September 6, 1816, Foreign Office Report 146/13/81, Public Record Office, Kew, United Kingdom [hereafter FO 146].

5. Wellington to Richelieu, July 18, 1816, Wellington Papers 1/514.

6. Richelieu to Osmond, July 15, 1816, Fonds Richelieu 147.

7. Wellington to Castlereagh, August 30, 1816, Wellington Papers 1/517.

8. Hardenberg, Charles-Auguste (1750–1822), Hanoverian, 1810 Chancellor of State, Prussia; 1815, Prussian envoy to Allied Council of Ambassadors; represented Prussia at Congresses of Vienna, Aix-la-Chapelle, and Carlsbad.

9. Richelieu to Wellington, September 7, 1816, Wellington Papers 1/520.

10. Ibid., Wellington to Richelieu, October 10, 1816, 1/522. Wellington's delay in a reply resulted from a series of inspections in Alsace.

11. Richelieu to Osmond, October 13, 1816, Fonds Richelieu 147.

12. Charles Stuart to Castlereagh, December 12, 1816, FO 146/11/471.

13. Wellington to Richelieu, October 19, 1816, Wellington Papers 1/522; Charles William Vane, editor, *Correspondence, Despatches, and other Papers of Viscount Castlereagh, Second Marquess of Londonderry*, 12 volumes (London: William Shoberl, 1852), 11:321, Stuart to Castlereagh, December 2, 1816.

14. Richelieu to Osmond, October 24, 1816, Fonds Richelieu 147.

15. There had been another outbreak of Luddite violence in 1816, and England had also suffered an agricultural uprising.

16. *The Times* (London), July 15, 1817.

17. Cathcart to Stewart, December 31, 1816, the Londonderry Papers D/LO/C-49/6, Durham County Record Office, County Hall, Durham, United Kingdom.

18. Castlereagh to Stuart, September 6, 1817, FO 146/13/81; and Castlereagh to Stuart, December 28, 1816, FO 146/13/117.

19. The Prince Regent's confidential memorandum on the Holy Alliance, May 28, 1816, Londonderry Papers D/LO/C-16/4.

20. Pierre de la Gorce, *Louis XVIII* (Paris: Librairie Plon, 1926), 113; Pierre Rain, *L'Europe et la Restauration des Bourbons, 1814–1818* (Paris: Perrin et Cie, 1908), appendix III.

21. R. B. Mowat, *The States of Europe, 1815–1871* (New York: Longmans, Green and Company, 1932), 27.

22. Philip Guedalla, *Wellington* (New York: The Literary Guild, 1931), 304.

23. Wellington to Charles Stuart, December 24, 1816, Wellington Papers 1/526.

24. Richelieu to Osmond, November 28, 1816, Fonds Richelieu 147. Richelieu writes that France cannot sustain the drain on her economy; see also Comtesse de Boigne, *Memoirs of the Countess de*

Boigne, edited by Charles Nicoullaud, 2 volumes (New York: Charles Scribner's Sons, 1908), 2:199.

25. Wellington to Czar Alexander I, January 9, 1817, Wellington Papers 1/533.

26. Ibid., Wellington to Castlereagh, January 13, 1817.

27. Ibid., Wellington to Castlereagh, February 4, 1817, 1/535.

28. Ibid., Wellington to Charles Stuart, Memorandum of a note on the reduction of the Army of Occupation, January 9, 1817, 1/533.

29. Ibid.

30. Ibid.

31. Louis de Viel-Castel, *Histoire de la Restauration* (Paris: 1860–1878), 5:452, citing Richelieu's speech.

32. Fouques-DuParc, *Le Troisième Richelieu*, 111.

33. Wellington to the Duke of York, February 5, 1817, Wellington Papers 1/535.

34. The Duke of York and Wellington were not on the closest terms. Wellington was known to have disagreed with the role of the king's brother as commander-in-chief during the campaign against France in the Low Countries in 1794–1795. Wellington commanded the 33^d Regiment of Foot in Holland, and the campaign ended in failure. The Duke of York felt Wellington gave himself too much credit for Waterloo and not enough to his subordinates.

35. The Duke of York to Wellington, February 13, 1817, Wellington Papers 1/536.

36. Ibid., the Duke of York to Wellington, February 28, 1817.

37. Ibid., the Duke of York to Wellington, January 31, 1817, 1/532. All forces were to proceed to Cork, Ireland with the exception of the Royal Scots. The Duke of York's brother, the Duke of Kent, urged Wellington to keep the Royal Scots in France because it was a unit filled with soldiers of unlimited service and he feared the regiment would be broken up if it returned home. The Duke of Kent to Wellington, February 9, 1817, Wellington Papers 1/534; and the Duke of Kent to Wellington, March 5, 1817, Wellington Papers 1/536.

38. Sir George Murray Papers 46.7.4/142, March 15, 1817, National Library of Scotland, Edinburgh, United Kingdom.

39. Ibid., March 18, 1817, 46.7.4/77.

40. Weekly Returns of the State of the Forces, State of the British Forces, September 1818, Wellington Papers 9/7/2, reflects the reorganization caused by the departure.

41. Ibid.

42. Austrian order of battle, April 3, 1817, Murray Papers 46.7.5/28.

43. Ibid., The Saxon departure, 46.7.4/154. The Saxons did not complete their departure until well into April.

44. Ibid., Count de Scheler to Wellington on the Würtemberg departure, March 1817, 46.7.4/167.

45. Ibid., Count Alten to Murray, March 24, 1817, 46.7.4/195. The Hanoverians did not start to leave until March 30, very close to the required date of departure.

46. Report of Charles Stuart, February 6, 1817, FO 146/16/50.

47. Woronzoff to Wellington, March 13, 1817, Wellington Papers 1/536.

48. Report of Charles Stuart, April 10, 1817, FO 146/16/132. Stuart notes in his report the nervousness of the Austrians over the slow Russian departure.

49. Report of Charles Stuart, April 17, 1817, FO 146/16/140. Stuart reported that Russian ships would go to Cherbourg or Le Havre.

50. May 20, 1817, Murray Papers 46.7.5/174.

51. Wellington memorandum of January 8, 1817, FO 146/16/10.

52. General Colville to Lieutenant Colonel Wallace, Records of the Connaught Rangers, WO 79/46, Public Record Office.

9

French Internal Reforms

In order to create the conditions inside France that would fulfill the second *Treaty of Paris*, the Richelieu ministry undertook necessary legislative programs which would lead to the evacuation of the country.[1] By instituting those reforms, France indicated to the allies that she was earnest in her desire to sustain peace and participate as an active member of the European community, and thus was entitled to an allied departure.[2] If France failed to reform, Richelieu believed that she would continue to appear as the leader of unrest on the continent, and thus the allies would be justified in maintaining the occupation for the full five years allotted. The allies would also remain poised to use force to subdue the French should any outbreak of revolutionary ideas arise again. The Richelieu government, already committed to ending the occupation at the earliest moment while restoring France to her rightful place among the other major powers, undertook a reform program dedicated to stating the new intentions of France.

The Richelieu ministry concentrated principally on three areas that needed attention. First, a new election law was required. Richelieu believed that if France kept its existing law, the ultra-royalists would retain control of the French parliament. While the allies may have wanted an end to revolutionary thought inside France, ultra-royalism created conditions for a potential backlash that might aggravate revolutionary fervor. France needed to build a system whereby political moderates could assume the leadership in French politics. Secondly, French military forces needed to be rebuilt. A stated purpose of the allied occupation was to remain in France until Louis XVIII had the backing of a loyal army. The Richelieu government had to build a loyal army that would find a role for the Napoleonic veterans, and that would accommodate the royalist faction, while not raising fear among the European powers. With the recent memory of the 1814 and 1815 debacles, this was not an easy task. Finally, France needed to institute a press law that would mitigate attacks against the crown but would not be viewed as censorship by the British. This constituted the basic domestic program of the Richelieu ministry.

In addition to these internal reforms, France had to make arrangements for reparation payments owed to the allied powers. The allies believed that the presence of their occupation army served as the means of insuring these payments. Until such arrangements were concluded, the allies had no intention of withdrawing their forces from France. In the end, the allies looked to the Duke of Wellington to resolve the open pecuniary issues.

The Legal Terror

In the elections held in August, 1815, the French electors turned their backs on the experience of the Revolution by casting their votes in support of royalism. Nine of every ten deputies elected to the Chamber of Deputies were confirmed royalists. Their sense of purpose was so strong that Louis XVIII gave the newly seated house the title of *Chambre Introuvable*.[3] The chamber was absolutely opposed to the ideas of the revolution and the empire. This legislature was certain to run into trouble with the moderation sought by the ministry Richelieu formed in late September. The chamber membership actually consisted of more commoners than Old Regime nobles, and many of the *émigrés* seated had served the empire. The first sign of a political grouping arose from the right which formed an amorphous group known as the ultra-royalists.

The period of July–August, 1815 witnessed the institution of the "White Terror," a period of reaction against supporters of the Hundred Days. The *Chambre Introuvable* participated in the terror by passing a series of four repressive measures between October, 1815 and January, 1816 designed to legalize the reaction. The first law, the law of public security, allowed the detention of anyone suspected of plotting against state security or the royal family.[4] A second law forbade seditious writing and speechmaking.[5] This law was directed against words or demonstrations which called for the overthrow of the government or threatened the royal family. The law also forbade anything that merely weakened respect for the monarchy such as flying the tricolor or cries for the emperor. A third law permitted the re-establishment of special provost courts.[6] Provost courts had been used under the Old Regime and the Empire and had jurisdiction over political crimes of all types, from the holding of seditious meetings to the conduct of armed violence aimed at the overthrow of the monarchy. The provost courts had no jury, there was no appeal of conviction, and punishments were executed within twenty-four hours. The chamber passed a fourth law concerned with the amnesty question.[7] Amid the debate over this bill, the famous Napoleonic marshal, Michel Ney, was executed.[8] Louis XVIII refused to step in and commute the sentence of Ney.[9]

The legalized "White Terror" led the government to dismiss many of its civil servants at the cost of disruption of services. An estimated fifty to eighty thousand servants, roughly a quarter to a third of government administrators, were removed from office. Eventually the legal terror caused a breakdown in political alliance between the Chamber of Deputies and the Richelieu ministry. The government advocated moderation; it found support from the monarch, but not from the deputies. Richelieu found his legislative support from the chamber's liberal wing, and both joined together to build support for the crown. Oddly then, the ultras assumed the role of supporters for parliamentary authority, a place where they were in the ascendancy, and from which they could best restore France to its previous system.[10]

Towards the summer of 1816 the allies, particularly the Duke of Wellington and the Russian ambassador to Paris, Pozzo di Borgo, were concerned with the continuing debate in the Chamber of Deputies over the French budget. This debate raised fears that the French deputies intended to renege on the payment of indemnities to the allies. The allies indicated that the French monarch should somehow discipline the legislature. Wellington hinted that the allies might have to act to somehow save France from its own legislature. Czar Alexander I warned that the chamber had to be eliminated, stating, "Either send your deputies home, or we'll keep all our troops in France,"[11] a clear assertion that the allies would not consider a troop withdrawal in 1816 unless things changed. Minister of the Interior Elie Decazes, an opponent of the ultras, diligently worked for a dissolution. Richelieu had no use for allied interference in his country's internal affairs, but he was strongly influenced by Decazes' argument that continued opposition from the chamber would inevitably serve as an obstacle to an early departure by the army of occupation, a departure which was the great hope of Richelieu's administration. Decazes won over both Louis XVIII and Richelieu for dissolution of the chamber.[12] In great secrecy, the king issued an order to dissolve the Chamber of Deputies, currently out of session, on September 5, 1816.[13] Even the King's brother, the Count of Artois, so closely connected with the ultras, was not informed of the order until after it was issued. The pretense for the dissolution was that the chamber needed to be reduced to the constitutionally prescribed membership and age requirements as stated in the *Charte Constitutionelle.* Though new elections were called for, the Richelieu ministry had to win seats in a chamber based on the same election law that had produced the *Chambre Introuvable*, since no new election law had been passed. The Richelieu government was dubious that it could win a working majority in the parliament.[14]

In spite of the small electorate, a heated campaign followed. A number of voters of the left, encouraged by Decazes, participated in the voting. Decazes successfully portrayed the ultras as so afraid of a liberal government that they actually favored continued allied occupation. The ultras attempted to boycott the election when they discovered defeat was imminent. Some of the seats in the upcoming chamber went unfilled due to lack of participation. Only two hundred thirty-eight seats were filled, with the ultras gaining only ninety-two seats, while moderates in support of the government captured one hundred forty-six seats.[15] The Richelieu ministry, thanks to the efforts of Decazes, won a working majority in the legislature for policies of moderation. The ultras discovered their power greatly reduced. Richelieu was then able to pursue the moderate program he had outlined to achieve his objective of removing the allied army and freeing France from the onerous treaty. French political parties became more sharply defined over the next two years, but this did not affect the ultimate mission of the Duke of Richelieu.

The Election Law of 1816

The first piece of legislation consisted of electoral reform. In November, 1816, the Richelieu ministry submitted an electoral bill which promised to revamp the political system.[16] The bill, supported by Richelieu and Decazes, was written by the new minister of the interior, M. Joseph Laine,[17] who had replaced a favorite of the ultras, Count Vaublanc. Louis XVIII dismissed Vaublanc in May, 1816, at the request of Richelieu. Though the electoral bill further restricted the size of the voting public, the political right wing attacked it as an attempt to return to a republic. The *Charte* had required a deputy to be thirty years of age. The new law raised the age to forty. The law also deprived local committees of their power to nominate members to the district committee which was charged with the actual election of parliamentary representatives. The rural nobility dominated these local committees, and it was there that the power of the ultra-royalists in the Chamber of Deputies originated. By disposing of the committees, the government successfully diminished the influence of the ultras. By the new election law, department colleges, meeting in the most important town in the department, would elect deputies through a voting process that would take place over several days, usually two. Liberal power was centered in the urban areas and was sure to grow under the new law. The government possessed strong control over these meetings when it reserved for itself the right to appoint the presidents of the colleges. In them, the ministry should be able to bring all its weight to bear on the choice of the electors, and create a more sympathetic legislative body.[18]

To be eligible to vote, the law required a citizen to pay three hundred francs in direct taxation. A candidate for office had to pay one thousand francs in direct taxes. These requirements restricted the right to vote to some ninety thousand Frenchmen, out of twenty-nine million, while only sixteen thousand were eligible to run for office.[19] Under such a system the wealthy urban bourgeoisie gained a preponderant influence, and they could more than hold their own against the nobility in the next election. By passing control to the bourgeoisie, any possibility of a relapse of power to the ultras seemed impossible. Having secured its political position, this class would not challenge the authority of the crown. The monarchy would enjoy a guarantee of support it so badly needed. Allied with the crown and the ministry, the bourgeoisie would exercise power over the next few years by restoring the financial stability of France through budgets regularly audited.[20]

The new election law confirmed the number of deputies at two hundred fifty-eight. The final important provision of the electoral bill was the requirement which provided for a partial renewal of the Chamber of Deputies every year. The term of office was established at five years, with one-fifth of all seats renewed every year. The chamber would achieve a certain continuity without the possibility of a radical changeover in deputies in any given election. The ministry hoped that the new law would achieved political stability with its provisions; instead the ministry would find itself occupied continually with elections.

A stormy debate followed in the legislature over the election bill, but it became law in February, 1817, just as negotiations for a reduction in the occupation forces opened.[21] The passage of the law enabled Richelieu to enter his negotiations with Wellington for a troop reduction with a new spirit of confidence.

In September, 1817, the first of the new elections under the bill took place. One-fifth of the deputy seats were up for election. In the newly formed house, seventy-five members could be classified as ultras, twenty-five as independents, and one hundred fifty-five could be counted as supporting the ministry.[22] With a legislative majority secured, the Richelieu ministry proceeded with its plans for freeing French territory; it wasted little time. Soon after the first session of the new chamber, the government submitted a bill for the restructuring of the French army.

Changes in the French election laws did not necessarily bring an end to the widespread political spectrum. The ultras did not accept a dilution of their political power in quiet solitude. They decided that the best way to restore their political position was to undermine the Richelieu government in the eyes of the allies through a series of secret notes passed through Europe.[23] The allies never acknowledged the validity of the ultra arguments against Richelieu but sensed that they were attempts to maintain a deteriorating political posture. Wellington predicted the future problems of the French dynasty when he wrote, "I entertain no doubt how this contest will end. The descendants of Louis XV will not reign in France; and I must say, it is the fault of Monsieur [the Count of Artois] and his adherents [the ultras]."[24]

The French Army Bill of 1817

In November, 1817, the Richelieu ministry submitted to the reconstituted chamber a bill for the resurrection of the French army.[25] The failure of the 1814 restoration may be explained in part by a decision to maintain the existing French army, an army that lacked loyalty for the Bourbons. It may also be argued that, in 1815, Louis XVIII and Napoleon enjoyed about equal support amongst the French populace, with each having the backing of particular regions of the country. When most of the army rallied to the emperor in March, 1815, the monarch fled to Ghent. The treachery of Marshal Ney is well documented, and most of the other Napoleonic marshals, with notable exceptions, deserted the royal cause.[26] In the minds of the royalists (and Wellington's as well), the army had deserted the monarch, not the French people. Louis XVIII wrote to Talleyrand as he fled to Lille that, based on his observations enroute into exile, Bonaparte had force of arms on his side while French hearts were with the Bourbons.[27] The defections in the French army to Napoleon made Louis XVIII's decision to flee to Belgium his most viable choice. The lack of loyalty should not have surprised anyone. Louis had regained his throne in 1814 only when the allied armies had defeated the French army in battle.

Even as Louis XVIII went into exile in 1815, a renewed army supporting the monarch had begun to develop out of the most loyal soldiers, the king's household troops. Some of the royal volunteers, which the crown had called for as Napoleon marched on Paris in March, 1815, departed for Belgium with the king. A limited number of regular troops also rallied to the king. By June Louis XVIII could muster at Ghent some twenty-one hundred loyal army troops.[28] This was small consolation for the monarch. The triumphant Napoleonic return from Elba clearly demonstrated to Louis and the allies where the sympathies of the French army lay. In establishing the peace-keeping army in 1815, one of the stated allied goals was to provide security for the French monarch during a period of transition while he rebuilt a loyal army which could guarantee his throne. Thus the occupation could not logically come to an end until such a military force was operational. If the allies departed without a dependable French army, the allies risked another failed Bourbon restoration.

On September 12, 1817, Marshal Gouvion-Saint-Cyr[29] replaced the Duke of Feltre, the first minister of war under Richelieu.[30] While serving as war minister for a short period in 1815, Saint-Cyr began the military reform process by developing a system of department legions. Each of the eighty-six French departments had the responsibility to raise its own legion. The number of battalions in each legion was based on the number of soldiers the department recruited. The army was authorized forty-seven regiments of cavalry, with each department or, in some cases, two departments combined, again responsible for the recruitment of troops. The best troops were organized into a royal guard, some twenty-six thousand strong. The guard consisted of eight infantry regiments, two of them Swiss, eight cavalry regiments, and three artillery regiments. The royal guard was created as an elite unit, receiving higher pay, and its ranks were officially recognized as one grade higher than the corresponding rank in the regular legions.[31] Conscription was banned by the *Charte*. The 1815 system was considered a failure, and with the return of Saint-Cyr, the government ordered a replacement program. The war ministry abandoned the recruiting system for lack of volunteers since the army totaled 117 thousand in 1817.[32] The government needed a new army program to create a force that would meet the allied criteria to end their occupation. Saint-Cyr authored the new army bill and arranged for its introduction into the legislature.

The proposed army law included two major provisions, one which created an active army while the other formed an inactive reserve. The active army would recruit by two methods, through the raising of volunteers or by choosing men through lots drawn on the names of men aged twenty. The French army inducted those men picked by the lottery unless the recruit could pay for a substitute. Though conscription was limited, the vestiges of equality begun with the revolutionary armies remained. Each year the army raised another forty thousand inductees with a term of service set at six years. The government aimed at establishing a regular army of 240 thousand men, though in fact this goal was never met. At the end of the six-year term of service the active army transferred the soldier to the inactive reserve for an additional six-year period. The government could call the reserve force to active duty only in case of war. Europe remembered French armies marching across the continent for a generation. Europe wished for calm, and the new French army bill attempted to reassure the allies by stating that no part of a recruit's military service would take place outside the territorial limits of France.[33]

The legislature considered several major questions during debate over the bill. Among these issues, the chamber debated the methods by which officer commissions were to be awarded and officers promoted. The bill granted commissions only to those men who had served as non-commissioned officers for at least two years, or those who had graduated from a military school which admitted students by competitive examination.[34] Marshal Saint-Cyr planned to prevent those ambitious young noblemen who relied on their lineage and who had no military expertise from commanding battalions and brigades in the new French army. All officers now had to earn their higher ranks. With this program, Saint-Cyr surely pushed the ideals he had observed during the empire at the expense of royalist desires to control officer ranks.[35]

Royalist deputies attacked the proposed promotion plan. The army bill based promotion on seniority in the case of two-thirds of all officers up to the grade of lieutenant colonel. Advancement to higher grades was to be based solely on merit.[36] According to the *Charte*, the royalist deputies reasoned that the chambers had a right to legislate on the matter of recruitment, but as the king, also in accordance with the *Charte*, served as commander-in-chief of the army, he did not need any law which stipulated a method of promotion. Simple royal ordinance could cover advancements.[37] In reality, the nobility defended privilege in the belief that the profession of officer should belonged exclusively to them, as it had during the Old Regime. Likewise, automatic promotion could create an officer class which would not be politically reliable.[38]

The French chambers entered into extended debate on two other points. First, fear was expressed that the Napoleonic veterans would dominate the reserve forces, especially during the first years after implementation of the bill. Consequently, this would give the veterans a controlling hand in the event that the reserves were activated.[39] Secondly, the ultras opposed any planned conscription since it was in violation of the *Charte* and was reminiscent of revolutionary France.[40] Richelieu reviewed Saint-Cyr's proposals and, though he felt sympathy for the rationale behind royal prerogative of promotion, he supported the army bill from the beginning and refused to desert his war minister.[41]

The president of the lower chamber described the debate on the proposed bill as a meeting between "the old and the new regimes, the former trying to re-establish privilege and the latter trying to maintain equality." The Duke of Broglie described the debate over the army bill as a "battlefield between the ministry and the royalist opposition." Saint-Cyr, a Napoleonic veteran, dominated the discussions. He envisioned an army organized in such a way that it would be capable of maintaining the independence of France both from within and without. The bill designed an army that could effectively perform its mission though small in numbers. Quality would count in this army, service was limited to six years, and advancement regulated.[42]

Saint-Cyr addressed the chambers and confronted the question of the Napoleonic veterans serving France. He refused to renounce their services, saying:

> We must decide whether we will once again call to the defence of the fatherland soldiers who have made its glory, or whether we will declare them once and for all dangerous to its tranquillity. The latter would be harsh and unjust, for these soldiers were admirable on the day of battle: they were moved by indefatigable ardour, upheld by heroic patience; they never ceased to believe that they were sacrificing their lives for the glory of France; and when they left their colours, they still had to offer vast treasures of strength and bravery![43]

On the issue of recruitment, Saint-Cyr stated to the legislature that conscription was a "fundamental principle of obligation...a fundamental principle in every political society, a principle indispensable to its existence."[44] The bill recognized that conscription was not in accordance with the *Charte*, but the bill's first article stated, "The army relies entirely on volunteers but resorts to the following rules when understaffed."[45] Since the Bourbons had not recruited more than thirty-five hundred men in any one year, the army should have been considered "understaffed."[46] The army requirement of forty thousand recruits per year made conscription virtually mandatory.

Saint-Cyr spoke to the deputies concerning the defensive nature of the proposed French army. He proclaimed it an army designed only for France's true defensive needs. The bill proposed a military system built in the interests of France's national institutions and in harmony with the desires of the great powers. The ministry had dedicated itself to the removal of the allied army, and the bill satisfied conditions so that the ministry could accomplish its objectives. The bill did not create an army so weak it would threaten the throne, nor would its strength arouse suspicion. Saint-Cyr asked the deputies to reconcile themselves to necessity.[47]

The debate in the chambers was heated. The Count of Artois wrote to his brother, Louis XVIII, and called for the dismissal of Decazes, a favorite of the king, because Decazes encouraged Saint-Cyr's appointment as minister of war. The king rejected Artois' intervention into the debate and seemed intent on supporting the Cabinet.[48] Louis XVIII became directly involved in the final decision when the vote reached the Chamber of Peers. Some of the peers, known to oppose the bill, held positions in the king's court and normally attended Louis' daily drive. On the day and time of the vote, Louis intentionally prolonged his ride so that three dukes could not get to the chamber to cast votes. Without having to change their minds, Louis enabled the bill to pass by preventing the three opponents from voting and thereby causing it to fail.[49] The army bill passed on March 12, 1818.[50]

The National Guard also came up for reorganization in 1818. The guard was a cross between an army and a police force, and since 1815 it had been the private domain of the king's brother, Artois. As commander-in-chief, Artois recruited for the guard amongst his friends and their dependents, who were given commissions or who served as the rank and file. Artois and his ultra friends turned the guard into a private militia supporting their political ideas. The National Guard was particularly important in 1815 and 1816 when recruiting for the French army faltered. The minister of war, the Duke of Feltre, warned in April, 1816 that the army was incapable of sufficiently garrisoning French fortresses. Feltre denounced the ever-growing tendency of the National Guard to "overstep the bounds of their duties" and stated that it posed a threat to royal authority.[51] As time passed, the guard acted less as militia and more as Artois' private army. The guard was far too independent of civil authority.[52] If France allowed the National Guard to continue as organized, it would surely cause problems for the new French army as well as political problems for both Louis XVIII and the Duke of Richelieu.

On September 30, 1818, Count Decazes successfully used his influence with Louis to get the king to issue a royal ordinance concerning the National Guard. The Count of Artois lost most of his power over the guard and his central office was abolished. The ordinance made the post of colonel-general largely honorary. The ordinance placed the guard under the local control of mayors and prefects, reporting to the minister of the interior.[53] Decazes thereby made the guard a more middle class armed force since its membership was now open. But at the same time he limited its ranks to those who paid direct taxes and to their sons. In addition, the reorganization of the National Guard had an immediate effect as its influence in the

October, 1818 elections became greatly reduced. In 1818, the ultras lost all fifteen seats they had up for re-election.[54]

Those such as the Duke of Wellington, who feared a reserve army dominated by Napoleonic veterans, discovered their concerns unfounded since reserve units were never formed.[55] Deputies who feared a disloyal officer corps made up of Napoleonic veterans discovered that most of the corps remained largely royalist in viewpoint, with only a third considered doubtful or disloyal. After the departure of Saint-Cyr from the war ministry in 1819, promotion by king's choice was re-established.[56] Saint-Cyr replaced only a few of Feltre's royalist appointees, some of whom were of questionable competence. The army command dismissed only twenty-one of one hundred thirty-seven infantry and cavalry regimental colonels between 1817 and 1819. Saint-Cyr helped restore army morale by returning many competent imperial officers to active service in order to create a general staff for the French army.[57] The newly established army thus had a fair selection of officers of both Napoleonic and royalist background.

Europe keenly observed the debate through its representatives sitting in the parliamentary galleries. The allies were much concerned over any army bill that would create an effective army for a country that had waged war for a generation, although they also realized that Louis needed a loyal force. The assembled ambassadors and generals left the chambers pleased that the discussions were conducted over internal matters and not on any thoughts of revenge. The Richelieu ministry saw its influence grow during the course of the debate, and many royalist deputies joined with the government in support of the bill, and thus the chambers presented Europe with an expression of cooperation between legislators and government.[58] With passage of the bill, France possessed the outline for a loyal army, a condition required by the allies for the end of occupation.

The Press Laws

Though the 1814 *Charte* proclaimed freedom of the press, it developed slowly. Louis XVIII and his government were concerned that this freedom might get out of hand if not restricted in some way. If the government allowed criticism in the press to run uncontrolled, it might threaten the stability and support the government desired. At the same time, if the government harshly subdued the press, it would surely bring criticism from the liberals at home and Great Britain abroad. The ministry had to locate some *modus vivendi* between those two positions.

The *Chambre Introuvable* stated the ultra position in the legislation of 1815 whereby it made any seditious writing a crime. Those who threatened the king or royal family, those who urged an overthrow of the government or a change in the succession of the throne through their published works, those who hoisted a flag other than the White Flag, and those who uttered seditious cries against the king were subject to deportation.[59] The so-called "white terror" brought on as many as six thousand convictions between 1815 and 1817 for writings and cries against the royal family.[60] In order to avoid the restrictions, anti-government and anti-royalist authors went elsewhere to publish their material. Many ex-patriots went off to the Netherlands to publish their venom under the protection of the Dutch king. The French king and the allies approached the Duke of Wellington to speak with the Dutch monarch about bringing these writers under control. This was an unusual responsibility for a military commander to assume, but Wellington was on excellent terms with both monarchs and all parties counted on the duke to act impartially.

The British ambassador in Paris, Charles Stuart, warned foreign secretary Castlereagh in 1816 of the threat to the French crown from the writings coming out of the Netherlands. There were numerous exiles in the Low Countries, and France wanted restraints placed upon them. The Dutch king did little to prevent publication of attacks against Louis XVIII as *The Fundamental Law* also guaranteed freedom of the press. As a result, the Dutch authorities seemed uninterested in taking any measures to restrain publications directed against the French throne, in spite of requests from the Allied Council of Ambassadors.[61] Stuart feared that the Netherlands would bring ruin upon themselves if they did not prevent the press from causing "mischief."[62] Stuart urged that Castlereagh instruct Wellington to speak with the Dutch king because of the duke's knowledge of affairs in both the Netherlands and France. Stuart stated that Wellington could make a decision "analogous to the principles of the Alliance." Only the duke carried enough weight to influence the Dutch crown to cooperate on this touchy issue.[63] The Council of Ambassadors eventually referred the entire question to Wellington since they had exhausted all attempts to alert the Netherlands to the threat of discontented French ex-patriots to allied peacemaking efforts.[64]

Wellington's meetings with the Dutch king succeeded in achieving the allied aims. The king stated that he would attend to the desires of the allied courts and take measures that would reduce published attacks against the French throne. He promised to take action against those exiles who attacked France. He also assured Wellington that the most libelous writers would be prosecuted and, if that failed, he would seek a law from the States General against them. The king also promised to extradite those individuals not protected by the French amnesty law passed by the *Chambre Introuvable*. Yet, the Dutch government said that it would not deport those regicides forced out of France by the Law of General Amnesty, but it promised that the regicides would no longer be allowed to reside in the southern provinces of the Netherlands, i.e., Belgium. If an individual had his passport revoked by the French government, the Dutch authorities would ask him to leave the country.[65] The Duke of Wellington urged the Dutch to expel anyone whose writings provoked the French ministry. The Dutch king appeared to understand the threat of continued intrigue by French refugees.[66] It was essential that the Netherlands accede to allied requests. For if it failed to do so, the Dutch might weaken the position of the French monarch. Wellington grasped the issue and successfully pointed out the long-term threat to the Dutch king if seditious material continued to flow out of his country.

At the same time in 1817 and 1818, the government of Richelieu sponsored a series of provisional laws which liberalized the rules on publishing political material. The public seemed to desire writings which supported their political positions as the political spectrum, from the ultras of the right to the moderates in support of Richelieu over to the liberal left of the independents, was becoming more sharply defined. More structured political parties organized and gathered their supporters. Political organizations created a number of publications in support of their beliefs and openly distributed them.

Occasionally, the French government interfered directly with freedom of the press. The Duke of Decazes, minister of police, seized Chateaubriand's *La Monarchie selon la Charte*, and ordered two other writers, Comte and Dunoyer, placed in jail for one year for their material, even though they were considered liberal and not anti-crown. The *Nain Jaune*, a publication in opposition to the Richelieu ministry, was printed out in the Netherlands and was circulated under secrecy for protection. Ironically, the ultras found themselves supporting of freedom for the press in order to maintain their position and circulate their own publications. On the left, liberals created the *Society of the Friends of Freedom of the Press* in 1818 to awaken France to their ideals. Eventually, in 1819, the minister of justice, the Count de Serre, steered a series of laws through the chambers which firmly established liberal rules concerning the press. The laws established the freedom to express one's opinion and insured the right to trial by jury for crimes involving the press.[67]

The Richelieu ministry gradually relaxed press laws to allow free expression to become more firmly rooted. The whole attitude of France towards this question should have pleased the allies. The initial actions against seditious writings were harsh, yet rules became more relaxed during the years 1816–1818. When discussion of the final troop departure came up, the allies retained no questions about the press issue inside France.[68]

French Reparations

The allied powers would never have even considered withdrawing their forces from France until she had successfully concluded arrangements for full payment of all moneys owed them. British foreign secretary Lord Castlereagh was clear in his assertion that "all money accounts arising out of the treaty [of November 20, 1815] be settled and closed" by the time the army of occupation withdrew.[69] Reparations payments covered two categories, a war indemnity and claims by private citizens against France. The war indemnity costs were listed in the second *Treaty of Paris*[70] and totaled 700 million francs, without interest. Payments were due quarterly. The allies also required France to discharge European claims made against her for debts contracted by previous French governments in countries occupied by French troops during the course of the recent wars. The allies and France originally estimated these claims to to total approximately 200 million francs.[71] Compounding France's financial requirements were the heavy costs involved in the support payments due for the army of occupation.[72] The war indemnity and support payments for the occupation army were unavoidable costs, while the issue of claims remained open pending submission of charges. All these costs promised to saddle French finances for years.

France and the allies ultimately settled the war indemnity issue at the Conference of Aix-la-Chapelle.[73] France had paid a total of 368 million francs of the 700 million owed. In a strike for economy as well as to have the evacuation effected, Richelieu offered 265 million francs to be paid immediately in lieu of the still-owed 332 million francs. The allies accepted this proposal. France negotiated additional loans from the London-Amsterdam based financial house of Hope and Baring, and thus transferred her obligations from the allied powers to a banking house. Since the allies would receive their indemnity, they could no longer use that subject as a reason to keep their troops inside France.[74]

The issue of claims had become much more serious for France when actual claims submitted surpassed the expected 200 million francs. The figure grew to over 1,600 million francs.[75] The claims far exceeded France's ability to pay. In September, 1817, Richelieu announced that France could not possibly pay more than the original estimate of 200 million francs.[76] Once again, the allied powers turned to the Duke of Wellington to solve an issue. Czar Alexander I suggested that the allies name Wellington to arbitrate all claims submitted. The czar called Wellington the only alternative to solving the issue in the interests of both the allies and France.[77] The Prussians, Austrians, and Saxons all agreed to defer the subject to Wellington.[78] Richelieu agreed to accept his arbitration. Castlereagh wrote Wellington that the subject of claims is "left entirely to you to decide as you may find best for the general question."[79]

The British ambassador in Paris, Charles Stuart, also saw danger in the issue of claims. He called the subject "an instrument of mischief" which might raise national pride to the point that France might choose war as more economical than submission to outrageous claims. Stuart thought it would be very bad if the army of occupation remained for even a day because of pecuniary issues when all other motives for the occupation had ceased to exist. Stuart called for moderation on the part of the allies.[80]

The subject of claims threatened the question of when the allies would withdraw their forces from France. The British prime minister, Lord Liverpool, believed that the evacuation depended upon France's satisfaction with a claims settlement. He realized it would be difficult to remain simply because France did not have the money to meet the demands, but with a "reasonable compromise" on private claims, the Hope-Baring House would arranged for French payments. Liverpool believed France had the ability to pay and the allies "should call upon her to do so before we evacuate."[81] The British prince regent, George, informed Wellington that a final settlement was required prior to an allied departure.[82]

The Duke of Wellington eventually accepted a figure of valid claims totaling 240 million francs.[83] Richelieu sought even further reductions based on the opposition he believed he would receive in the French chambers. The field marshal refused to alter his decision. Wellington submitted the results of his arbitration decision to the Council of Ambassadors in Paris. He determined that interest claims could only go back two years, i.e., ten percent of the allowed claim. Ambassador Stuart informed Castlereagh of French feelings of "irritation" over the work of Wellington. Stuart also believed that Wellington had successfully concluded the issue in France's favor, considering the "overwhelming mass of demands" brought against her.[84] Wellington later revised his position and allowed interest charges to accrue only from March 22, 1818.[85]

On April 25, 1818, a convention was signed for payment of the claims issue.[86] By the agreement France agreed to inscribed upon its Great Book of Public Debt, with interest from March 22, 1818, *rentes* totaling 12,040,000 francs representing a capital of 240,800,000 francs to cover the allowable claims.[87] With the settlement, Richelieu expressed his thanks to Wellington for his work in bringing about a settlement and for his "moderation."[88]

Conclusions

Since France desired an early allied evacuation, the government moderated its stances in several areas. Richelieu understood what France needed to accomplish, and he began to formulate policies designed to achieve his aims. His choice as chief minister by Louis XVIII had been critical to the nation. Just as he sought to achieve a reduction of the initial allied demands in the second *Treaty of Paris*, he directed himself and his ministry to create the conditions for removal of foreign troops. The election law successfully brought about a removal of the ultras from a controlling position in the Chamber of Deputies, and the law gained for Richelieu the working majority he needed in the French legislature. The ultras did not regain their political status until after the assassination of the Duke of Berri in 1820.

The allies required other reforms. The French government had to reform its army after the debacle of the Hundred Days. The army bill successfully built a loyal force which employed many of the veterans of the Napoleonic Wars, while a royal ordinance restructured the organization of the National Guard, a para-military force too loyal to the king's brother, the Count of Artois. The allies specifically required army reform when they agreed to conduct the military occupation of France. The allies promised not to leave until a loyal army was created; Richelieu and Gouvion-Saint-Cyr built one. The issue over press control also needed attention. The French monarchy needed to build support for its rule, so censorship of seditious material was warranted in the early days of the Restoration. Allied interests required a suppression of exile publications and the powers dispatched Wellington to the Netherlands to solicit support from the Dutch king. Once support for the monarchy was demonstrated, the French government passed a new press law to protect the writings of the entire political spectrum operating inside France. Wellington successfully concluded the open issue of private claims against France. He arbitrated a fair settlement for both France and Europe. With French reforms underway and with reparation payments settled, Richelieu removed whatever objections the allies could possibly muster over French internal affairs in order to avoid evacuation at the end of three years.

NOTES

1. Several of these reforms were initiated prior to the troop reduction of 1817, but for style format reasons, the author groups all reforms into this chapter.

2. In 1815, Castlereagh wrote that France was entitled to an allied guarantee of evacuation at the conclusion of the planned occupation period if she had met the conditions stipulated for her in the peace treaty. Charles William Vane, editor, *Correspondence, Despatches, and other Papers of Viscount Castlereagh, Second Marquess of Londonderry*, 12 volumes (London: William Shoberl, 1852), 10:457, Castlereagh to Liverpool, August 3, 1815 [hereafter *Correspondence of Castlereagh*].

3. Name given by Louis XVIII to the royalist dominated Chamber of Deputies which served from October, 1815 until it was dissolved by the king in September, 1816. The name translates roughly to the "unexpected" chamber or the chamber "so good as to be unexpected." The chamber was at odds with the Richelieu ministry over a number of issues. For a quantitative analysis of the makeup of Chamber of Deputies for the period 1815–1820, see Thomas D. Beck, *French Legislators, 1800–1834* (Berkeley: University of California Press, 1974), chapters V and VI.

4. *Bulletin des Lois du Royaume de France*, 7th serie (Paris: De L'Imprimerie Royale, 1816), bulletin 36(189), October 29, 1815, 1:379–81 [hereafter *Bulletin de Lois*].

5. Ibid., bulletin 40(204), November 9, 1815, I:415–19; *Archives Parlementaires de 1787 á 1860, Deuxième Série 1800 à 1860*, 95 volumes (Paris: Librairie Administrative De Paul DuPont, 1869), 15:77–78 and 15:154–58 [hereafter *Archives Parlementaires*]. The law was submitted October 16, 1815 and approved October 28, 1815.

6. *Bulletin des Lois*, bulletin 52(311), December 20, 1815, I:519–28; *Archives Parlementaires*, 15:248–50 and 15:388–90. The law was submitted November 17, 1815 and approved December 5, 1815.

7. *Archives Parlementaires*, 15:422–23 and 15:712–14. The law was submitted on December 9, 1815 and approved January 6, 1816.

8. Marshal Michel Ney, Prince of Moscow and Duke of Elchingen (1769–1815), saw actions in all major Napoleonic campaigns including Russia and Spain. Ney had promised to return Napoleon to Paris in a cage upon his return to France from Elba but defected to the Emperor. After Waterloo, he attempted to go into retirement but was arrested. He was found guilty of treason and executed by firing squad on December 7.

9. Guillaume de Bertier de Sauvigny, *The Bourbon Restoration*,

translated by Lynn M. Case (Philadelphia: University of Pennsylvania Press, 1966), 130. Wellington refused all requests to get involved with efforts to commute the Ney sentence.

10. Ibid., 135.

11. Gordon Wright, *France in Modern Times: 1760 to the Present* (Chicago: Rand McNally and Company, 1966), 129.

12. In his memoirs, François Guizot states that the king informed the ministers of his decision to dissolve the chamber on August 14, 1816, and requested absolute secrecy from them. François Guizot, *Memoirs to Illustrate the History of My Times*, 8 volumes (London: Richard Bentley, 1858), 1:147–48. Louis told his ministers at the meeting of August 14, "From this moment you may regard the chamber dissolved." Cited in Louis Viel-Castel, *Histoire de la Restauration*, 20 volumes (Paris: Michel Lévy, Frères, 1867), 5:210–11.

13. Article 2 of the Royal Ordinance of September 5, 1816. See *The Morning Chronicle*, September 11, 1816; also Viel-Castel, *Histoire de la Restauration*, 5:227.

14. Bertier de Sauvigny, *Bourbon Restoration*, 138–39.

15. Ibid., 138–45, 150.

16. *Archives Parlementaires*, November 25, 1816, 17:563–64.

17. Joseph-Louis-Joachim Laine, Viscount (1767–1835), legislator and minister. He served in Napoleon's Legislative corps where he attacked the Emperor on the evils of the continuing wars. He serve as president of the Chamber of Deputies under the Restoration and as Interior Minister from 1816 to 1818. He was considered to be fully loyal to Richelieu.

18. *Archives Parlementaires*, November 25, 1816, 17:563–564; Alphonse Marie de Lamartine, *Histoire de la Restauration*, 8 volumes (Paris: Fagnerre, Lecou, Fourne et Cie, 1852), 3:337–38; J. Lucas-Dubreton, *The Restoration and the July Monarchy*, translated by E. F. Buckley (New York: G.P. Putnam's Sons, 1929), 54; Bertier de Sauvigny, *Bourbon Restoration*, 146.

19. *Archives Parlementaires*, November 25, 1816, 17:563–64.

20. Lucas-Dubreton, *Restoration*, 54.

21. *Archives Parlementaires*, January 30, 1817, 18:460–64.

22. John R. Hall, *The Bourbon Restoration* (New York: Houghton Mifflin Company, 1909), 212.

23. See chapter 10 for a review of these notes.

24. Philip Guedalla, *Wellington* (New York: The Literary Guild, 1931), 305; Frederick B. Artz, in his article "The Electoral System in France during the Bourbon Restoration, 1815–1830" concludes that in spite of the lack of participation, the small electorate, and government manipulation which made the Chamber of Deputies

hardly representative of the French people, the restoration elections were the first extended French experience in democratic government during a time of peace. *Journal of Modern History*, 1 (June 1969), 218.

25. *Archives Parlementaires*, Chamber of Deputies, November 29, 1817, 19:650–51.

26. Among those marshals who did not rally to the emperor were Victor, Marmont, Oudinot, Macdonald, Berthier, and Saint-Cyr. Napoleon's loss of his chief of staff, Berthier, who committed suicide, was crucial considering the French lack of battlefield coordination at Waterloo.

27. Philip Mansel, *Louis XVIII* (London: Blond and Briggs Ltd., 1981), 232. Louis' letter to Talleyrand is quoted.

28. Ibid., 243.

29. Marshal Laurent Gouvion-Saint-Cyr (1764–1830) rose rapidly and was a general by age thirty. He was disgraced in Spain in 1809 for leaving his command before his successor's arrival. He regained his stature in Russia and earned his marshal's baton for his battlefield actions. He returned to France in June, 1814 and reconciled with the Bourbons. He served as minister for war and for marine in the Second Restoration. Saint-Cyr helped restore many of marshals to their ranks and returned their estates. He voted for Ney's conviction in 1815 but not for his execution, voting instead for banishment.

30. Feltre resigned to avoid criticism of excess expenditures in the war ministry. British ambassador Stuart privately suspected that the influence of Pozzo di Borgo on Richelieu led to Feltre's resignation. Vane, *Correspondence of Castlereagh*, 11:376–77, Stuart to Castlereagh, September 15, 1817.

31. Bertier de Sauvigny, *The Bourbon Restoration*, 282–84.

32. Mansel, *Louis XVIII*, 353.

33. *Archives Parlementaires*, November 29, 1817, 19:651; Louis Madelin, *Deux Relevements Francais, 1815–1818, 1871–1878* (Paris: Flammarion, 1951), 83; Viel-Castel, *Histoire de la Restauration* (Paris, 1860–1878), 6:333–35.

34. Andre Jardin and Andre-Jean Tudesq, *Restoration and Reaction, 1815–1848*, translated by Elborg Forster (London: Cambridge University Press, 1983), 36. The military schools were Saint-Cyr for infantry officers and Metz for artillery officers.

35. *Archives Parlementaires*, November 29, 1817, 19:650–55.

36. Madelin, *Deux Relevements Francais*, 84; Lucas-Dubreton, *The Restoration*, 55.

37. *Archives Parlementaires*, January 14, 1818, 20:236, and February 5, 1818, 20:624–36; Antoine Francois Claude Ferrand,

Mémoires du Comte Ferrand (Paris: Alphonse Picarde et Fils, 1897), 211.

38. Bertier de Sauvigny, *Bourbon Restoration*, 148.

39. Madelin, *Deux Relevements Francais*, 84; Viel-Castel, *Histoire de la Restauration*, 6:342–56.

40. *Archives Parlementaires*, January 14, 1818, 20:236, and February 5, 1818, 20:642–99.

41. Viel-Castel, *Histoire de la Restauration*, 6:342–56.

42. Bernard Combes de Patris, *Le Comte de Serre* (Paris: Auguste Picard, 1932), 116.

43. *Archives Parlementaires*, address of Gouvion-Saint-Cyr to the Chamber of Deputies, January 26, 1818, 20:513; Jardin, *Restoration and Reaction*, 37.

44. *Archives Parlementaires*, January 26, 1818, 20:510.

45. Ibid., article 1 of proposed army bill, November 29, 1817, 19:653.

46. Douglas Porch, *Army and Revolution, France 1815–1848* (London: Routledge and Kegan Paul, 1974), 3.

47. *Archives Parlementaires*, Saint-Cyr speech to Chamber of Deputies, February 9, 1818, 20:704–05.

48. Mary D. R. Leys, *Between Two Empires. A History of French Politicians and People between 1814 and 1848* (London: Longmans, Green and Company, 1955), 92.

49. Bertier de Sauvigny, *Bourbon Restoration*, 148; Leys, *Two Empires*, 92

50. Guizot states that the chambers debated the new army bill in depth because it was an attack against the monarchy. In the end, he believed that the law actually created an army that was "devotedly monarchical." Guizot, *Memoirs*, 1:168.

51. Mansel, *Louis XVIII*, 337.

52. Viel-Castel, *Histoire de la Restauration*, 7:98–99.

53. Ibid., VII:98–99; *The Morning Chronicle*, October 7, 1818.

54. Bertier de Sauvigny, *Bourbon Restoration*, 152; Leys, *Two Empires*, 92.

55. Jardin, *Restoration and Reaction*, 37.

56. Bertier de Sauvigny, *Bourbon Restoration*, 148.

57. Mansel, *Louis XVIII*, 354.

58. Madelin, *Deux Relevements Francais*, 85.

59. *Archives Parlementaires*, projected law on seditious writings, articles 1–3, November 9, 1815, 15:77–78.

60. Mansel, *Louis XVIII*, 324.

61. Stuart to Castlereagh, April 18, 1816, Foreign Office Report 146/8/142, Public Record Office, Kew, United Kingdom [hereafter FO 146].

62. Vane, *Correspondence of Castlereagh*, 11:290–92, Castlereagh to Wellington, September 6, 1816.

63. Stuart to Castlereagh, April 4, 1816, FO 146/8/128.

64. Stuart Memorandum, August 26, 1816, FO 146/10/320.

65. Stuart to Castlereagh, April 29, 1816, FO 146/6/153.

66. Stuart to Castlereagh, June 10, 1816, FO 146/9/207; Stuart to Castlereagh, July 1, 1816, FO 146/9/239.

67. Jardin, *Restoration and Reaction*, 38.

68. The Chamber of Deputies passed its major press reform legislation in May–June, 1819, after the departure of the allied army. The legislation was directed by the new minister of justice, Count de Serre, who believed that opinions did not become criminal if merely expressed publicly.

69. Castlereagh to Stuart, November 11, 1817, FO 146/21/103.

70. *Archives Parlementaires*, 15:312, article I of the Convention Relative to the Pecuniary Indemnity Payment owed by France to the Allied Powers.

71. Bertier de Sauvigny, *The Bourbon Restoration*, 154–56.

72. As required by the second *Treaty of Paris*.

73. See chapter 10 concerning the conference at Aix-la-Chapelle.

74. *The Morning Chronicle*, October 9, 1818, spoke of the great influence of the Hope–Baring financial house, and claimed that the allied powers could not resolve the financial questions that were vital to the peace and prosperity of all Europe without the help of commercial interests.

75. Bertier de Sauvigny, *Bourbon Restoration*, 154–56. Some claims were preposterous. The Duke of Anhalt-Bernburg placed a claim for a contract by which one of his ancestors furnished mercenary troops to Henry IV. Webster states that the claims reached 1,200 million francs. See C. K. Webster, *The Congress of Vienna, 1814–1815* (London: G. Bell and Sons, 1945), 141.

76. Ibid., 154–56.

77. Alexander I to Wellington, October 30, 1817, Wellington Papers 1/558, University of Southampton, Southampton, United Kingdom; Stuart to Castlereagh, December 8, 1817, FO 146/19/489.

78. Stuart to Castlereagh, January 19, 1818, FO 146/24/26; and Stuart to Castlereagh, January 26, 1818, FO 146/24/33.

79. Castlereagh to Wellington, March 17, 1818, Wellington Papers 1/574.

80. Charles Stuart Memorandum on French debts, October 1817, MD, France 709.

81. Liverpool to Wellington, March 6, 1818, Wellington Papers 1/573.

82. Castlereagh to Stuart, March 20, 1818, FO 146/28/10.

83. Wellington to Castlereagh, April 19, 1818, Wellington Papers 1/578. Wellington allowed Prussia the largest claim, over 52 million francs. The smallest claim allowed, fourteen thousand francs, belonged to Hesse Electorale and Saxe Weimar.

84. Stuart to Castlereagh, April 20, 1818, FO 146/25/148.

85. Stuart to Castlereagh, April 23, 1818, FO 146/25/151.

86. Convention between Great Britain, Austria, Prussia, Russia, and France for the Final Liquidation of Private Claims upon the French Government, signed at Paris, April 25, 1818. United Kingdom, Foreign Office, *British and Foreign State Papers*, compiled by Sir Edward Hertslet, 170 volumes (London: James Ridgeway, 1869), 5:179–81.

87. *Rentes* are dividend payments on bonds. Corvetto floated a bond inside France for the *rentes* at the same time he was negotiating a further loan from Hope and Baring to cover indemnity payments. The French responded far beyond the expectations of the finance minister. Bertier de Sauvigny, *Bourbon Restoration*, 155.

88. Richelieu to Wellington, April 27, 1818, FO 146/25/160.

10

The Allied Departure from France

According to the *Treaty of Paris* of November 20, 1815, the allies agreed that the army of occupation would remain in France for a maximum period of five years. The allied sovereigns also agreed to review the issue of continuing the occupation after three years had passed. It was in France's interest that the earliest possible departure date be secured. Perhaps more importantly, Louis XVIII and the Duke of Richelieu had a vested interest in producing an early departure to demonstrate, just as they had with the partial reduction of 1817, their ability to govern effectively France and restore her to her position of greatness. The troop diminution had given a renewed popularity to the king's rule. Negotiating a final removal for a date prior to the stated five-year occupation program would add a further sense of stability to the Bourbon monarchy.

Richelieu, embarrassed with the November 1815 treaty, spent three years directing France toward a stable internal situation acceptable to the allied leadership. He refused to leave the allies any valid reason for their continued occupation of France. The popularity of the Richelieu ministry approached a new peak in 1818. The Chamber of Deputies, via changes in the election laws, became more moderate in accordance with the desires of Richelieu and Louis XVIII, a posture approved by Europe. The chamber dedicated itself to reconciling the nation's diverse factions. The government designed and then rebuilt the French army so that it was capable of insuring domestic order and tranquillity. Richelieu's ministry successfully negotiated loans to enable France to meet the financial obligations imposed on her. By doing so Richelieu assured Europe of France's intention to live up to the second *Treaty of Paris*. The value of government bonds rose. Richelieu did not limit his efforts to restoring internal order, but he also planned to return France to an equal footing with the other great powers. France had to meet the conditions of the November, 1815 treaty or the duke's goals could not be achieved. Those conditions depended on the status of the internal affairs of France. When the minister settled France's financial and political affairs, the question of complete evacuation could be discussed.[1] Richelieu had succeeded to a great extent, and France seemed to be on the verge of an era of peace and stability, if the allies departed in a timely fashion.

Not all elements in France were reconciled. The ultras watched their political power diminish beginning with Louis XVIII's legislative dissolution ordinance of September 5, 1816, and the subsequent elections. They then rallied behind the Count of Artois and sought a means of attempting a coup d'etat to restore their power. The ultras convinced themselves that an allied departure might signal the start of another revolution and crush the monarchy forever. For the ultras, the liberation of France from allied occupation was a step closer to captivity. They believed it pointless to address their grievances to Louis XVIII since they regarded him as a prisoner of the revolutionary spirit. The ultras decided to portray the danger by means of a circular letter addressed to the European powers which would present the true French political situation.[2]

The ultras previously tried the same approach on two earlier occasions with no success. In August, 1816 a *Note Secrete* bemoaned the fact the the ministry was not cooperating with the Chamber of Deputies. The note insinuated that the Richelieu ministry was dominated by revolutionaries and others sympathetic to the ideology of the French Revolution. The note portrayed Richelieu as a dupe led astray by his colleagues. Accredited French ambassadors to European courts were reportedly under the influence of those with revolutionary ideas, and they presented foreign governments with a false picture of conditions existing in France.[3] A second note, in August, 1817, repeated the first, though in a much stronger tone. This note lamented the royalist political losses over the past year and it charged the Richelieu ministry with being openly revolutionary. In their view, Louis XVIII was a complete captive of the ministry. The royalists, of course, considered themselves as the true representatives of all Frenchmen.[4] Both of these efforts ended in failure. For the third effort, the ultras commissioned the Count of Vitrolles to write a note that would play upon the anxieties of the allied courts.

The Count of Vitrolles directed the third note primarily at the Prussians, thought to be the most receptive for the report since they were uneasy that an allied evacuation might allow France to avoid further indemnity payments. The Vitrolles note needed to appeal to both Austria and Britain, since Prussia would not act alone. Considering the close relationship between the czar and Richelieu, dating back to the duke's service under the czar, any attempt to influence Russian thinking appeared doomed to failure.

The third *Note Secrète* also failed to achieve the ultra goals. The Austrian foreign minister, Prince Metternich, gave little attention to the approach, though the note painted France's internal situation as grave.[5] The British cabinet rejected the envoy of the Count of Artois and his arguments, after having received an appraisal of the French situation from the Duke of Wellington. Having heard the gloomy picture of France from the envoy carrying the Vitrolles note, British Foreign Secretary Viscount Castlereagh commented:

> If this description is exact, we should be obliged to recall our troops forthwith, form a cordon around France and leave the inhabitants to devour one another. Fortunately, my lord, we have less terrifying information to oppose to yours.[6]

The ultras, however, were not satisfied with merely making protestations and appeals through the Secret Notes. They even went so far as to create a conspiracy in June, 1818, known as "The Conspiracy at the Water's Edge." The conspiracy, or planned coup d'état, foresaw the capture and imprisonment of Louis XVIII and the Richelieu ministry. It would force the monarch either to appoint an ultra cabinet or to accept exile in favor of a regency for his brother, Artois. The plot was discovered and smashed.[7] The minister of police, Decazes, wanted to make examples of the ultras involved in the plot, particularly Vitrolles, but this was impossible due to the importance of those implicated. The privy council dismissed Vitrolles. The implication of the Count of Artois led to the September, 1818 legislation which eliminated his position as head of the National Guard.[8] The plot resulted in disaster in the next election for the ultras. They lost every contested seat that they held. The attempts by the ultras to convince the allies that an evacuation was not in their interests was an abject failure. The plot largely discredited the ultras, and the allied courts and Richelieu continued the negotiations required to launch the next European conference, a conference that would agree to end the occupation.

Colonel Sir Henry Hardinge,[9] British liaison officer long assigned to the Prussian forces, wrote to the Duke of Wellington's Chief of Staff, Sir George Murray, in early 1818 concerning the attitudes of the French public in the Prussian sector. Hardinge stated that the French inhabitants expressed "more impatience" towards the occupation than previously recognized. Colonel Hardinge warned that he considered the attachment between the French public and the Bourbons deteriorating. An allied troop departure would bring France a step closer towards regaining her status as a major power and bring her nearer to re-entering European diplomacy as a full fledged member. If the European peace process ultimately sought stability and legitimacy, then the incentive for the allies to seek a conclusion to the occupation existed. Hardinge wrote Murray stating that ultimate goal of the French people was to bring an end to the occupation.

Rumors spread wildly throughout 1818 about an impending allied departure. *The Times* of London reported that the French Chamber of Deputies secretly requested that Louis XVIII seek support from the allied sovereigns for a complete withdrawal.[10] *The Times* reported that the smaller contingents would abandon France in the spring of 1818, leaving only the four powers.[11] The paper stated flatly that the Duke of Wellington and Russian General Woronzoff had declared that the allies would be out of France by October.[12] Rumors also stated that the Russians were ready to pay in order to keep six thousand men in France until 1819 and, in turn, they would sell their horses to the French upon departure.[13] After a full summer of gossip circulated by the Parisian newspapers, *The Times* voiced its support for the final withdrawal in its September 15 edition.[14]

Though the allied plenipotentiaries meeting at Aix-la-Chapelle in the fall of 1818 issued the order to evacuate France, once again the allied governments looked to the Duke of Wellington for his guidance about the removal of their soldiers. Wellington held in his hands the military rationale for either sustaining or discontinuing the occupation, just as he had during the discussion of the troop reduction the previous year. The duke's knowledge of events, beyond pure military issues, guided him to a decision.

Wellington took a firm approach in his analysis of whether the peacekeeping operation should terminate. His review led him to ask four questions which he wanted answered satisfactorily before he would rule in favor of the final withdrawal. First, did the circumstances that the November 20, 1815 peace treaty sought to achieve currently exist? Second, should the allies expect guarantees of payment of French debts for years four and five of occupation in jeopardy since the army was leaving? Third, what military precautions, required to insure tranquillity, would replace the army of occupation? Fourth, what alterations would take place in the diplomatic relationship between France and the Quadruple Alliance?[15] Since Wellington participated in both the allied political and military decisions, he enjoyed access to all information needed to answer these questions.

Wellington enjoyed access to many French politicians, and he was aware of what their feelings were on the subject. The duke believed that, if Louis XVIII, the French legislature, and the political parties all favored an end to the occupation, retaining it posed a threat to public tranquillity. One of the objectives that the allies had held in placing an occupation army in France was to achieve internal quiet. Maintaining an unwanted presence threatened all that the army had already achieved. A longer occupation would add to France's payment problems since France still had the responsibility of logistical support of Wellington's army. Added economic woes caused by the army of occupation would increase the potential for public unrest. Wellington spoke with the French leadership, including her military officers, and they all agreed that it was inadvisable to continue the occupation. The allied ministers in Paris expressed the same feelings to the duke. Whatever the danger to internal tranquillity, keeping the army in place would increase rather than diminish the threat of unrest. In answer to his first question, the duke concluded that the conditions expected by the powers from the occupation had been achieved, but they were endangered unless the army departed. French national resentment posed a real threat if there were two more years of occupation.[16]

In the area of reparations, the French contracted with the House of Baring to raise the funds necessary to pay off their indemnity. Removal of the army entailed some risks concerning further French payments. Without the army's presence, the allies could experience difficulty insuring loan repayment. But the duke's keen insight into the French government's drive for legitimacy meant that France wanted to pay its owed amounts. The French government wanted to maintain public credibility, especially from its own citizens, and it was not worth the risk to provoke further allied intervention with bad faith. Bad faith created by a France unwilling or unable to pay its indemnity posed as big a threat as an act of violence in causing a possible allied military response. Wellington grasped the need to remove the issue in question at the earliest possible moment, so he recommended a short period be established for French repayments.[17]

Wellington addressed the question of whether it was necessary that some type of permanent military protection for Europe replace the army of occupation. In many minds, the army may have emerged as the only deterrent which kept France within her borders. If it departed, renewed European warfare might again erupt. Rumors spread which called for the creation of an new allied army to be deployed across the frontier in the Kingdom of the Netherlands and designed to serve as a corps of observation. The British cabinet was hesitant on agreeing to end the occupation and suggested a special observation corps quartered on the Dutch frontier.[18] Reportedly, negotiations were already underway between the British and Dutch which would allow the British army to occupy positions in the Netherlands when the occupation ended. These troops would remain until the rebuilding of the Dutch barrier fortresses was completed.

The proposal was firmly rejected by the allies, and the Dutch wanted no part of it. Wellington noted that should hostilities become imminent, the German Confederation could field an army of 300 thousand almost immediately, while France's standing army numbered only eighty thousand.[19] By the time France could mobilize sufficient forces to fight a successful war, the allies could reconstitute their armies just as quickly as they had in June, 1815. The best military result France could expect was another defeat.[20]

Officials of the French government insisted that there was no need for a large standing army. If the allies maintained expensive military readiness, it could result in an arms race by all of Europe, and give grounds for increased French military preparations. Wellington pointed out that without continued allied concentration of forces, French military adventures would not generate popular support. The allies may have been slow in reacting to Napoleon's return in 1815, but with the size of the German forces and with the Bourbons on the French throne, a permanent presence seemed unnecessary. In 1815, the allies created another deterrent to the possibility of renewed French aggression when they awarded Prussia territory on the west bank of the Rhine River. Wellington believed, however, that any preventive strike by a corps of observation would only discredit the allies.[21] Russia pushed for a European military headquarters at Brussels with Wellington as commander, but Wellington wanted the subject forgotten.[22] The Dutch barrier fortresses, though behind schedule, upon reaching completion would better serve as the type of military *cordon sanitaire* that Europe desired. The barrier renovation program was sufficiently close to completion that it would not delay the allied departure from France after three years. The Dutch barrier was the permanent military precaution which replaced the army of occupation.

Wellington then addressed the issue of France's diplomatic status. If Europe desired a lasting peace established through the use of diplomacy rather than the sword, she had to admit France to full membership in the congress system. By the *Treaty of Chaumont* and the Quadruple Alliance, each European nation knew its responsibilities should the Bonapartists try to regain the French throne. But if France remained under a continued occupation, she could not enter the peacekeeping process or the congress system, for if she did, Louis XVIII and Richelieu would appear to act as agents of the occupation of their own country. The king might find his political base destroyed. Wellington wanted France to participate fully in the alliance systems which grew out of the conclusion of peace; if she met her financial obligations, she could and would join this system. If the powers prevented this, the result would pose a much greater threat to the peace. Wellington believed France stood against revolutionary ideas and Europe should accept her as an equal diplomatic player. Failure to do so would indicate that the alliance remained aimed against France.[23]

Diplomats such as Viscount Castlereagh of Britain and Prince Metternich of Austria designed the conference system as a quasi-European assembly to provide the powers with a system to discuss peacefully the obstacles to peace rather than to have to resort to war to redress grievances. Prior to 1818, conferences already functioned, albeit on a small scale, to address rather restricted questions. For example, the Allied Council of Ambassadors met in Paris from 1815 to 1818 to solve problems associated with the occupation army.[24] If a congress was now warranted, the allies needed to agree under what provisions it would meet. Viscount Castlereagh informed the allies in a memorandum on March 27, 1818 of England's position favoring a conference, but not a congress on the scale of Vienna. The British foreign minister wanted to meet on a strict interpretation of Article VI of the alliance, not Article V of the November 20, 1815 *Treaty of Paris*. Under Article VI, the sovereigns could debate issues and questions beyond those strictly related to France. At the same time, meeting under this article did not require the presence of any other European nation.[25]

The Russian czar, Alexander I, and his government initially hoped for a more expanded conference under Article VI of the Quadruple Alliance that would include Spain and Portugal.[26] The Austrians, however, opposed any expansion of participation or agenda, and Prince Metternich directed an effort to persuade Prussia to take a similar stand.[27] Metternich issued a memorandum on April 5, 1818, calling for a restricted conference. The Russians went along with Prince Metternich when the czar realized that a broadened conference might make it appear that the powers aspired to direct the affairs of other smaller nations.[28]

The French signature on a protocol dated April 25, 1818, regulating payments of claims removed the last obstacle for a gathering of nations. The Council of Ambassadors communicated the decision of the allied powers to meet in conference to the rest of Europe via a circular issued from Paris dated May 25, 1818.[29] The circular stated that Article V of the *Treaty of Paris* of November 20, 1815 was the basis for the upcoming discussions. The allies selected Aix-la-Chapelle as their meeting site. The selection of a site caused a minor delay. It was believed that holding it inside France might cause that nation further humiliation. If the allies desired to conduct their talks in a smaller state, they might discover it necessary to invite at least one additional sovereign. Metternich suggested Aix-

la-Chapelle, located in Prussian territory, because of its proximity
to France. This would allow Wellington to attend and furnish his
ideas to the decision-makers.[30]

The allies spent the months of August and early September ex-
changing notes between their chancelleries for arrangement of the
final details concerning the time of the meeting and those participating. All of the major representatives would attend. Viscount
Castlereagh represented Britain, although Wellington also attended.
As commander-in-chief of the occupation forces and representative of
all of Europe, he was expected to remain neutral. The Austrian Emperor attended the conference along with his chief minister, Prince
Metternich. Metternich's aide, Gentz, served as the conference secretary, just as he had at Vienna. The King of Prussia arrived accompanied by Prince Hardenberg and Count Bernstorff. Czar Alexander
I attended and was joined by several aides, the Greek, John Capo
d'Istria, and Count Nesselrode, and by his ambassador to Paris,
Pozzo di Borgo.[31] Louis XVIII, though invited to attend, opted not
to appear for reasons of bad health.[32] The Duke of Richelieu represented France, assisted by the French ambassador to Austria, Victor-
Louis de Caraman.

On September 16, Richelieu and Louis XVIII met to discuss
French policy to be followed at the upcoming conference. The two
directed French strategy to achieving two objectives. They first
planned to obtain a total evacuation of French territory, then restore complete sovereignty to France and to the king.[33] They claimed
that France had faithfully fulfilled each and every provision imposed
by the *Treaty of Paris* of November 20, 1815. The paying of allied claims remained the only open question, but progress on the
issue was readily apparent. The 1815 treaty provided an indemnity
payment totaling 700 million francs over a period of five years, without interest. At the time of the Aix-la-Chapelle conference, France
had successfully paid a total of 368 million francs of the indemnity.
France owed payment of the remaining 332 million francs no later
than November 20, 1820. Richelieu, recognizing the financial needs
of Russia and Prussia, planned to offer 265 millions to be paid immediately, with France obtaining the greater portion of this amount by
arranging further loans from the Houses of Baring and Labouchère
in exchange for French government bonds.[34]

The second French goal addressed concerns related to her position in the European community. Louis XVIII and the Duke of
Richelieu hoped they could put to rest the alliance created by the
Treaty of Chaumont which had been renewed by separate agreement
on November 20, 1815. The two men regarded the alliance not as
hostile to France, but rather as prejudicial to her dignity.[35] Richelieu

intended to emphasize to the powers that, if they left France isolated with a union directed against her, there was a good possibility for the revival of revolutionary ideas. He decided he would recommend a more general alliance of all major powers aimed at the general pacification of Europe.

Louis XVIII left no doubt in the mind of his minister as to what he considered the most important task:

> M. de Richelieu, make every kind of sacrifice in order to obtain the evacuation of the territory. It is the first condition of our independence...Explain to my allies how difficult the position of my government will be as long as one attributes to it the misfortunes of the country and the military occupation...Obtain the best conditions possible, but at any price let us not have any more foreigners on our soil.[36]

On September 29, Richelieu wrote to Decazes on the same matter and informed him that, before anything else, he intended to see French territory evacuated. When that was settled, he could approach the question of France's international standing. "The evacuation will be the first thing which shall be treated by the Conference. I have let completely sleep the idea of a Quintuple Alliance in order to first complete the evacuation of our land and the solidification of our finances."[37] Richelieu considered no other subject more important to his nation than the freeing of French soil from occupation, and he would not compromise on the issue. France had fulfilled the conditions imposed upon her by the second *Treaty of Paris*, and now Richelieu wanted the allies to fulfill their part.

Based on the instructions prepared for the British mission to Aix-la-Chapelle, the British government clearly favored an allied departure. The British cabinet formed their position when the Duke of Wellington spoke before them that a continued occupation was "against the declared wish of the King [Louis XVIII] and every political party in France and would increase rather than decrease the danger."

On the evening of September 30, 1818, Czar Alexander I and Richelieu met privately. The czar pressed Richelieu as to whether France was ready for an evacuation and if her government was "firmly consolidated."[38] Richelieu did not hesitate. He assured the czar that royal authority was fully established with the loyalty of French citizens.[39] Austria also favored a departure. With the stand of the other three powers, the Prussians would surely go along.[40] The czar told Richelieu "Prussia is very hard pressed for money, she would like to see a prompt liquidation,"[41] clearly an indication of where

Prussia stood on the evacuation issue.

Later that same evening, the allied plenipotentiaries held their first meeting. They invited Richelieu to the meeting and questioned him as to the state of French internal affairs, specifically on extremism in the Chamber of Deputies and on freedom of the press. The foreign minister assured the allies that radical wings in the chamber were of little influence. He also stated that a certain freedom of correspondence was a must and that the press should not be suppressed. The meeting resulted in a formal declaration from the allies stating that the occupation should come to an end by the close of the year.[42] The allies required, however, that France would have to insure money payments so that the clauses of the November 20, 1815 *Treaty of Paris* were fulfilled. The allied plenipotentiaries ordered the Duke of Wellington to report back on the matter.

Richelieu wrote to his sovereign the next day about the allied decision to evacuate France and stated that the allies remained only concerned with the liquidation of French debts.[43] Louis XVIII expressed his joy to the minister. "I have lived long enough, for I have seen France free and the French flag floating from all the French cities."[44] The allies made their official announcement of the end of the occupation to the French foreign minister on October 9. They declared that all foreign troops would leave France no later than November 30, 1818. The French requirement to supply the occupation army would end that day, regardless of where the allied troops were located. As the allied army withdrew from its cantonments, the French army was given permission to reoccupy its former fortresses.[45]

The French financial questions were also solved. On October 8, the Houses of Hope-Baring and the five powers signed a convention regulating the payment of the remaining 265 million francs, which allowed the formal announcement ending the occupation on October 9. This action disposed of the second of the two questions for which the conference had been called. With the issue of evacuation of France and indemnities disposed of, the future relationship between France and the alliance remained the only open subject of interest to France.

The Duke of Richelieu now turned his attention towards the re-admittance of France into the European community of nations on an equal footing with the other major powers. Doing so would restore the real sovereignty of his country, and it would remove any personal embarrassment Richelieu may have experienced when he signed the *Treaty of Paris*. Richelieu proposed that the Quadruple Alliance be extended to include France as an equal partner. The powers rejected this request, since inclusion of France in a treaty system that was actually directed against her was unacceptable.[46]

Castlereagh acknowledged that the French king could not become a member of "a league avowedly pointed at France."[47] On October 12 the allies agreed in secret protocol to adhere to their alliance and not to allow France to join.[48] France was allowed to continue in the conference deliberations, however, in accordance with Article VI of the treaty. Therefore, the Quintuple Alliance never existed.

On October 14, Alexander I issued a memorandum which called for allying the powers into a "common league mutually guaranteeing the existing order of things, thrones as well as territories."[49] The allies discussed the plan for the remainder of the month. Prince Metternich gave merit to the plan since it supposedly guaranteed the status quo of Europe. But he also knew full well that Britain was not going to make that type of commitment, and he too decided not to support the Russian proposal.[50] Viscount Castlereagh insisted that Britain was bound to the settlements of Vienna and Paris, and she would meet with the other powers according to Article VI of the alliance. Beyond that, Britain would make no further commitment. Castlereagh recognized that any plan of guarantee was impractical due to the difficulties in determining what conditions made intervention in the internal affairs of another country acceptable. In some cases, the British minister felt revolution within a particular country might be justified. Until an international system was created, the powers could not guarantee European borders.[51] In spite of all these reservations, it was imperative for the great powers to place France back on equal status with themselves. Failure to do so could force France to seek an alliance with one power which might precipitate a breakup of the congress system.

In a note to Richelieu on November 4, the plenipotentiaries invited France to participate with the allies in the present and in the future in "deliberations consecrated to the maintenance of peace."[52] The note remarked that the allies had investigated conditions inside France and, with France having fulfilled the provisions of the November 20, 1815 treaty, they were willing to restore France to her rightful international position. With this note, the allies in effect accepted France as a full partner in the congress system. Nothing remained for the Aix-la-Chapelle conferees except to make the official announcements to Europe of what transpired at the conference. The allies issued their proclamation on November 15, 1818.

Both the Duke of Richelieu and Viscount Castlereagh achieved victory at Aix-la-Chapelle. Richelieu obtained both of his major goals, the liberation of French territory and the right to participate in allied deliberations, though France was not admitted by treaty into the European concert. Castlereagh won his victory by keeping Great Britain committed to a policy of European cooperation without having to sign any further agreements which the British cabinet might find unacceptable.

The Allied Departure

With the issuance of the note of October 9 to Richelieu, allied plans for evacuation of France went into operation. Just as Sir George Murray had predicted a year earlier, the troop reduction of 1817 served as training for the eventual departure of the allies, except more was at stake. During the departures of the previous year, if the allied units stayed longer than agreed to, the allies faced only the problem of added logistical support costs. No physical or military danger threatened the remaining forces. With the final departure now forthcoming, any delayed departure would cost the allies much more. If there was any threat of violence to the departing troops, the Duke of Wellington and his commanders could no longer count on 120 thousand men to protect their movement out of France. In addition, the French army would enter the demilitarized zone and the allied occupation sector, and increase the possibility of confrontation between the two sides. With a force four times the size of those of 1817 now leaving, along with their artillery, support wagons, and baggage trains, the allied troops would strain the French road network to its fullest.[53] Wellington's army had to deal with rigid time constraints which were much more restrictive, since the announcement from Aix-la-Chapelle conference allowed only a month and a half before the final departure date.

The allies began preparations for departure almost immediately after the official announcement of the end of the occupation. Time schedules for departures and allotting roads for movements assumed a new significance. With the decision to hold another set of fall maneuvers, Sir George Murray faced a more difficult situation. Colonel Henry Hardinge wrote to Murray on October 13 stating that it was essential to "save the evacuation from the appearance and hurry of a flight."[54] Should the abandonment take on the appearance of a retreat under pressure, then the allied capability to maintain European security would come into question.

With the short preparation period, each allied contingent submitted its evacuation plans to Sir George Murray. On October 7, Wellington ordered Murray to begin the planning of routes, even before the allies made the official announcement from Aix-la-Chapelle. Wellington wanted the Russians to follow the Prussians out, insisting that the Prussians march with "celerity the moment I order it."[55] The duke gave Murray specific dates for contingents to leave, but his hopes for a quick departure were just not possible. Wellington hoped to accomplish the departure as rapidly as possible to encourage prompt indemnity payments from the French. The autumn review posed the major obstacle. Those units participating moved to the training site and then returned to their cantonments to get their baggage trains, all within the short period between the Aix declaration and November 30. They were unable to move as early as the duke had desired.

The British, having participated along with the Russians and the smaller commands in the last of the autumn reviews, began their embarkation on October 29 when the 4th Regiment of Foot departed from Calais. Wellington wanted to use the ports at Boulogne and Dunkirk, but the Royal Navy opted to use only Calais.[56] Much of the artillery was moved during the early days, a signal that this was a concern of George Murray. The infantry units preceded the cavalry regiments,[57] presumably because the cavalry could move faster during the last days of the occupation. Sir Manley Power, 2d Brigade Commander of the 1st Division, was given the responsibility of control of the embarkation point at Calais.[58] The British organized an orderly departure. Movement into and out of Calais went smoothly.[59] General Power reported that, as of November 29, all commands had left, and only a few horses and some required personnel remained in France.[60] The assistant quartermaster general in Calais announced the formal departure of the British command on December 5, and the end of British demands on the local populace.[61]

The other commands began their movements at the appropriate times. Henry Hardinge wrote to George Murray that the Prussians discovered the major obstacle was to maintain movement timetables in consideration of the heavy road traffic. Hardinge feared that the foreign contingents would run into each other due to the limited road network and, in the rush to get home, confrontations would occur.[62] The Russians began their movements on October 27, with the last unit departing their cantonments on November 13. The first unit departing arrived in the German town of Kaiserslautern on November 18, and the last unit reached that town on December 4.

The Prussians moved their forces in five columns along five routes, with each column containing between three and five main force units. The Prussians had four different final stops outside of France, at the cities of Koblenz, Treves, Cologne, and Luxembourg. Departures began on November 4, with a normal travel time to leave France of approximately ten days. The final march unit arrived in Cologne on December 9.[63] The Saxons planned to depart in two columns from the city of Charleville on November 14 and 16 in order to give the Russians time to pass that town. They changed their order of march once, but the two columns arrived in the German town of Homburg, just over the French border, on November 29 and December 1.[64] The Danes started their movements on November 8 in six columns, planning to reach the Belgian town of Mons by November 19.[65] The Bavarians, with the shortest distance to travel, commenced movement on November 12 according to their commander, General de la Motte, and evacuated French territory on November 15.[66] The Hanoverians moved on October 20, immediately following the autumn review.[67] The Austrians began crossing the frontier on November 1, and the last unit departed France by the eleventh of the month.[68]

With the departure of the allies from their cantonments, a real threat of incidents existed between the withdrawing troops and the French army as it moved forward into the demilitarized zone and finally into the former allied sector. The French troop movements started immediately after the allied departure announcement of October 9. On October 16, the Duke of Wellington wrote to George Murray that he had no objection to the French movements.[69] Wellington acknowledged the reality of the situation because he had no way of preventing the French from doing so. After all, the allies were moving in the opposite direction and, in any case, the effect of the arrival of French troops on the local population would evoke a burst of support for the French government, a desired goal of the allied sovereigns. In anticipation of the departure, the French army had already started recruitment procedures in the occupied departments, a program which Wellington had not attempted to halt, though two years earlier he had expressly forbidden it. The French war minister Saint-Cyr kept Wellington advised of all the movements of his army.[70] He identified all units and their objectives. Saint-Cyr clearly attempted to prevent incidents between the French army and the evacuating allies. As the French army reached their assigned locations, the British Royal Engineers were able to turn over a number of fortresses over to them with little or no complaint.[71] The French obviously wanted the allies out of France and their fortresses back without delays.

As the withdrawal continued, the allies concerned themselves with the rather large number of sick soldiers that were left behind until they could travel. The number of sick amounted to over sixteen hundred men, of which the Austrians and Russians totaled fourteen hundred. The French agreed they would care for these unfortunate soldiers starting on December 1, with the expense to be agreed to between the French and appropriate national government.[72] For some time, the French had cared for the Prussian sick, and the Duke of Wellington requested that records of the cost of care be forwarded to him so that he could accurately assess medical costs for the soldiers left behind. The expected expense amounted to two francs seventy-five centimes per day per individual, which included food, medicine, bedding, bandages, energy costs, and hospital attendants. The allies left behind seventy-four officers and almost two hundred and fifty enlisted men to assist in the care of the sick.[73]

The last of the military measures resulting from the Napoleonic Wars ended as scheduled. What of the attitude of the British army as it left France after all the years of fighting the emperor and the three years of occupation? A feeling of satisfaction must have existed after victory on the battlefield and participation in the occupation translated into a few years of peace. Surely the men and officers were glad to go home, albeit for many only a short period back in the British Isles prior to reassignment elsewhere.

The Duke of Wellington, not always remembered for his favorable attitude towards his men, took the time to thank his soldiers for their service in France prior to the final breakup of the army. The duke wrote his officers and men a letter of thanks:

> The Field Marshal cannot take leave of the troops which he has had the Honor of commanding without returning their thanks for their uniform good conduct. Three years have now elapsed since the Allied Sovereigns were pleased to entrust to the Field Marshal the command of their troops which the circumstances of the times had rendered it necessary to detain in France. This measure has been carried into execution in a manner satisfactory to their Majesties, and has been successful to a degree beyond what the most sanguine expectations of any could anticipate, its success must be attributed to the conciliating dispositions of their excellencies the General Officers commanding the several contingents to the example set by them to the General Officers and Officers under their command respectively and to the strict discipline which they have maintained in their several corps.
>
> The Field Marshal regrets that the cessation of the occupation will discontinue the Intercourse which he has had with their excellencies and those under their command from which he has derived so much advantage. But he begs to assure them that he will always reflect with satisfaction upon the three years which has passed and will be always happy to hear of their success.[74]

Wellington later expressed his thanks again to his officers and men upon their return to England. He thanked them for the example they set for others by their own conduct.

After a service of ten years' duration, almost without inter-
ruption, with the same officers and troops, the Field Marshal separates from them with regret; but he trusts that
they will believe that he will never cease to feel a concern
for their honour and interest.[75]

Count Alten of the Hanoverian contingent wrote to Sir George
Murray to express his satisfaction with the success of the occupation
and of having the pleasure of serving under the Duke of Wellington.
Alten felt he could not leave

without expressing the sentiments of gratitude manifested
by the officers of that [Hanoverian] Corps for all the kindness they have experienced from Field Marshal the Duke
of Wellington, during the time they had the honor to serve
under His Grace's command.[76]

Meanwhile, the French vigorously celebrated the final removal
of the allies from their sacred territory. As the British departed,
a French lieutenant overseeing the embarkation at Calais wrote to
Saint-Cyr that the process was nearly completed. He stated, "The
Reign of England died yesterday [17 November 1818] at one hour
past noon."[77] The Prefect of the Haut-Rhin wrote to Feltre that the
orderly evacuation of his province was complete. He noted that ev-
erywhere the departure of foreign troops had given the inhabitants
great joy. He reminded the minister that his residents had expressed
good dispositions towards the Austrians over the past period, however difficult, and that insults and provocations had always been
minimized.[78] The great joy of France over the foreign departure was
subdued until the date of departure arrived, the date the Duke of
Richelieu eagerly sought for his nation and for his family name. A
Scottish magazine wrote, "The government of France being now left
to itself, a new experiment is, therefore, begun."[79]

NOTES

1. C. K. Webster, *The Foreign Policy of Castlereagh, 1815–1822*
(London: G. Bell and Sons, Ltd., 1947), 123.
    2. Pierre Rain, *L'Europe et la Restauration des Bourbons, 1814–
1818* (Paris: Perrin et Cie, 1908), 453–54.
    3. Eugène Francois Auguste d'Armond, Baron de Vitrolles,
Mémoires et Relations Politiques, 3 volumes (Paris: G. Charpentier, et Cie, 1884), 3:459–67.
    4. Ibid., 468–493.

5. Rain, *Restauration*, 454–55.

6. Comtesse de Boigne, *Memoirs of the Countess de Boigne*, edited by Charles Nicoullaud, 2 volumes (New York: Charles Scribner's Sons, 1908), 2:313–14.

7. Rain, *Restauration*, 449–58.

8. Boigne, *Mémoirs*, 2:315; François Guizot and Madame Guizot de Witt, *The History of France from Earliest Times to 1848*, translated by Robert Black, 8 volumes (New York: John B. Alden, 1884), 8:232.

9. Colonel Henry Hardinge (1785–1856), later Field Marshal and Viscount, served as a quartermaster for Wellington in the Peninsular War, and was attached to the Prussian forces as liaison officer during the Waterloo campaign. He remained in that post until 1818. He had a long political career after 1820, including service as governor-general of India.

10. *The Times* (London), November 24, 1817.

11. Ibid., December 2, 1817; December 18, 1817.

12. Ibid., January 9, 1818.

13. Stuart to Castlereagh, March 30, 1818, Foreign Office Report 146/24/118, Public Record Office, Kew, United Kingdom states that Richelieu had been asked to make this concession to Russia.

14. *The Times*, September 15, 1818.

15. Wellington Memorandum on the projected conference at Aix-la-Chapelle, Wellington Papers 1/602.

16. Ibid.

17. Ibid.

18. The cabinet discussed a corps of observation in a memorandum on March 27, 1818. See Webster, *Foreign Policy*, 87.

19. Actually the French army numbered over 100 thousand and was in the process of rebuilding in accordance with the Army Bill of 1817.

20. Wellington Memorandum, Wellington Papers 1/602.

21. Ibid.

22. Webster, *Foreign Policy*, 164.

23. Wellington Memorandum, Wellington Papers 1/602.

24. The functioning of the council is the primary objective of Pierre Rain's *La Restauration*.

25. Castlereagh to Lord Cathcart, March 27, 1818 (enclosure to Castlereagh letter to Wellington, March 31, 1818), Wellington Papers 1/575.

26. Webster, *Foreign Policy*, 126.

27. Rain, *Restauration*, 449.

28. Webster, *Foreign Policy*, 126–27.

29. J. B. de Capefigue, *Histoire de la Restauration*, 5 volumes (Paris: Dufey et Vezard, 1832), 5:357.

30. Ibid., 5:357–60.

31. Webster, *Foreign Policy*, 131–33; Rain, *La Restauration*, 462–465.

32. Rain, *Restauration*, 452.

33. Armand-Emmanuel-Sophie Richelieu, *Le Duc de Richelieu, Sa Correspondence*, edited by Raoul de Cisternes (Paris: Calmann Levy, 1898), 17–34.

34. R. B. Mowat, *The States of Europe, 1815–1871* (New York: Longmans, Green and Company, 1932), 28.

35. Richelieu, *Le Duc de Richelieu*, 18 ff.

36. Louis XVIII cited by Capefigue, *Histoire de la Restauration*, 5:366–67.

37. Letter cited by E. Daudet, "Le Duc de Richelieu au Congrès d'Aix-la-Chapelle, 1818," *La Nouvelle Revue* 114 (1898): 206.

38. Alphonse Marie de Lamartine, *Histoire de la Restauration*, 8 volumes (Paris: Fagnerre, Lecou, Fourne et Cie, 1852), 6:160–61. Richelieu also related his audience with the Emperor in a letter to Louis on September 30, 1818, Richelieu, *Le Duc de Richelieu*, 46–47.

39. Louis Madelin, *Deux Relevements Francais, 1815–1818, 1871–1878* (Paris: Flammarion, 1951), 90.

40. Webster, *Foreign Policy*, 134–35.

41. Capefigue, *Histoire de la Restauration*, 5:369–70.

42. Richelieu, *Le Duc de Richelieu*, 49.

43. Ibid., 50–55.

44. Capefigue, *Histoire de la Restauration*, V:372.

45. Convention between Great Britain, Austria, Prussia, and Russia for the Evacuation of the French Territory by the Allied Troops, October 9, 1818. *British and Foreign State Papers*, 6:6–10.

46. Sir A. W. Ward and G. P. Gooch, *The Cambridge History of British Foreign Policy, 1783–1919*, 3 volumes (New York: The MacMillan Company, 1923), 1:23.

47. Webster, *Foreign Policy*, 137.

48. Ibid., 145.

49. Ibid.

50. Clemens Lothar Metternich, *Memoirs of Prince Metternich, 1773–1815*, edited by Prince Richard Metternich, translated by Mrs. Alexander Napier, 5 volumes (New York: H. Fertig, 1970), 3:183–88.

51. Webster, *Foreign Policy*, 150–51.

52. *The Annual Register or a View of the History, Politics, and Literature for the Year 1818* (London: Baldwin, Cradock, and Joy, 1819), 157–59.

53. *The Morning Chronicle*, October 17, 1818.

54. Murray Papers 46.7.12/94, Hardinge to Murray, October 13, 1818.

55. Murray Papers 46.7.12/23, Wellington to Murray, October 7, 1818.

56. Murray Papers 46.7.12/137, Murray to Wellington, October 16, 1818; Bathurst to Wellington, October 12, 1818, WO 6/16/84, comments on the unsuitability of Boulogne at this time of the year.

57. Murray Papers 46.7.13/146.

58. Murray to Manley Power, October 25, 1818, Wellington Papers 1/592.

59. *The Morning Chronicle*, November 9, 1818. The newspaper also reported the warm welcome that returning soldiers received at Dover, November 2, 1818.

60. Murray Papers 46.7.13/213, Manley Power to Murray, December 3, 1818.

61. Murray Papers 46.7.13/219, from Major Shaw, Assistant Quartermaster at Calais, to Murray, December 5, 1818.

62. Murray Papers 46.7.13/129, Hardinge to Murray, November 13, 1818.

63. Murray Papers 46.7.12/249 and 168; 46.7.13/25–26.

64. Murray Papers 46.7.13/1 and 46.7.13/46.

65. Murray Papers 46.7.12/275.

66. Murray Papers 46.7.12/279, de la Motte to Murray, October 30, 1818.

67. Murray Papers 46.7.12/108, October 14, 1818.

68. Baron Frimont to Wellington, October 23, 1818, Wellington Papers 1/592.

69. Murray Papers 46.7.12/137, Wellington to Murray, October 16, 1818.

70. Murray Papers 46.7.12/281, Saint-Cyr to Wellington, October 30, 1818; 46.7.13/92 and 108–09, November 1818.

71. Murray Papers 46.7.12, October 1818.

72. Murray Papers 46.7.13/82, Murray to Hardinge, November 9, 1818.

73. Murray Papers 46.7.13/152–53, Wellington to Murray, November 16, 1818; 46.7.13/209, November 23, 1818; 46.7.13/211, November 26, 1818.

74. Murray Papers 46.7.14, Wellington Order of the Day, Number 21, October 1818, on the breakup of the army of occupation.

75. General Order, November 10, 1818, Wellington Papers 1/596.

76. Murray Papers 46.7.13/57, Count Alten to Murray, November 5, 1818.

77. Lieutenant of the king at Calais to the Minister of War, November 18, 1818, General Military Correspondence of the Second Restoration, 1815–1830, *Archives de l'armée de terre*, D3-57, Château de Vincennes, France [hereafter War Ministry Archives].

78. Prefect of the Haut-Rhin to the Minister of War, November 14, 1818, War Ministry Archives D3-57.

79. *The Edinburgh Magazine and Literary Miscellany*, November, 1818, 175.

11

Conclusions

The allied occupation army stands as history's first joint multinational peacekeeping command. Prior to 1815, monarchs had never committed themselves to integration of their soldiers into a force that would enforce the conditions of peace upon a vanquished foe. Though the occupation army of 1815–1818 did not approach the total integration of forces that exists in today's NATO alliance, it deserves study as the first effort. Wellington's army was thus an experiment in peacekeeping which established standards and revealed problems that would be beneficial for future equivalent operations.[1] At the same time, it must be remembered this army was only a part of a general program, itself unique. The allied occupation army served as only a part of a European process designed to insure peace and tranquillity, and it accomplished its assigned role. The army played an important role in assisting in the re-establishment of European security. In part this was done by helping to secure the Bourbons on the French throne. The occupation army, under its commander-in-chief the Duke of Wellington, served in France as peacekeeper for three years while the French government, under the leadership of the Duke of Richelieu, simultaneously attempted to create the political, economic, and social conditions which enabled France to fulfill the stipulations stated in the second *Treaty of Paris*. When the French met the provisions of the treaty, the allied troops departed. France then entered a diplomatic system dedicated to European peace and returned to her rightful place among the major powers. Ending a generation of war, the occupation army formed a key part of a much larger system that would successfully prevent a general European war for another century. This study focused primarily upon the military role of the army, and considered diplomacy, economics, and politics only when they had a direct bearing on the military mission. The success of the allied occupation army is based on three factors: the dominant role of the Duke of Wellington, the rationale upon which the army was established and operated, and the efforts of Richelieu in directing France to meeting the allied requirements to end the occupation.

As a result of his victories in the Peninsular War, but above all due to his success at Waterloo, Wellington commanded the full respect and support of the major powers of Europe. Once they decided to occupy France jointly, the allied powers agreed to name the duke to command the army. Over the next three years, Wellington's leadership on a variety of issues reflected the esteem in which he was held. The duke's role went well beyond that of occupation army commander-in-chief as he involved himself in the more significant political, military, and economic issues. For example, he inspected the Dutch barrier fortresses; he decided when and if a troop reduction would take place; he arbitrated private claims against France; and he served as intermediary over press attacks against France originating in the Netherlands. His efforts in both the political and military arenas normally met the needs of both his army and the nations of Europe. The lessons he learned as commander of the army served as building blocks for his political career. He served in a position where he was an equal with the allied diplomats, with many of whom he would negotiate when he became Britain's prime minister. In many respects, Wellington performed tasks as army commander which many statesmen should experience prior to assuming high office. General Dwight Eisenhower's career would in some ways make a suitable comparison with Wellington's experiences. Eisenhower's command of the allied expeditionary forces in World War II resulted in him acting as a conciliator over alliance military problems; it gave him the opportunity of meeting many of the statesmen of the day and thus provided useful training for his two terms as president.

Any military officer must fully understand the objectives of his superiors in order that he correctly guide his own unit in support of those goals. The earmark of a commander is that he must possess an even broader vision of what his force is to accomplish. Wellington understood that his army was deployed in France in support of the general European interests of peace and tranquillity as espoused by the four powers of Great Britain, Austria, Prussia, and Russia. He organized his command, established goals, and personally acted as a standard bearer, all in support of the goal of European stability. When the duke ordered his officers to control intoxication or when he announced his reasons supporting the troop withdrawal of 1817, he consciously acted in the interests of Europe. Wellington's disciplinary actions helped to reduce the levels of plundering. He made his decisions within the strategic aims of the second *Treaty of Paris*, even though they might not necessarily have been in the best interest of his military command. From 1815 to 1818, Wellington used his office to direct the army of occupation to support the much broader aims of Europe's sovereigns. When he recognized the burden that allied troops placed on France, the duke supported the removal of the army at the earliest date possible.

The allied occupation army met many of the requirements considered essential for successful peacekeeping operations.[2] A peacekeeping force should have a single commander who simultaneously acts as the interface between the military command and the states authorizing the effort. Wellington, with the full respect of the allied powers as well as with the confidence of Louis XVIII, served as this interface successfully. Wellington did not command the occupation army in the manner he had on the battlefield where he enjoyed full control of his military efforts. He worked through the offices of each of the contingent commanders, because forces were not fully integrated into a command structure completely under Wellington's command and control.

A peacekeeping force requires unqualified sponsor support, and Wellington and his army enjoyed this backing. The duke had the support of the allied powers at a time when integration of national forces was unknown. Yet the allies turned to him and gave him the backing needed to conduct a successful peacekeeping operation. During any crisis situation, the responsibility for employment of the army was left entirely to the field marshal. He could make his decisions without outside interference, but he was subject to later review on the part of the allied sovereigns though their Council of Ambassadors sitting in Paris.

The army of occupation enjoyed the support of both parties, that is, the victorious allies on one hand and Bourbon France on the other, for the conduct of the operation. The four major powers that had battled Napoleon were willing to contribute to the peace effort and provide thirty thousand men each to Wellington's command. After Waterloo, Wellington had been their obvious choice. The powers encouraged five smaller countries, Bavaria, Denmark, Saxony, Hanover, and Würtemburg, to participate in the occupation, for they too had fought against France and had much at stake. In short, it was a European operation. These contributions, of major powers with the support of minor states, achieved a unity of effort directed towards the ultimate goal of insuring European tranquillity and introduced the concert system.

The host nation, France, also had much to gain from the allied presence. The Bonapartists were prevented from returning to power. The Bourbons were able to rebuild support for their rule and maintain their throne. France was able to fulfill the requirements of the second *Treaty of Paris*. Without the consent of the French government, the army would have served instead as a continuing source of animosity between the allies and France. In turn, the allied departure would have allowed a return of the attitudes prevalent during the revolutionary era. Wellington never jeopardized French backing for the army's presence by using it to interfere with decisions of the French government or to enforce peace. Had Wellington employed the army to suppress French citizens over some isolated incident, the army would have lost its status as a peacekeeping operation and the sense of neutrality that it enjoyed. Such an action would have jeopardized the support the army received from the French government.

All elements of the occupation army were important to the accomplishment of the assigned tasks. When the army was reduced in size in 1817, France and Russia wished to eliminate the smaller contingents entirely. These requests were rejected by Wellington, who insisted that the one-fifth reduction be taken by each occupying force. The smaller powers benefited from the presence of the army, and Wellington desired them to continue their contribution. European peace, even if directed by the allied powers, was a continental goal which demanded pan-European participation.

Peacekeeping forces require freedom of movement throughout their area of responsibility. Wellington's army of occupation did not have the ability to move throughout France, but the occupation army did not require this authority. The army of occupation was posted where it was needed, along the traditional invasion route into and out of France. The army moved as needed within its assigned region. Because of its limited size, the allied army could never have occupied all of France. Its primary objective was to restrict France to its own borders, not to quell internal revolt, and that goal was met with a limited zone of operations. Enforcement of France's obligation to pay reparations was achieved via diplomacy. Restraint on the part of the allied contingents was encouraged at all times, and complaints made by both parties were investigated fully.

The allied army was not the sole method of achieving and maintaining peace after the long years of war. It was part of a much larger and sustained effort seeking respite from war. Some form of concurrent action was needed to create permanent conditions for peace. Had it been the only effort at re-establishing peace, the occupation army's success would have been limited merely to the period of its presence inside France. Instead the army acted as part of a larger security system which included concurrent actions such as the development of the congress system, the French payment of reparations, territorial adjustments, restoration of legitimate rulers, and construction of the Dutch barrier fortifications.

The peace treaty of 1815 may have lacked the generosity of the first *Treaty of Paris* of May 30, 1814, but it was not so severe that it made France a permanently dissatisfied power. The territories lost to France did not create any *irredenta* which had to be avenged by resorting to war. Thanks to loans received from the financial houses of Hope and Baring, France was able to pay off its indemnity. With successful conclusion of the financial issue, the allies remained true to their words and ended the occupation. The European powers agreed to a moderate peace settlement and admit France to the concert system. In the aftermath of France's defeat, the allies resisted the temptations of total victory which could have led to a dictated peace agreement including a dismemberment. For this they are to be commended. Subsequent European history reflects the correctness of the route taken by the allied statesmen.

The Duke of Richelieu also played an important role by his efforts to end the occupation of his homeland at the earliest possible moment. He had been personally humiliated when he signed the second *Treaty of Paris*, even though he had succeeded in reducing some of the allied demands. Richelieu spent the next three years trying to reduce the allied extractions on France, as well as fulfilling the provisions of the treaty so that the allies would end their occupation. France achieved tranquillity and stability under his ministry. The monarchy appeared to be firmly re-established. A working government was in place. The French chambers passed legislation to rebuild a loyal French army. Even with the enormous financial costs placed on France, the indemnity was in the process of being paid off and claims were settled. (In 1815 it had appeared that France would be paying these huge debts indefinitely.[3]) The Dutch barrier fortresses were nearing completion. They would stand as the permanent replacement to the army of occupation and prevent future French expansion into central Europe. Wellington had pronounced himself satisfied with the military arrangements. Thanks to the efforts of Richelieu, by the time the allies met at Aix-la-Chapelle in 1818, all that remained was to announce a date of departure, the completion of the final indemnity payment, and the restoration of France's diplomatic standing. When this was accomplished, Richelieu returned home in triumph.

Triumph did not greet the foreign minister. Richelieu returned home to face the latest French election results. Another heated campaign had seen the ultras lose all fifteen of their seats contested in the election, while the government had lost four seats. Independents and republicans picked up some twenty representatives. The percentage of independent deputies had risen and a distinct move to the left could been observed with the election of a number of former revolutionaries to the chamber, a number of them known to oppose the monarchy.[4] Richelieu attempted a reconciliation with the right. Richelieu's ministry abruptly split over this move, and Elie Decazes, the king's favorite who was tied to the center-left, broke with the duke. The issue of a new election law came up, with the ultras favoring the idea and the independents rejecting it. Dissension in the cabinet was readily apparent. A full-fledged crisis was at hand. The king begged Richelieu to attempt to form a new government. Unsuccessful, Richelieu submitted his resignation on December 23. Louis refused it and again ordered the duke to try a form a ministry. For a second time he was unsuccessful and submitted his resignation the day after Christmas. There was no way the duke could form a government without Decazes.[5] Richelieu, in his note to the king, reminded his sovereign that he never considered himself fitted for the "management of internal affairs." He could safely point out that he had served France well at Aix-la-Chapelle, stating, "my mission was properly at an end at the moment of concluding the negotiations with the foreign powers." The king accepted his resignation with deep regret.[6] The allies, too, noted his passing from power with misgivings, having just settled with him at the conference. Prince Metternich summarized the allied feelings: "The [Austrian] Emperor regrets the dismissal of the Ministry of the Duke of Richelieu, because the just and conciliating spirit of the duke was able to serve as a guarantee of the relations between France and the powers."[7] The powers had negotiated the evacuation with Richelieu, and now, a month after his signature on the evacuation protocols, he was out of office. The French crown fared somewhat better than Richelieu: Louis XVIII maintained his throne until his death in 1824, and the 1830 demise of his brother Charles X can be attributed to factors other than those resulting from the occupation.

Under the guiding hand of the Duke of Wellington, the allied army of occupation achieved its assigned tasks. At a time when the allies enjoyed overwhelming military advantage, the army was wisely employed and did not create any lasting feelings of frustration on the part of France which might have led to desires for revenge. The army was never used as an instrument of a conqueror against a vanquished foe. French military expansionism came under control and remained that way after the departure of the allies in 1818. The threat of French domination of the European continent disappeared, and a general system of maintaining peace was placed into operation.

The British prince regent probably most cogently expressed the feelings of everyone associated with the planning, operation, and conclusion of the occupation when he thanked Wellington for his service. The prince declared that the duke had performed the difficult task of commanding many different nationalities of troops located in a country with which they had long been at war. This had "presented difficulties of no ordinary magnitude which could be surmounted by no ordinary measure of judgment and discretion."[8] The prince thanked Wellington for sustaining good discipline in an army away from home for such a long period, for keeping harmonious relations in the multinational army, and for doing so while acting in the best interests of France. He concluded his remarks by stating that these "achievements which will carry your name and the glory of the British Empire down to the latest posterity" were part of a command unexampled in its character.[9]

This command was Wellington's last active military post, though he remained commander-in-chief of the British army until 1852. However, in 1818, his political career was just beginning. He returned to Britain and was appointed Master General of the Ordnance with a seat on the Cabinet until 1827. He became prime minister in 1828 as a Tory. This final command had been more, much more, than a simple military command. He had achieved such a level of importance that his role was greater than that of a general. The lessons he learned in his three years in Paris and Cambrai would serve him well in his long political career.

The roles of both Wellington and Richelieu demonstrate the type of leadership necessary to make the army of occupation a success. Wellington exceeded the normal expectations of his office as commander-in-chief of an army. He supported the interests and aims of all Europe. Richelieu's performance served his nation well, which in turn served Europe well. Rather than dwelling on the hardships of occupation and allowing resentment to build, Richelieu directed his ministry to achieving those goals required to bring the occupation to an end. In their positions of power, both men worked for the peace of Europe, and it is this work which makes both true leaders.

The occupation army stands as an example for all future equivalent operations; its success had a great impact on Europe's direction over the next century. A generation of conflict had devastated the continent. The struggles needed to end. Europe joined together to accomplish this goal, and the peacekeeping force became part of a larger effort to prevent war. The allied army of occupation of 1815–1818 stands as a successful commitment of nations to peace.

NOTES

1. Richard W. Nelson, in his study of the successful peacekeeping force in the Sinai Peninsula, 1981 to the present, and the

failed American/European operation in Lebanon, 1983–1984, calls peacekeeping "a concept still in its infancy." "Multinational Peacekeeping in the Middle East and the United Nations Model," *International Affairs*, 1 (Winter 1984–1985), 61:89. Today's politics apparently rules out superpower participation in peacekeeping operations, yet the European powers contributed eighty percent of Wellington's army. Surely there is something to be learned from the occupation of France.

2. United States Army, Field Circular 100–20, *Low Intensity Conflict* (Fort Leavenworth, Kansas: United States Army Command and General Staff College, 1981.) See chapter six for a primer on peacekeeping operations.

3. Mary D. R. Leys, *Between Two Empires. A History of French Politicians and People between 1814 and 1848* (London: Longmans, Green and Company, 1955), 94. France paid over 633 million francs to support the army of occupation, while indemnities and claims reached 1,200 million francs.

4. Guillaume de Bertier de Sauvigny, *The Bourbon Restoration*, translated by Lynn M. Case (Philadelphia: University of Pennsylvania Press, 1966), 153.

5. Ibid., 157.

6. Alphonse Marie de Lamartine, *Histoire de la Restauration*, 8 volumes (Paris: Fagnerre, Lecou, Fourne et Cie, 1852), 3:406.

7. Clemens Lothar Metternich, *Lettres du Metternich à la Comtesse de Lieven*, edited by Jean Hanoteau (Paris: Plon Nourrit et Cie, 1909), 115.

8. His Royal Highness the Prince Regent to the Duke of Wellington, November 27, 1818, War Office Report 6/16/12, Public Record Office, London, United Kingdom [hereafter WO 6].

9. George Prince Regent to Wellington, November 27, 1818, WO 6/16/12.

Appendix A

The Treaty of Paris
November 20, 1815

In the Name of the Most Holy and Undivided Trinity

The Allied Powers having by their united efforts and by the success of their arms, preserved France and Europe from the convulsions with which they were menaced by the late enterprise of Napoleon Bonaparte, and by the revolutionary system re-produced in France to promote its success; participating at present with his Most Christian Majesty in the desire to consolidate, by maintaining inviolate the Royal authority, and by restoring the operation of the constitutional charter, the order of things which had been happily reestablished in France, as also in the object of restoring between France and her neighbors those relations of reciprocal confidence and goodwill, which the fatal effects of the revolutions and of the system of conquest had for so long a time disturbed; persuaded, at the same time, that this last object can only be obtained by an arrangement framed to secure to the Allies proper indemnities for the past and solid guarantees for the future, they have in concert with his Majesty the King of France taken into consideration the means of giving indemnity due to the Allied Powers cannot be either entirely territorial or entirely pecuniary, without prejudice to France in the one or other of her essential interests, and that it would be more fit to combine both the modes, in order to avoid the inconveniences which would result, were either resorted to separately: their Imperial and Royal Majesties have adopted this basis for their present transactions; and agreeing alike as to the necessity of retaining for a fixed time in the frontier Provinces of France, a certain number of allied troops they have determined to combine their different arrangements, founded upon these bases in a Definitive Treaty. For this purpose and to this effect, his Majesty the King of the United Kingdom of Great Britain and Ireland, for himself his Allies on the one part, and his Majesty the King of France and Navarre on the other part have named their plenipotentiaries to discuss, settle, and sign the said Definitive Treaty; namely his Majesty the King of the United Kingdom and Ireland, the Right Hon. Robert Stewart Viscount Castlereagh, &c; and the most illustrious and most noble Lord Arthur, Duke, Marquis, and Earl of Wellington, &c; and his Majesty the King of France and of Navarre, the Sieur Armand Emmanuel du Plessis Richelieu, Duke of Richelieu, &c. who, having exchanged their full powers, found to be in good and due form, have signed the following Articles:

ARTICLE I. The frontiers of France shall be the same as they were in the year 1790, save and except the modifications on the one side and on the other, which are detailed in the present Article. First on the northern frontiers, the line of demarkation shall remain as it was fixed by the Treaty of Paris, as far as opposite to Quivreain, from thence it shall follow the ancient limits of the Belgian Provinces, of the late Bishopric of Liege and the Duchy of Bouillon, as they existed in the year 1790, leaving the territories included within that line, of Phillipeville, and Marienbourg, with the fortresses so called, together with the whole of the Duchy of Bouillon, without the frontiers of France. From Villers near Orval upon the confines of the Department Des Ardennes and of the Grand Duchy of Luxembourg as far as Perle, upon the great road leading from Thionville to Treves the line shall remain as it was laid down by the Treaty of Paris. From Perle it shall pass by Laududorff, Walwich, Schardorff, Niederveiling, Pelweiler (all these places with their Banlieues or dependencies remaining to France) to Houvre; and shall follow from thence the old limits of the district of Sarrebruck, leaving Sarrelouis, and the course of the Sarre, together with the places situated to the right of the line above described, and their Banlieues or dependencies without the limits of France. From the limits of the district of Sarrebruck the line of demarkation shall be the same which at present separates from Germany the departments of the Moselle and the Lower Rhine, as far as to the Lauter, which river shall from thence serve as the frontier until it shall fall into the Rhine. All of the territory on the left bank of the Lauter, including the fortress of Landau, shall form part of Germany.

The town of Weissenbourg, however, through which that river runs, shall remain entirely to France, with a rayon on the left bank, not exceeding a thousand toises, and which shall be more particularly determined by the Commissioners who shall be charged with the approaching designation of the boundaries. Secondly, leaving the mouth of the Lauder, and continuing along the departments of the Lower Rhine, the Upper Rhine, the Doubs, and the Jura, to the Canton de Vaud, the frontiers shall remain as fixed by the Treaty of

Paris. The Thalweg of the Rhine shall form the boundary between France and the States of Germany, but the property of the islands shall remain in perpetuity, as it shall be fixed by a new survey of the course of that river, and continue unchanged whatever variation that course may undergo in the lapse of time. Commissioners shall be named on both sides, by the High Contracting Parties, within the space of three months to proceed upon the said survey. On half of the bridge between Strasbourg and Kehl shall belong to France, and the other half to the Grand Duchy of Baden. Thirdly, in order to establish a direct communication between the Canton of Geneva and Switzerland, that part of the Pays de Gex, bounded on the east by Lake Leman; on the south by the territory of the Canton of Geneva; on the north by that of the Canton of Vaud; on the west by the course of the Versoix, and by a line which comprehends the communes of Collex, Bossy, and Keyrin, leaving the commune of Ferney to France, shall be ceded to the Helvetic Confederacy, in order to be united to the Canton of Geneva. The line of the French custom-houses shall be placed to the west of the Jura, so that the whole of the Pays de Gex shall be without that line. Fourthly, from the frontiers of the Canton of Geneva, as far as the Mediterranean the line of demarkation shall be that which in the year 1790, separated France from Savoy, and from the country of Nice. The relations which the Treaty of Paris of 1814 had reestablished between France and the Principality of Monaco, shall cease forever and the same relations shall exist between that Principality and his Majesty the King of Sardinia. Fifthly, all of the territories and districts included within the boundary of the French territory, as determined by the present Articles, shall remain united to France. Sixthly, the High Contracting Parties shall name within three months after the signature of the present Treaty, Commissioners to regulate everything relating to the designation of the boundaries of the respective countries, and as soon as the labours of the Commissioners shall have terminated, maps shall be drawn and landmarks shall be erected, which shall point out the respective limits.

ARTICLE II. The fortresses, places and districts, which according to the preceding Article, are no longer to form part of the French territory, shall be placed at the disposal of the Allied Powers, at the periods fixed by the 9th Article of the Military Convention annexed to the present Treaty; and his Majesty the King of France renounces for himself, his heirs, and successors forever the rights of sovereignty and property, which he has hitherto exercised over the said fortresses, places and districts.

ARTICLE III. The fortifications of Huningen have been constantly an object of uneasiness to the town of Basel, the High Contracting Parties, in order to give to the Helvetic Confederacy a new proof of their good will, and of their solicitude for its welfare, have agreed among themselves to demolish the fortifications of Huningen, and the French government engages from the same motive not to reestablish them at any time, and not to replace them by other fortifications, at a distance less than that of three leagues from the town of Basel. The neutrality of Switzerland shall be extended to the territory situated to the north of a line to be drawn from Ugine, that town being included, to the south of the Lake of Annecy, by Paverge, as far as Lecheraine, and from thence, by the Lake of Bourget, as far as the Rhone, in like manner as it was extended to the Province of Chablais and Faucigny, by the 92^d Article of the final Act of the Congress of Vienna.

ARTICLE IV. The pecuniary part of the indemnity to be furnished by France to the Allied Powers, is fixed at the sum of seven hundred millions of francs. The mode, the periods, and the guarantees for the payment of this sum, shall be regulated by a Special Convention, which shall have the force and effect as if it were inserted, word for word in the present treaty.

ARTICLE V. The state of uneasiness and of fermentation, which after so many violent convulsions, and particularly after the last catastrophe, France must still experience, notwithstanding the paternal intentions of her King, and the advantages accrued to every class of his subjects by the constitutional charter, requiring, for the securing of the neighboring States, certain measures of precaution and of temporary guarantee, it has been judged indispensable to occupy, during a fixed time, by a corps of allied troops certain military positions along the frontiers of France, under express reserve, that such occupations shall in no way prejudice the sovereignty of his Most Christian Majesty, nor the state of possession, which as it is recognized and confirmed by the present Treaty. The number of these troops shall not exceed one hundred and fifty thousand men. The commander in chief of this army shall be nominated by the Allied Powers. This army shall occupy the fortresses of Conde, Valenciennes, Bouchain, Cambray, Le Quesnoy, Maubeuge, Landrecies, Avesnes, Rocroy, Givet with Charlemont, Meziers, Sedan, Montmedy, Thionville, Longwy, Bitsch, and the Tetade-Pont of Fort Louis. As the maintenance of the army destined for this service is to be provided by France, a Special Convention shall regulate everything which may relate to that object. This convention, which shall have the same force and effect as if it were inserted word for word in the present Treaty, shall also regulate the relations of the army of occupation with the civil and military authorities of the country. The utmost extent of the duration of this military operation, is fixed at five years, the Allied Sovereigns, after having in concert with his Majesty the King of France, maturely examined their reciprocal situation and interests, and the progress which shall have been made in France in the reestablishment of order and tranquillity, shall agree to acknowledge that the motives which led them to that measure have ceased to exist. But whatever may be the result of this deliberation, all the fortresses and positions occupied by the allied troops shall at the expiration of five years, be evacuated without further delay, and give up to his Most Christian Majesty, or to his heirs and successors.

ARTICLE VI. The foreign troops, not forming part of the army of occupation shall evacuate the French territory within the term fixed by the 9th Article of the Military Convention annexed to the present Treaty.

ARTICLE VII. In all countries which shall change Sovereigns, as well in virtue of the present Treaty, as of the arrangements which are to be made in consequence thereof, a period of six years from the date of the exchange of the ratifications shall be allowed to the inhabitants, natives or foreigners, of whatever condition and nation they may be, to dispose of their property, if they should think fit to do so, and to retire to whatever country they may choose.

ARTICLE VIII. All the dispositions of the Treaty of Paris of the 30th of May 1814, relative to the countries ceded by that treaty shall equally apply to the several territories and districts ceded by the present Treaty.

ARTICLE IX. The High Contracting Parties having caused representation to be made of the different claims arising out of the nonexecution of the 19th and the following Articles of the Treaty of the 30th of May 1814, as well as of the Additional Articles of that Treaty signed between Great Britain and France, desiring to render more efficacious the stipulations made thereby, and having determined by two separate Conventions, the line to be pursued on each side for that purpose, the said two Conventions, as annexed to the present Treaty, shall in order to secure the complete execution of the above mentioned Articles, have the same force and effect as if the same were inserted word for word, herein.

ARTICLE X. All prisoners taken during the hostilities, as well as all hostages which may have been carried off or given, shall be restored in the shortest time possible. The same shall be the case with respect to the prisoners taken previously to the Treaty of the 30th of May 1814, and who shall not already have been restored.

ARTICLE XI. The Treaty of Paris of the 30th of May 1814, and the final Act of the Congress of Vienna of the 9th of June 1815, are confirmed and shall be maintained in all such of their enactments as shall not have been modified by the ARTICLES of the present Treaty.

ARTICLE XII. The present Treaty, with the Conventions annexed thereto, shall be ratified in one act, and the ratifications thereof shall be exchanged in the space of two months, or sooner, if possible.

In witness whereof, the respective Plenipotentiaries have signed the same, and have affixed thereunto the seals of their arms.

Done at Paris this 20th day of November in the year of our Lord 1815.

(signed)

Castlereagh
Wellington
Richelieu

Appendix B

Military Convention of the
Second Treaty of Paris

Convention between Great Britain, Austria, Prussia, Russia, and France, relative to the Occupation of a Military Line in France by an Allied Army, signed at Paris November 20, 1815.

ARTICLE I. The composition of the army of 150,000 men, which, in virtue of the Vth article of the treaty of this day, is to occupy a military line along the frontiers of France, the force and nature of the contingents to be furnished by each power, as well as the choice of the generals who are to command those troops, shall be determined by the allied sovereigns.

ARTICLE II. This army shall be maintained by the French government in the manner following:

The lodging, the fuel, and lighting, the provisions and forage are to be furnished in kind.

It is agreed that the total amount of daily rations shall never exceed 200,000 for men, and 50,000 for horses, and that they shall be issued according to the tariff annexed to the present convention.

With respect to the pay, the equipment, the clothing, and other incidental matters, the French government will provide for such expense, by the payment of a sum of 50,000,000 of francs per annum, payable in specie from month to month, from the 1st of December of the year 1815, into the hands of the allied commissioners.

But the allied powers, in order to concur as much as possible in every thing which can satisfy His Majesty the King of France, and relieve his subjects, consent that only 30,000,000 of francs, on account of pay, shall be paid in the 1st year, on condition of the difference being made up in the subsequent years of the occupation.

ARTICLE III. France engages equally to provide for the keeping up of the fortifications, and of the buildings of the military and civil administrations, as well as for the arming and provisioning the fortresses which, in virtue of the Vth article of the treaty of this day, are to remain as a deposit in the hands of the allied troops.

These respective services, which are to be regulated upon the principles adopted by the French administration of the war department, shall be executed upon a demand, addressed to the French government by the commander-in-chief of the allied troops, with whom some plan shall be agreed upon for ascertaining what may be needful, and concerting the measures necessary to remove all difficulties which may also arise, and for accomplishing the object of this stipulation, in a manner equally satisfactory to the interests of the respective parties.

The French government will take such measures as it shall judge to be the most effectual, for securing the accomplishment of the different services stated in this and the preceding article; and will concert to that effect with the commander-in-chief of the allied troops.

ARTICLE IV. In conformity with the Vth article of the principal treaty, the military line to be occupied by the allied troops, shall extend along the frontiers which separate the Departments of the Pas de Calais, of the North, of the Ardennes, of the Meuse, of the Moselle, of the Lower Rhine, and of the Upper Rhine, from the interior of France.

It is further agreed, that neither the allied troops nor the French troops shall occupy (except it be for particular reasons, and by common consent) the territories and districts hereafter named;

In the Department of the Somme, all the country north of that river from Ham to where it falls into the sea; In the Department of the Aisne, the districts of St. Quentin, Vervins and Laón; In the Department of the Marne, those of Rheims, St. Ménéhould, and Vitry; In the Department of the Upper Marne those of St. Dizier and Joinville; In the Department of the Meurthe, those of Toul, Dieuze, Sarrebourg and Blamout; In the Department of the Vôsges, those of St. Diez, Brugères and Remiremont; The District of Lure, in the Department of the Upper Saône, and that of St. Hyppolite, in the Department of the Doubs.

Notwithstanding the occupation by the allies, of the portion of territory fixed by the principal treaty, and by the present convention, His Most Christian Majesty may, in the towns situated within the territory occupied, maintain garrisons, the number of which, however, shall not exceed what is laid down in the following enumeration:

City	Troops	City	Troops
Calais	1000	Lille	3000
Gravelines	500	Verdun	500
Bergues	500	Metz	3000
St. Omer	1500	Lauterbourg	200
Béthune	500	Weissenberg	150
Montreuil	500	Lichtenberg	150

Hesdin	250	Petite Pierre	100
Ardres	150	Phalsburg	600
Aire	500	Strasburg	3000
Arras	1000	Schlestadt	1000
Boulogne	300	Belfort	1000
St. Venant	300		

Dunkirk and its forts	1000
Douay/Ft de Scarpe	1000
Neuf Brisach/Ft Mortier	1000

It is, however, well understood, that the *materiel* belonging to the engineer and artillery departments, as well as such articles of military equipment as do not belong to those fortresses, shall be withdrawn from them, and shall be transported to such places as the French government shall think fit, provided those places are situated without the line occupied by the allied troops, and without the districts in which it is agreed not to leave any troops, either allied or French.

If any infraction of the above stipulations should come to the knowledge of the commander-in-chief of the allied armies, he shall make his representations on the subject to the French government, which engages to do what is right thereupon.

The fortresses abovementioned, being, at this moment, unprovided with garrisons, the French government may place therein, as soon as it shall think fit, the number of troops fixed as above; appraising always before hand the commander-in-chief of the allied troops, in order to avoid any difficulty and delay which the French troops might experience in their march.

ARTICLE V. The military command in the whole extent of the departments which shall remain occupied by the allied troops, shall belong to the general-in-chief of those troops: it is, however, distinctly understood, that it shall not extend to the fortresses which the French troops are about to occupy, in virtue of the IVth article of the present convention, nor to a rayon of 1,000 toises[1] around each of those places.

ARTICLE VI. The civil administration, the administration of justice, and the collection of taxes and contributions of all sorts, shall remain in the hands of the agents of His Majesty the King of France.

The same shall be the case with respect to customs. They shall remain in their present state, and the commanders of the allied troops shall throw no obstacle in the way of the measures to be taken, by the officers employed in that service, to prevent frauds: they shall even give them, in case of need, succour and assistance.

ARTICLE VII. To prevent all abuses which might affect the regulations of the customs, the clothing and the equipments, and other necessary articles, destined for the allied troops, shall not be allowed to enter, except they be furnished with a certificate of origin, and in pursuance of a communication to be made, by the commanding officer of the different corps, to the general-in-chief of the allied army, who will, on his part, cause information to be given thereof to the French government, who will, in consequence thereof, issue the proper orders to their officers employed in the administration of the customs.

ARTICLE VIII. The service of the *gendarmerie* being acknowledged as necessary to the maintenance of order and public tranquillity, shall continue, as hitherto, in the countries occupied by the allied troops.

ARTICLE IX. The allied troops, with the exception of those that are to form the army of occupation, shall evacuate the territory of France in 21 days, after the signature of the principal treaty.

The territories which, according to that treaty, are to be ceded to the allies, as well as the fortresses of Landau and Sarre-Louis, shall be delivered up by the French authorities and troops, in 10 days, from the date of the signature of the treaty.

Those places shall be given up in the state in which they were on the 20th of September last.

Commissioners shall be named on both sides, to ascertain and declare that state, and to deliver and receive respectively the artillery, the military stores, plans, models, and archives, belonging as well to the said places as to the different districts ceded by France, according to the treaty of this day.

Commissioners shall also be named, to examine and ascertain the state of those places still occupied by the French troops, and which, according to the Vth article of the principle treaty, are to be held in deposit, for a certain time, by the allies.

These places shall also be delivered up to the allied troops in 10 days, from the date of the signature of the treaty.

Commissioners shall also be named by the French government, on the one part, and by the general commanding-in-chief of the allied troops destined to remain in France, on the other; also by the general commanding the allied troops which are at present in possession of the fortresses of Avesnes, Landrecy, Maubeuge, Rocroy, Givet, Montmedy, Longwy, Mezières, and Sedan, to ascertain and declare the state of those places, and of military stores, maps, plans, models, etc., which they shall contain, at the moment which shall be considered as that of the occupation in virtue of the treaty.

The allied powers engage to restore, at the expiration of the temporary occupation, all the places named in the Vth article of the principle treaty, in the state in which they shall have been found at the time of that occupation, save and except the damages which may have been caused by time, and which the French government should not have provided against by the necessary repairs.

Done at Paris, this 20th day of November, in the year of our Lord, 1815.

(signed)

Castlereagh
Wellington
Richelieu

NOTE

1. A rayon is a radius of a fort's firing ability; a toise is a distance of just under two meters.

Appendix C

Official Note Relative to

the Diminution of the Army of Occupation

Paris, February 10, 1817

The Courts of Austria, England, Prussia, and Russia, having taken into consideration the desire manifested by His Most Christian Majesty to have the numbers of the Army of Occupation diminished, and proportionally the amount of charge occasioned by its presence on the French territory, have authorized the undersigned to make the following communication to his Excellency the Duke de Richelieu, President of the Council of Ministers, and Secretary of State for the Department of Foreign Affairs:

At the time when the King re-established upon his throne and put in possession of his legitimate and constitutional authority, endeavoured to discover, in concert with the other powers, the most efficacious means of consolidating internal order in France, and of associating his kingdom to the system of good understanding and general pacification interrupted by the troubles which were scarcely put an end to; it was found that the temporary presence of an Allied Army was absolutely necessary both to secure Europe against the consequences of agitations, the renewal of which were threatened, and to afford the opportunity of exercising in tranquillity its benevolent influence, and of strengthening itself by the attachment and submission of all Frenchmen.

The solicitude of His Most Christian Majesty to render this indispensable expedient the least onerous to his subjects, and the wisdom which directed all the arrangements stipulated at that period, led them to anticipate by common accord the case in which the diminution of the Army of Occupation might take place without weakening the motives, or injuring the great interests, which had rendered its presence necessary.

These conditions the undersigned have great satisfaction in retracing; they consist in the firm establishment of the legitimate dynasty, and in the success of the efforts, and endeavours of His Most

Christian Majesty to compress factions, dissipate errors, tranquilize passions, and unite all Frenchmen around the throne by the same wishes and the same interests.

The great result desired and looked to by all Europe could be neither the work of a moment, nor the effect of a single effort. The Allied Powers have observed with a constant attention, but not with astonishment, the differences of opinion which have prevailed as the mode of obtaining it. In this attitude they have looked to the superior wisdom of the King for the measures proper to fix uncertainty, and to give to his administration a firm and regular march; not doubting that he would unite with the dignity of the throne and the rights of his crown, that magnanimity which, after civil discord, assures and encourages the weak; and, by an enlightened confidence, excite the zeal of all his other subjects.

Experience having already happily fulfilled, as far as the nature of things will allow, the hopes of Europe upon this subject, the Allied Sovereigns, eager to contribute to this great work, and to give to the nation the means of enjoying all the benefits which the efforts and the wisdom of the King are preparing for it, do not hesitate to regard the present state of affairs as sufficient to determine the question which they have been called upon to decide.

The good faith with which the King's government has hitherto fulfilled the engagements entered into with the Allies, and the care which has been taken to provide for the different services of the current year, by adding to the resources arising from the revenues of the state those of a credit, guaranteed by foreign and national banking-houses the most considerable in Europe, have also removed the difficulties which might otherwise have justly arisen upon this point of the proposed question.

These considerations have at the same time been strengthened by the opinion which his Excellency Marshal the Duke of Wellington has been requested to give respecting an object of such great importance.

The favourable opinion and the authority of a personage so eminent have added, to the motives already stated, all those which human prudence can unite to justify a measure demanded and consented to with sentiments of sincere and reciprocal kindness.

The undersigned are therefore authorized by their respective courts to notify to his Excellency the Duke de Richelieu:

1. That the reduction of the Army of Occupation will be carried into effect.

2. That the amount of the diminution of the whole army shall be 30,000 men.

3. That this amount shall be proportioned to that of each con-

tingent; that is to say, it shall be a fifth of each corps d'armée.

4. That it shall take place from the 1st of April next.

5. That from that period the 200,000 rations per day, furnished for the troops by the French government, shall be reduced to 160,000, without, however, in any respect altering the 50,000 rations of forage destined for the feed of the horses.

6. Lastly, that from the same period France shall otherwise enjoy all the advantages arising from the said reduction, conformably to existing treaties and conventions.

In communicating so marked a testimony of friendship and confidence to His Most Christian Majesty, on the part of their august masters, the undersigned have at the same time to declare to his Excellency the Duke de Richelieu, how much the principles of the ministry over which he presides, and those which are personal to himself, have contributed to establish that mutual good will, which, directed by the spirit and the letter of existing treaties, has hitherto served to arrange so many delicate affairs, and which affords for the future the most satisfactory pledges of a definitive and satisfactory conclusion.

They seize this opportunity of renewing to the Duke de Richelieu the assurances of their high consideration.

(signed)

The Baron de Vincent
Charles Stuart
The Count de Goltz
Pozzo di Borgo

Appendix D

Convention for the Evacuation of France

Convention between Great Britain, Austria, Prussia, and Russia for the Evacuation of French Territory by the Allied Troops. Signed at Aix-la-Chapelle, October 9, 1818.

Their Majesties the Emperor of Austria, the King of Prussia, and the Emperor of all the Russians, having repaired to Aix-la-Chapelle; and their Majesties the King of the United Kingdom of Great Britain and Ireland, and the King of France and Navarre, having sent thither their plenipotentiaries; the Ministers of the 5 Courts have assembled in Conference together; and the plenipotentiary of France having intimated that in consequence of the state of France, and the faithful execution of the Treaty of November 20th, 1815, His Most Christian Majesty was desirous that the military occupation stipulated by the Vth Article of the said treaty, should cease as soon as possible; the Ministers of the Courts of Austria, Great Britain, Prussia, and Russia, after having, in concert with the said Plenipotentiary of France, maturely examined every thing that could have an influence on such an important decision, have declared, that their Sovereigns would admit the principle of the evacuation of the French Territory at the end of the 3^{d} year of the Occupation; and wishing to confirm this resolution by a formal Convention, and to secure, at the same time, the definitive execution of the said Treaty of November 20th, 1815,—His Majesty the King of the United Kingdom of Great Britain and Ireland on the one part, and His Majesty the King of France and Navarre, on the other part, have named as their plenipotentiaries, (Castlereagh, Wellington, and Richelieu).

Who, after having mutually communicated to each other their respective Full Powers, found to be in good and due form, have agreed upon the following Articles:

ARTICLE I. The Troops composing the Army of Occupation shall be withdrawn from the Territory of France by the 30th of November next, or sooner, if possible.

ARTICLE II. The strong Places and Fortresses which the said Troops occupy, shall be given up to Commissioners named for that purpose by His Most Christian Majesty, in the state in which they were at the time of their occupation, conforming to the IXth Article of the Convention concluded in execution of the Vth Article of the Treaty of November 20th, 1815.

ARTICLE III. The sum destined to provide for the pay, the equipment, and the clothing of the Troops of the Army of Occupation, shall be paid, in all cases, up to the 30th of November next, on the same footing on which it has existed since the 1st of December, 1817.

ARTICLE IV. All the accounts between France and the Allied Powers having been regulated and settled, the sum to be paid by France, to complete the execution of the IVth Article of the Treaty of 20th November, 1815, is definitely fixed at 265,000,000 of francs.

ARTICLE V. Of this sum the amount of 100,000,000, effective value, shall be paid by Inscriptions of *Rentes* on the great book of the Public Debt of France, bearing interest from the 22^{d} of September, 1818. The said Inscriptions shall be received at the rate of the funds on Monday the 5th of October, 1818.

ARTICLE VI. The remaining 165,000,000 shall be paid by 9 monthly installments, commencing on the 6th of January next, by Bills on the Houses of Hope and Co. and Baring, Brothers and Co., which as well as the Inscriptions of *Rentes* mentioned in the above Article, shall be delivered to Commissioners of the Courts of Austria, Great Britain, Prussia, and Russia, by the Royal Treasury of France, at the time of the complete and definitive evacuation of the French Territory.

ARTICLE VII. At the same period, the Commissioners of the said Courts shall deliver to the Royal Treasury of France, the 6 Bonds not yet discharged, which shall remain in their hands, of the 15 Bonds delivered conformably to the II^{d} Article of the Convention concluded for the execution of the IVth Article of the Treaty of 20th November, 1815. The said Commissioners shall, at the same time, deliver the Inscription of 7,000,000 of *Rentes*, created in virtue of the VIIIth Article of the said Convention.

ARTICLE VIII. The present Convention shall be ratified, and the Ratifications thereof exchanged at Aix-la-Chapelle in the space of a fortnight, or sooner if possible.

In witness whereof, the respective Plenipotentiaries have signed the same, and have thereunto affixed the Seal of their Arms.

Done at Aix-la-Chapelle, the 9th day of October, in the Year of our Lord 1818.

(signed)

Castlereagh
Wellington
Richelieu

Appendix E

Allied Military Commanders

Commander-in-Chief: The Duke of Wellington
Chief of Staff: Sir George Murray

Great Britain

Commander-in-Chief:	The Duke of Wellington
Infantry Commander:	Lord Rowland Hill
Cavalry Commander:	Sir Stapleton Cotton, Lord Combermere
Adjutant General:	Maj. Gen. E. Barnes
Quartermaster General:	Sir George Murray
Infantry Division Commanders:	Sir Lowry Cole
	Sir Henry Clinton
	Sir Charles Colville
Infantry Brigade Commanders:	James Kempt
	Thomas Brisbane
	Denis Pack
	Peregrine Maitland
	John Lambert
	R. W. O'Callaghan
	Thomas Bradford
	Manley Power
	John Keane
Cavalry Brigade Commanders:	Richard Hussay Vivian
	Colquhoun Grant
	Edward Somerset
Staff Corps of Cavalry:	George Scovill

Russia

Commander-in-Chief:	Lt. Gen. Count Woronzov
Division Commanders:	Lt. Gen. Alexeieff
	Maj. Gen. Oudom
	Maj. Gen. Lissanevitch

Chief of Staff:	Maj. Gen. Poucet
Brigade Commanders:	Maj. Gen. Balabine
	Maj. Gen. Kobloukoff
	Maj. Gen. Achlestnhoff
	Maj. Gen. Ivanoff
	Maj. Gen. Bagdanofski
	Maj. Gen. Gourieff
	Maj. Gen. Pantzenbitter
	Maj. Gen. Poltoratsky

Austria

Commander-in-Chief:	General Baron de Frimont
Division Commanders:	Lt. Gen. Baron Mohr
	Lt. Gen. Baron Lederer
	Lt. Gen. Baron Marschall
Chief of Staff:	Major Baron Hauer
Brigade Commanders:	Maj. Gen. Count Desfours
	Maj. Gen. Count Raigecourt
	Maj. Gen. Baron Senitzer
	Maj. Gen. Baron Folseis
	Maj. Gen. Baron Wrede
	Maj. Gen. Count Latour

Prussia

Commander-in-Chief:	General Zeiten
Cavalry Commander:	Maj. Gen. de Wahlen Furgass
Chief of Staff:	Colonel de Reiche
Cavalry Brigade Commanders:	Colonel Borstell
	Colonel Count Lehndorff
Infantry Brigade Commanders:	Lt. Gen. Pirch
	Maj. Gen. de Borke
	Maj. Gen. Ryssel
	Maj. Gen. Lassau

Bavaria

Commnader in Chief:	Lt. Gen. de la Motte
Chief of Staff:	Maj. Baron Horn
Cavalry Brigade Commander:	Maj. Gen. Count Seydewitz
Infantry Brigade Commander:	Maj. Gen. de Barnklau

Denmark

Commander-in-Chief:	Prince Frederick of Hesse
Chief of Staff:	Maj. de Lesser
Brigade Commanders:	Colonel de Waldeck
	Colonel Prince Guillaume of Hesse

Saxony

Commander-in-Chief:	Maj. Gen. Gablenz
Chief of Staff:	Colonel de Zezochwitz
Infantry Brigade Commander:	Colonel Seydewitz
Hussar Regiment Commander:	Lt. Col. de Stunzer

Würtemburg

Commander-in-Chief:	Lt. Gen. Baron de Woellworth [later de Scheler, Dec 1816]
Chief of Staff:	Captain Araud
Infantry Brigade Commander:	Maj. Gen. Messani [later de Hupeden, Feb 1817]
Cavalry Regiment Commander:	Colonel Reinhard

Hanover

Commander-in-Chief:	Maj. Gen. Sir James Lyon [later Count Alten, Dec 1816]
Adjutant General:	Lt. Col. Hetle
Infantry Brigade Commanders:	Colonel Halkett
	Colonel Berger
Hussar Regiment Commander:	Col. Count Kielmannsegge

The British Army in France:
Battalion and Squadron Commanders

Cavalry Regiments

2nd Dragoon Guards:	LTC James Kearney
3^{d} Dragoons:	LTC Charles Manners
7th Hussars:	LTC Edward Kerrison
11th Light Dragoons:	LTC James Wallace Sleigh
12th Lancers:	LTC Frederick Ponsonby
18th Hussars:	LTC Henry Murray

Infantry Regiments

2nd Battalion, Coldstream Guards:	MAJ Alex. Woodford
3^{d} Battalion, Grenadier Guards:	MAJ William Stuart
3^{d} Battalion, The Royal Scots:	LTC Frederick Muller
1st Battalion, 3^{d} Regiment of Foot:	LTC William Stewart
1st Battalion, 4th Regiment of Foot:	LTC Francis Brooke
1st Battalion, 5th Regiment of Foot:	LTC Charles Pratt
1st Battalion, 6th Regiment of Foot:	LTC Archibald Campbell
1st Battalion, 7th Regiment of Foot:	LTC Edward Blakeney
1st Battalion, 9th Regiment of Foot:	LTC John Cameron
1st Battalion, 21st Regiment of Foot:	LTC William Paterson
1st Battalion, 23^{d} Regiment of Foot:	LTC Thomas Palmer
1st Battalion, 27th Regiment of Foot:	LTC Lemuel Warren
1st Battalion, 29th Regiment of Foot:	LTC John Tucker
1st Battalion, 39th Regiment of Foot:	LTC Cavendish Sturt
1st Battalion, 40th Regiment of Foot:	LTC Henry Thornton
1st Battalion, 43^{d} Regiment of Foot:	LTC Christ Patrickson
1st Battalion, 52nd Regiment of Foot:	LTC John Colborne
1st Battalion, 57th Regiment of Foot:	LTC Collis Spring
1st Battalion, 71st Regiment of Foot:	LTC Thomas Reynell
1st Battalion, 79th Regiment of Foot:	LTC Neil Douglas
1st Battalion, 81st Regiment of Foot:	LTC Patrick McKenzie

1st Battalion, 88th Regiment of Foot: LTC Alex. Wallace
1st Battalion, 91st Regiment of Foot: LTC William Douglas
1st Battalion, The Rifle Brigade: LTC Andrew Barnard
2nd Battalion, The Rifle Brigade: LTC Dugald Gilmour

Author's Note: These were the commanders in charge for the longest period of time during the occupation. Often they were able to go on leave for extended periods and the ranking major would take command.

Appendix G

Memorandum on the 1816 Autumn Review

Bouchain is supposed in possession of the enemy, his army in position on the heights in front of Escoudain, the right at Denain, the left at Abscon. The attacking force assembles between Avluy and Helesmes. After the first attack, the enemy retires across the Scheldt, covering his movement by a position connecting Lourche and Roulx. The third position has the right on Douchy; the center in rear of Neuville, and the left at Lieu St. Amaud. The Danish and Saxon Corps are consequently directed to threaten an attack along the front, whilst the British and Hanoverian troops make a movement to their left and passing the Scheldt by the bridges of Denain, Rouvigny, and pontoons laid near Wavrechin, both Corps are formed in three successive lines on the height above the right bank of the Selle. The enemy now finds his right turned, and immediately reinforces it by extending himself along the left bank of the Selle, occupying with considerable strength Douchy and Noyelle, but being forced both on the line of the Scheldt and the Selle, he retires, and makes a precipitate retreat in the direction of Cambrai.

(signed)

Murray
October 20, 1816

Bibliography

ARCHIVES AND MANUSCRIPT COLLECTIONS

Archives de l'armée de terre. Château de Vincennes, France.

General Military Correspondence of the Second Restoration, 1815–1830. D3-18 through D3-57.

Archives du Ministère des Affaires étrangères. Paris, France.

Mémoires et Documents. Fonds France.

702 Correspondence with Great Britain Relative to Occupation, 1815–1818.

703 Correspondence with Austria Relative to Occupation, 1815–1818.

706 Correspondence with Prussia Relative to Occupation, 1815–1818.

Bibliothèque de Victor Cousin. Paris, France.

Fonds Richelieu 147. Lettres du duc de Richelieu au marquis d'Osmond.

British Library. London, United Kingdom.

British Library MSS, War in Germany, France, and Belgium, 1813–1815.

The Papers of Lord Liverpool.

The Papers of Lord Rowland Hill.

Durham County Record Office. Durham, United Kingdom.

The Londonderry Papers.

National Army Museum. London, United Kingdom.

Sir Richard Hussay Vivian Papers.

W.B. Whitman Papers.

National Library of Scotland. Edinburgh, United Kingdom.

Sir George Murray Papers. ADV MSS 46.6.7–46.8.5, Occupation of France 1815–1818.

Baron Stuart de Rothesay Papers. MSS 6182-6186.

Public Record Office. Kew, Richmond, Surrey, United Kingdom.

Foreign Office Records.

FO 27 France.

FO 146 France Correspondence.

War Office Records.

WO 1 Secretary of State for War In Letters.

WO 6 Secretary of State for War Out Letters.

WO 17 Monthly Returns.

WO 28 Letters to and from Calais Assistant Quartermaster.

WO 27 Inspection Returns.

WO 37 George Scovill Papers.

WO 55 State of French Fortresses Occupied by Allied Troops.

WO 79 Records of Connaught Rangers.

WO 103 Establishments.

Public Record Office Records.

PRO 30 Papers of Sir Lowry Cole.

University of Southampton Library, United Kingdom.

The Wellington Papers.

PUBLISHED DOCUMENTS

The Annual Register or a View of the History, Politics, and Literature for the Year 1816. London: Baldwin, Cradock, and Joy, 1817.

The Annual Register or a View of the History, Politics, and Literature for the Year 1817. London: Baldwin, Cradock, and Joy, 1818.

The Annual Register or a View of the History, Politics, and Literature for the Year 1818. London: Baldwin, Cradock, and Joy, 1819.

Archives Parlementaires de 1787 a 1860. Deuxième Série 1800 à 1860. 95 volumes. Paris: Librairie Administrative De Paul DuPont, 1869.

Boigne, Comtesse de. *Memoirs of the Countess de Boigne.* Edited by Charles Nicoullaud. 2 volumes. New York: Charles Scribner's Sons, 1908.

Bulletin des Lois du Royaume de France. 7th Serie. Paris: De L'Imprimerie Royale, 1816.

Ferrand, Antoine Francois Claude. *Mémoires du Comte Ferrand.* Paris: Alphonse Picarde et Fils, 1897.

Guizot, François. *Memoirs to Illustrate the History of My Times.* 8 volumes. London: Richard Bentley, 1858. New York: AMS Press reprint, 1974.

Gurwood, Lt Colonel John, editor. *The General Orders of Field Marshal the Duke of Wellington in the Campaign of 1809 to 1818.* London: W. Clowes and Sons, 1837.

Jones, Sir Harry D., editor. *Reports Relating to the Re-establishment of the Fortresses in the Netherlands from 1814 to 1830.* London: Spottiswood and Company, 1861.

Metternich, Clemens Lothaire. *Lettres du Metternich à la Comtesse de Lieven.* Edited by Jean Hanoteau. Paris: Plon Nourrit et Cie, 1909.

———. *Memoirs of Prince Metternich.* Edited by Prince Richard Metternich. Translated by Mrs. Alexander Napier. 5 volumes. New York: H. Fertig, 1970.

Noailles, Marquis de. *Le Comte Molé, Sa Vie Ses Mémoires.* 4 volumes. Librarie Ancienne Adouard Champion, 1923.

Pasquier, Etienne Denis. *Mémoires du Chancelier Pasquier.* 4 volumes. Plon, Nourrit et Cie, 1896.

Richelieu, Armand-Emmanuel-Sophie. *Le Duc de Richelieu, Sa Correspondence.* Edited by Raoul de Cisternes. Paris: Calmann Levy, 1898.

Rouchechouart, Louis Victor Léon. *Memoirs of the Count of Rouchechouart.* Translated by Frances Jackson. New York: E.P. Dutton and Company, 1920.

Talleyrand. *Mémoires du Prince de Talleyrand.* 5 volumes. Paris: Calmann Levy, 1891.

United Kingdom. Foreign Office. *British and Foreign State Papers.* Compiled by Sir Edward Hertslet. 170 volumes. London: James Ridgway, 1841–1977.

United Kingdom. *The Parliamentary Debates from the Year 1803 to the Present Time.* 1st series, 41 volumes. London: T. C. Hansard, 1812–1830.

United Kingdom. *House of Commons Sessional Papers.* H.M.S.O. volumes XII and XVII, 1816. volumes XX, XXVI, and XLVIII, 1831–1832.

Vane, Charles William, editor. *Correspondence, Despatches, and Other Papers of Viscount Castlereagh, Second Marquess of Londonderry.* 12 volumes, London: William Shoberl, 1852.

Vitrolles, Eugene Francois Auguste d'Armand. *Mémoires et Relations Politiques.* Edited by Eugene Forques. 3 volumes. Paris: G. Charpentier et Cie, 1884.

Webster, C. K., editor. *British Diplomacy, 1813-1815. Select Docu-
    ments Dealing with the Reconstruction of Europe.* London: G.
    Bell and Sons, 1921.
Wellington, 2d Duke of. *Supplementary Despatches, Correspondence
    and Memoranda of Field Marshal the Duke of Wellington.* 15
    volumes. London: John Murray, 1864.

NEWSPAPERS AND PERIODICALS

*Anti-Jacobin Review; True Churchman's Magazine; and Protestant
    Advocate*
Cobbett's Weekly Political Register
*The Edinburgh Magazine and Literary Miscellany (also known as
    The Scots Magazine or Scottish Chronicle)*
The Examiner
The Morning Chronicle
The Times (London)

BOOKS

Regimental Histories

Atkinson, Christopher Thomas. *The Dorsetshire Regiment.* 2 vol-
    umes. Oxford: Oxford University Press, 1947.
Barrett, C. R. B. *History of the XIII Hussars.* 2 volumes. Edinburgh
    and London: William Blackwood and Sons, 1911.
Buchan John. *The History of the Royal Scots Fusiliers, 1678–1918.*
    London: Thomas NeCom and Sons, Ltd., 1925.
Cannon, Richard, compiler, Adjutant Generals Office, The Horse
    Guards. Historical Records of the British Army comprising the
    History of every Regiment (commonly known as the Cannon
    Series). *Historical Record of the First, or Royal Regiment of
    Foot.* London: Parker, Furnivall, and Parker, 1847.
——. *Historical Record of the Second Dragoon Guards, or Queen's
    Bays.* London: W. Clowes and Sons, 1837.
——. *Historical Record of the Third, or the King's Own Regiment of
    Light Dragoons.* London: Parker, Furnivall, and Parker, 1847.
——. *Historical Record of the Third Regiment of Foot, or the Buffs.*
    London: W. Clowes and Sons, 1839.
——. *Historical Record of the Fourth, or the King's Own, Regiment
    of Foot.* London: W. Clowes and Sons, 1839.
——. *Historical Record of the Fifth Regiment of Foot, or Northum-
    berland Fusiliers.* London: W. Clowes and Sons, 1839.

——. *Historical Record of the Sixth, or Royal Warwickshire Regiment of Foot.* London: W. Clowes and Sons, 1839.

——. *Historical Record of the Seventh, or the Queen's Own, Regiment of Hussars.* London: John W. Parker, 1842.

——. *Historical Record of the Seventh Regiment, or the Royal Fusiliers.* London: Parker, Furnivall, and Parker, 1847.

——. *Historical Record of the Ninth, or the East Norfolk Regiment of Foot.* London: Parker, Furnivall, and Parker, 1848.

——. *Historical Record of the Eleventh, or Prince Albert's Own, Regiment of Hussars.* London: John W. Parker, 1843.

——. *Historical Record of the Twelfth, or the Prince of Wales's Royal Regiment of Lancers.* London: John W. Parker, 1842.

——. *Historical Record of the Thirteenth Regiment of Light Dragoons.* London: John W. Parker, 1842.

——. *Historical Record of the Fifteenth, or the King's Regiment of Light Dragoons.* London: John W. Parker, 1841.

——. *Historical Record of the 21st Regiment, or the Royal North British Fusiliers.* London: Parker, Furnivall, and Parker, 1849.

——. *Historical Record of the 71st Regiment, Highland Light Infantry.* London: Parker, Furnivall, and Parker, 1852.

——. *Historical Record of the 88th Regiment of Foot, or Connaught Rangers.* London: W. Clowes and Sons, 1838.

Cope, Sir William Henry. *The History of the Rifle Brigade (The Prince Consort's Own), Formerly the 95th.* London: Chatto and Windus, Piccadilly, 1877.

Goff, Captain G.L. *Historical Records of the 91st Argyllshire Highlanders, now the 1st Battalion Princess Louise's Argyll and Sutherland Highlanders, 1794–1881.* London;: Richard Bentley and Son, 1891.

Groves, Percy. *Historical Records of the 7th or Royal Regiment of Fusiliers, 1685–1903.* United Kingdom, Guernsey: Frederick B. Guerin, 1903.

Hamilton, Lt. General Sir F. W. *The Origin and History of the First or Grenadier Guards.* 3 volumes. London: John Murray, 1874.

Kingsford, Charles Lethbridge. *The Story of the Royal Warwickshire Regiment (formerly the Sixth Foot).* London: George Newnes, Ltd., 1921.

Knight, C. R. B. *Historical Records of the Buffs East Kent Regiment (3d Foot) Formerly Designated the Holland Regiment and Prince George of Denmark's Regiment, 1704–1914.* 2 volumes. London: The Medici Society, Ltd., 1935.

Leask, J. C. and McCance, H. M. *The Regimental Records of the Royal Scots (The First or the Royal Regiment of Foot).* Dublin: Alexander Thom and Comapany, Ltd., 1915.

Levinge, Sir Richard George Augustus Bart. *Historical Records of the Forty-Third Regiment, Monmouthshire Light Infantry.* London: W. Clowes and Son, 1868.

Mackenzie, Captain T. A., Ewart, Lieutenant J. S., and Findlay, Lieutenant C. *Historical Records of the 79th Queen's Own Cameron Highlanders.* London: Hamilton, Adams and Company, 1887.

Malet, Colonel Harold, editor. *The Historical Memoirs of the XVIII (Princess of Wales's Own) Hussars.* London: Simpkin and Company, Ltd., 1907.

Maxwell, Sir Herbert, editor. *The Lowland Scots Regiments.* Glasgow: James MacLehose and Sons, 1918.

Moorson, William Scarth. *Historical Record of the Fifty-Second Regiment (Oxfordshire Light Infantry), 1755-1858.* London: Richard Bentley, 1860.

Petre, F. Loraine. *The History of the Norfolk Regiment, 1685-1918.* 2 volumes. Norwich: Jarrold and Sons, Ltd.

Ross of Bladensburg, Lt. Colonel John. *A History of the Coldstream Guards, 1815-1895.* London: A.D. Innes and Company, 1896. *The Royal Inniskilling Fusiliers. Being the History of the Regiment from December 1688 to July 1914.* London: Constable and Company, Ltd., 1928.

Smythies, Captain R. H. Raymond. *Historical Records of the 40th (2 Somersetshire) Regiment, now 1st Battalion The Prince of Wales Volunteers, 1717-1893.* United Kingdom, Devonport: A.H. Swiss, 1894.

Stewart, Captain P. F. *The History of the XII Royal Lancers (Prince of Wales's).* London: Oxford University Press, 1950.

Walker H. M. *A History of the Northumberland Fusiliers, 1674-1902.* London: John Murray, 1919.

Warre, Lt. General Henry James. *Historical Records of the Fifty-Seventh, or West Middlesex, Regiment of Foot.* London: W. Mitchell and Company, 1878.

White, Arthur S., compiler. *A Bibliography of Regimental Histories of the British Army.* London: The Society for Army Historical Research, 1965.

Woolright, H..H. *History of the Fifty-Seventh (West Middlesex) Regiment of Foot, 1755-1881.* London: Richard Bentley and Son, 1893.

The Duke of Wellington

Aldington, Richard. *The Duke.* New York: The Viking Press, 1943.

Brett, Oliver. *Wellington.* Garden City, New York: Doubleday, Doran and Company, 1929.

Davies, Godfrey. *Wellington and His Army.* Oxford: Basil Blackwell, 1954.

Glover, Michael. *Wellington as Military Commander.* London: B.T. Batsford, 1968.

Griffith, Paddy, editor. *Wellington Commander: The Iron Duke's Generalship.* United Kingdom: Antony Bird Publications Limited of Strettington House, Strettington, Chicester, Sussex.

Guedalla, Philip. *Wellington.* New York: The Literary Guild, 1931.

Longford, Elizabeth. *Wellington: Pillar of State.* London: Weidenfeld and Nicolson, 1972.

———. *Wellington: The Years of the Sword.* London: Weidenfeld and Nicolson, 1969.

Maxwell, Sir Herbert. *The Life of Wellington. The Restoration of the Martial Power of Great Britain.* 2 volumes. London: Sampson, Low, Marston and Company, Ltd., 1899.

Oman, Sir Charles. *Wellington's Army, 1809–1814.* London: Greenhill Books, reprint, 1986, first printed 1913.

Petrie, Sir Charles. *Wellington: A Reassessment.* London: Garden City Press, Ltd., 1956.

Ward, Stephen George Peregrine. *Wellington.* New York: Arco Publishing Company, Inc., 1965.

Wright, Reverend G. N. *Life and Campaigns of the Duke of Wellington.* 4 volumes. London: Fisher Son and Company, 1841.

Yonge, Charles Duke. *The Life of Arthur, Duke of Wellington.* London: Ward, Lock, Bowden and Company, 1892.

The Bourbon Restoration

Artz, Frederick B. *France Under the Bourbon Restoration, 1814–1830.* New York: Russell and Russell, Inc., 1963.

Bertier de Sauvigny, Guillaume de. *The Bourbon Restoration.* Translated by Lynn M. Case. Philadelphia: University of Pennsylvania Press, 1966.

Capefigue, J. B. de. *Histoire de la Restauration.* 5 volumes. Paris: Dufey et Vezard, 1832.

Gorce, Pierre de la. *Louis XVIII.* Paris: Librairie Plon, 1926.

Hall, John R. *The Bourbon Restoration.* New York: Houghton Mifflin Company, 1909.

Hudson, Nora E. *Ultra-Royalism and the French Restoration.* New York: Octagon Books, 1973.

Jardin, Andre and Tudesq, Andre-Jean. *Restoration and Reaction,*

1815-1848. Translated by Elborg Forster. Cambridge: Cambridge University Press, 1983.

Lamartine, Alphonse Marie de. *Histoire de la Restauration.* 8 volumes. Paris: Fagnerre, Lecou, Fourne et Cie, 1852.

Lucas-Dubreton, J. *The Restoration and the July Monarchy.* Translated by E.F. Buckley. New York: G.P. Putnam's Sons, 1929.

Mansel, Philip. *Louis XVIII.* London: Blond & Briggs Ltd., 1981.

Rain, Pierre. *L'Europe et la Restauration des Bourbons, 1814–1818.* Paris: Perrin et Cie, 1908.

Resnick, Daniel Philip. *The White Terror and the Political Reaction After Waterloo.* Cambridge, Massachusetts: Harvard University Press, 1966.

Stewart, John Hall. *The Restoration Era in France, 1814–1830.* Princeton: D. Van Nostrand Company, Inc., 1968.

Viel-Castel, Louis de. *Histoire de la Restauration.* 20 volumes. Paris: Michel Lévy, Frères, 1860–1878.

The Duke of Richelieu

Bertier de Sauvigny, Guillaume de. *France and the European Alliance 1816–1821. The Private Correspondence between Metternich and Richelieu.* Notre Dame, Indiana: University of Notre Dame Press, 1958.

Cox, Cynthia. *Talleyrand's Successor: Armand-Emmanuel du Plessis Duc de Richelieu 1766–1822.* London: Arthur Barker Ltd., 1959.

Fouques-Duparc, J. *Le Troisième Richelieu.* Lyon: H. Lardanchet, 1952.

Military History of the Period

Anglesey, The Marquess of. *A History of the British Cavalry, 1816–1919.* 3 volumes. London: Leo Cooper, 1973.

Bruce, A. P. C. *An Annotated Bibliography of the British Army, 1660–1914.* New York: Garland Publishing Inc., 1975.

Chandler, David G. *The Campaigns of Napoleon.* London: Weidenfeld and Nicolson, 1966.

———. *Dictionary of the Napoleonic Wars.* New York: MacMillan Publishing Company, Inc., 1979.

Craig, Gordon A. *Problems of Coalition Warfare: The Military Alliance Against Napoleon, 1813–1814.* From the Harmon Memorial Lectures in Military History. Colorado: United States Air Force Academy, 1965.

Fortescue, John W. *A History of the British Army.* London: Mac-
    Millan and Company, Ltd., 1920.
Keegan, John. *The Face of Battle.* New York: The Viking Press,
    1976.
——. *The Mask of Command.* New York: The Viking Press, 1987.
Rothenberg, Gunther E. *The Art of Warfare in the Age of Napoleon.*
    Bloomington, Indiana: Indiana University Press, 1980.
Segur, Count Philippe-Paul de. *Napoleon's Russian Campaign.*
    Translated by J. David Townsend. New York: Time Incor-
    porated, 1958.

Twentieth Century Occupations

Fraenkel, Ernst. *Military Occupation and the Rule of Law. Occupa-
    tion Government in the Rhineland, 1918–23.* London: Oxford
    University Press, 1944.
Friedmann, W. *The Allied Military Government of Germany.* Lon-
    don: Stevens and Sons, Ltd., 1947.
Hunt, I.L. *American Military Government of Occupied Germany,
    1918–1920.* Washington: Government Printing Office, 1943.
United States Army. Field Circular 100–20. *Low Intensity Conflict.*
    Fort Leavenworth, Kansas: United States Army Command
    and General Staff College, 1981.
Ziemke, Edward F. *The U.S. Army in the Occupation of Germany,
    1944–46.* Center Of Military History, Washington: U.S. Gov-
    ernment Printing Office, 1975.

Special Studies

Beck, Thomas D. *French Legislators, 1800–1834.* Berkeley: Univer-
    sity of California Press, 1974.
Brett-James Anthony, editor. *Edward Costello: Adventures of a
    Soldier.* London: Longmans, Green and Company, Ltd., 1967.
Bryant, Sir Arthur. *The Age of Elegance, 1812–1822.* London:
    Collins, 1950.
Bury, J. P. T. *France, 1814–1940.* London: Methuen and Company,
    Inc. 1949.
Collins, Irene, editor. *Government and Society in France, 1814–
    1818.* New York: St. Martin's Press, 1970.
Combes de Patris, Bernard. *Le Comte de Serre.* Paris: August
    Picard, 1932.
Cookson, J. E. *Lord Liverpool's Administration: The Crucial Years,
    1815–1822.* Hamden, Connecticut: Archon Books, 1975.

Cretineau-Joly, Jacques. *Histoire des Traités de 1815.* Paris: Colomb de Batines, 1842.

Gash, Norman. *Lord Liverpool: The Life and Political Career of Robert Banks Jenkinson Second Earl of Liverpool 1770-1828.* Cambridge, Massachusetts: Harvard University Press, 1984.

Geikie, Roderick and Montgomery, Isabel A. *The Dutch Barrier, 1705-1719.* Cambridge: Cambridge University Press, 1930.

Guizot, François Pierre Guillaume and Madame Guizot de Witt. *The History of France from Earliest Times to 1848.* Translated by Robert Black. 8 volumes. New York: John B. Alden, 1884.

Inventaire Sommaire des Archives du Départment des Affaires Étrangères. Mémoires et Documents Fonds France et Fond Divers Supplément. Paris: Imprimerie Nationale, 1896.

Kissinger, Henry. *A World Restored: Metternich, Castlereagh and the Problems of Peace, 1812-22.* Boston: Houghton Mifflin Company.

Lacour-Gayet, G. *Talleyrand.* 3 volumes. Paris: Payot, 1931.

Leys, Mary D. R. *Between Two Empires. A History of French Politicians and People between 1814 and 1848.* London: Longmans, Green and Company, Ltd., 1955.

Madelin, Louis. *Deux Relèvements Français, 1815-1818, 1871-1878.* Paris: Flammarion, 1951.

Mowat, R. B. *The States of Europe, 1815-1871.* New York: Longmans, Green and Company, 1932.

Newman, Edgar Leon, editor. *Historical Dictionary of France from the 1815 Restoration to the Second Empire.* 2 volumes. Westport, Conn.: Greenwood Press, 1987.

Pool, Bernard, editor. *The Croker Papers, 1808-1857.* London: B.T. Batsford, Ltd., abridged edition, 1967.

Porch, Douglas. *Army and Revolution, France 1815-1848.* London: Routledge and Kegan Paul, 1974.

Phillips, Walter Alison. *The Confederation of Europe. A Study of the European Alliance, 1813-1823.* New York: Howard Fertig, 1966.

Stephen, Sir Leslie and Lee, Sir Sidney, editors. *The Dictionary of National Biography.* 21 volumes and supplement. London: Oxford University Press Reprint, 1959-1960.

United Kingdom. *Guide to the Contents of the Public Record Office.* 3 volumes. London, 1963.

Ward, Sir A. W. and Gooch, G. P. *The Cambridge History of British Foreign Policy, 1783-1919.* 3 volumes. New York: The MacMillan Company, 1923.

Webster, Sir Charles Kingsley. *The Congress of Vienna, 1814-1815.* London: G. Bell and Sons, 1945.

——. *The European Alliance, 1815–1825.* University of Calcutta, 1929.

——. *The Foreign Policy of Castlereagh, 1815–1822. Britain and the European Alliance.* London: G. Bell and Sons, Ltd., reprinted 1963.

Wright, Gordon. *France in Modern Times: 1760 to the Present.* Chicago: Rand McNally and Company, 1966.

Yonge, Charles Duke. *The Life and Administration of Robert Banks, Second Earl of Liverpool, K.G.* 3 volumes. London: MacMillan and Company, 1868.

ARTICLES

Allen, John R. "Peacekeeping and 'Local Presence' Mission." Part 1 in *Defense Science 2003+* (December/January 1986): 54–62, part 2 in *Defense Science 2004+* (February/March 1986): 51–65.

Artz, Frederick B. "The Electoral System in France During the Bourbon Restoration, 1815–1830." *Journal of Modern History* 1 (June 1969):205–18.

Daudet, Ernest. "Le Duc de Richelieu au Congrès d'Aix-la-Chapelle." *La Nouvelle Revue* 114 (1898).

Garston, J. "Armies of Occupation, I: The British in France, 1815–1818." *History Today* 11 (July 1961):396–404.

Hamilton, Albert J. "'Une Position Nouvelle en Europe' The Duke of Wellington in France, 1815–1818." *Duquesne Review* 16(2):91–100.

Nelson, C. "The Duke of Wellington and The Barrier Fortresses after Waterloo." *The Journal of the Society for Army Historical Research* 42 (1964):36–43.

Nelson, Richard W. "Multinational peacekeeping in the Middle East and the United Nations Model." *International Affairs* 61 (Winter 1984–1985):67–89.

Rain, Pierre. "La France et Les Armees D'occupation, 1815–1818." *Revue des Questions Historiques* 81 (1907):229–39.

Robinson, Philip. "The Duke of Wellington." *Contemporary Review* 215 (September 1969):147–49.

Robson, William H. "New Light on Lord Castlereagh's Diplomacy." *The Journal of Modern History* 3 (1931):198–218.

Vovard, Andre. "Les soldats anglais en France en 1814 et 1816." *Revue des Études Napoléoniennes* 14 (July–December 1918):240–43.

Index

About the Author

THOMAS DWIGHT VEVE is Adjunct Faculty Instructor at Troy State University in Florida. His article "Wellington and the Army of Occupation in France, 1815-1818" appeared in *International History Review*.